The Columbia Comedy Shorts

Two-Reel Hollywood Film Comedies, 1933–1958

by
Ted Okuda

with
Edward Watz

FOREWORD BY
EMIL SITKA

INTRODUCTION BY
EDWARD BERNDS

McFarland
Classics

McFarland & Company, Inc., Publishers
Jefferson, North Carolina

For Vernon Dent (1895–1963)
"May you always be kept in the foreground"
(from an inscribed photo presented to Vernon by comedian Charley Chase)

McFarland Classics

1997
1. Michael R. Pitts. *Western Movies*
2. William C. Cline. *In the Nick of Time*
3. Bill Warren. *Keep Watching the Skies!*
4. Mark McGee. *Roger Corman*
5. R. M. Hayes. *Trick Cinematography*
6. David J. Hogan. *Dark Romance*
7. Spencer Selby. *Dark City: The Film Noir*
8. David K. Frasier. *Russ Meyer—The Life and Films*
9. Ted Holland. *B Western Actors Encyclopedia*
10. Franklin Jarlett. *Robert Ryan*

1998
11. R. M. Hayes. *3-D Movies*
12. Richard West. *Television Westerns*
13. Ted Okuda *with* Edward Watz. *The Columbia Comedy Shorts*
14. Steve Archer. *Willis O'Brien*

Front cover: Charley Chase and Ann Doran in *Pie à la Maid* (1938).
Back cover: Dudley Dickerson in *His Bridal Fright* (1940).

The present work is a reprint of the library bound edition of The Columbia Comedy Shorts, *first published in 1986.* **McFarland Classics** *is an imprint of McFarland & Company, Inc., Publishers, who also published the original edition.*

British Library Cataloguing-in-Publication data are available

Library of Congress Cataloguing-in-Publication Data
Okuda, Ted, 1953–   *The Columbia comedy shorts.*
Bibliography: p. 249.   Includes filmographies.   Includes index.
1. Comedy films—United States—History and criticism.   2. Short films—History and criticism.
3. Columbia Pictures Corporation.   I. Watz, Edward, 1958–   .   II. Title.
PN1995.9.C55048   1998   791.43'09'0917   84-43241

ISBN 978-0-7864-0577-0   (softcover : 50# alkaline paper) ∞

©1986 Ted Okuda and Edward Watz. All rights reserved. Printed in the United States of America

No part of this book, specifically including the index, may be reproduced or transmitted in any form or by any means, electronic or mechanical, including photocopying or recording, or by any information storage and retrieval system, without permission in writing from the publisher.

McFarland & Company, Inc., Publishers, Box 611, Jefferson, North Carolina 28640

Table of Contents

Acknowledgments

The most rewarding aspect of researching this book was the opportunity to get to know many of the creative people whose work we've enjoyed for years. Edward Bernds and Emil Sitka are deserving of far more praise than we have space to give. Ed went to great lengths to furnish us with the most accurate data possible; his encouragement and enthusiasm for our project never flagged. Emil also gave of himself one hundred percent; his trenchant comments gave us valuable insights into the operation of the comedy shorts unit and its personnel. We were graciously received by Jules White, who displayed a commendable faith in two neophyte scribes. Jules helped put us in touch with his brothers, Jack and Sam White, both of whom also made important contributions. Elwood Ullman provided us with perceptive observations on scripting the comedy shorts. We regret to report that Jules White, Jack White, and Elwood Ullman have all passed away since this book was completed. They will be sorely missed, and we will always remember their efforts on our behalf.

We are also deeply indebted to the following individuals who kindly shared their memories with us: Eddie Quillan, the late Richard Lane, Charles Lamont, Nell O'Day, Lois January, the late Harry Von Zell, Eunice Dent Friend, Adrian Booth (Lorna Gray), Lucille Ball, Bruce Bennett, the late Andrea Leeds Howard, Louise Currie, Emil Oster and Noah Beery, Jr.

For their assistance and moral support, we would like to thank Gregory and Mary Revak, Maurice Terenzio, Roy Kinnard, Alex Gordon, Tom Weaver, Joe Savage, Dick Andersen, Don Glut, Veto Stasiunaitis, Henry and Karen Ottinger, Larry Urbanski, Al Bielski, Mabel Langdon, Bill Cox, Eleanor Keaton, Dottie and Charlie Calderini, Danny Burk, John Aben, Sam Rubin, Robert Rosterman, Dan Aument, Gabe Taverny, Robert Miller, Brian Sawada, Kevin Graham, Tom Rose, Davis Sasaki, Tom Nicpon, Joe Nicpon, Bob Riskin, Ralph and Edith Schiller, and Ray Atherton.

Access to prints of some Columbia shorts was made possible through the following 16mm rental libraries: Union County Film Service, Budget Films, Kit Parker Films and Modern Sound Motion Picture Library.

Photograph credits: Mike Hawks, Eddie Brandt's Saturday Matinee, The Memory Shop, Movie Star News, Movie Memories, Emil Sitka, Edward Bernds, Erwin Dumbrille and Jules White.

We extend special thanks to Anthony Slide, Sam Gill, the late Carol Epstein and the staff of the Margaret Herrick Library of the Academy of Motion Picture Arts and Sciences, who patiently endured our inquiries and demands, supplying us with extensive reference material even at a moment's notice.

Last, and by no means least, a special debt of gratitude to Erwin Dumbrille, without whom this book would never have gotten beyond the planning stage. His excellent memory and exhaustive knowledge of film history helped to shape this volume every step of the way.

Foreword

We know the Siberian white tiger is disappearing, becoming extinct. The Great Plains bison have all but gone. Whooping cranes no longer darken the Mississippi flyways. The North American grizzly is vanishing from the Rocky Mountains.

It would be dismaying if amongst our film products, the comedy shorts made by Columbia Pictures were about to become as extinct as the California condor or the bald eagle. It's too horrifying to contemplate.

So we take solace from Ted Okuda and Ed Watz's meticulous pursuit of the facts in giving us a fine record of short comedy stories on film as Columbia made them. It's more than nostalgia — it's Americana. They have given us a comprehensive story of the colorful characters, incidents, data and details that vitalized these two-reelers.

We are provided a reference source with a nostalgic tug. The names of many who later became famous and great are a part of this wonderful history, as well as those of others whose fame and greatness ended with Columbia's memorable film shorts. We have here a wealth of material for film scholars and buffs of a bygone era, an era given to Hollywood largely by producers like Jules White.

Once these films were fillers on bills that presented one feature along with a newsreel. Now, in this book, they are preserved for all of us who hate to think they may become extinct, never to be recycled. Despite the archaic settings, topical references and styles of the day in these movies, the comedy remains undiluted. And when presented to audiences today, as are the popular Three Stooges films, they prove that what was funny then is still funny now.

Having worked as an actor in almost 100 of these films, I am proud to be so closely associated with them. Nevertheless, it's not for me, but rather for Ted and Ed to describe the comedy that Jules White, as producer, put on film for millions of appreciative viewers.

We have here a true picture of the factory where these movies were cranked out. Names like Lucille Ball, Buster Keaton, Andy Clyde, Charley Chase and The Three Stooges owe much to the creative genius of Jules White, Hugh McCollum, Elwood Ullman, Felix Adler, Ed Bernds, Del Lord, Jack White and all those other comedy practitioners who compressed their stories

vii

into two-reelers. Others in special effects, sound, stunts and casting are also mentioned. This book covers them all.

As an actor who witnessed the interesting and authentic creation of these pictures, I feel honored to have been called upon to supply my share to this worthy and wonderful history. It should be read by everyone who has seen any of these gems . . . and yes, even those of you who missed them!

—Emil Sitka

Preface

Today's generation of moviegoers, accustomed to sitting through a "No Smoking" warning, two or three trailers (previews of coming attractions), and perhaps a cartoon as a prelude to the feature presentation, may be surprised to learn that in Hollywood's Golden Age, the short subjects were often a highlight, or even *the* highlight, of the program. Comedy shorts (a two-reel "short" ran from sixteen to twenty minutes, on the average) were especially popular, and Columbia made some of the finest in the business.

By the time Columbia established their two-reel comedy unit in 1933, comedy shorts were already beginning to lose the prestige they had once enjoyed. Eventually, they came to be regarded as "fillers," a little something extra thrown in to add spice to the program. But, as this book reveals, sometimes they still meant as much to the box office receipts as the feature presentation did.

This, then, is the history of the Columbia comedy shorts.* Within these pages you'll find a historical survey of the comedy shorts department, a look at various aspects of production, critical appraisals of each series (accompanied by filmographies of all 526 two-reelers broken down by series), and selected biographies of writers, directors and performers. Quotes from cast and crew members provide illuminating insights, bringing to life the alternately joyful, tragic, infuriating and madcap activities that occurred behind the scenes at one of Hollywood's craziest fun factories. And you'll meet the colorful characters who pooled their talents in an effort to make people laugh.

That this volume overlaps previously published works shouldn't be surprising. When you're dealing with The Three Stooges, Buster Keaton, Charley Chase and others whose films and careers have been discussed at great length, there's bound to be repetition. However, we have done our best to inject new insights into familiar material while offering some never-before-published information.

One question that may cross the reader's mind is "How can I get to see some of these pictures?" We're sorry to say that there is no simple answer.

This volume concerns itself only with the Columbia two-reel comedies produced in Hollywood from 1933 to 1958. A cheaply-made series of two-reel musical comedies produced in New York by Ben K. Blake has been excluded.

With the exception of the still-popular Three Stooges series, the majority of
the Columbia comedy shorts (or, for that matter, short subjects in general)
remain inaccessible. Profits are and always have been the primary concern of
movie studios; since it's highly unlikely that the non–Stooge two-reelers will
generate enough income to justify having new prints struck, these films will
probably sit in the Columbia vaults indefinitely. So unless you can make arrangements with film archives, know private collectors, or are willing to go to
the expense of renting the handful of titles available through 16mm outlets,
there is no convenient way to view them.

   We hope that this book will spur a reinterest in these comedies. Not all
of them were gems—indeed, the bad often outweighed the good—but considering the creative talents involved and the sorry examples of what passes
for comedy today, the Columbia comedy shorts are certainly better than their
current obscurity would indicate.

                                                    —*Ted Okuda*
                                                    Edward Watz

Introduction

The short subjects department of Columbia Pictures was a lively place during the twenty-five years of its existence. From the beginning, the shorts department had strong links with the great days of silent comedy. When Mack Sennett's star began to decline, and when Hal Roach decided that the days of comedy shorts were ending, refugees, as it were, from the Sennett and the Roach studios came to Columbia; directors Harry Edwards, James Horne, Ray McCarey and Del Lord; writers Felix Adler, Arthur Ripley, Johnny Grey and Clyde Bruckman. And the actors—scarred veterans of many a rough-and-tumble silent film: Buster Keaton, Andy Clyde, Vernon Dent, Bud Jamison, Snub Pollard, and a host of bit players.

I was involved with Columbia's shorts program from the beginning. In 1934 I was the sound technician on *Woman Haters*, the first film the Three Stooges made for Columbia. Eleven years later, my first assignment as a director was a Three Stooges comedy, and in the seven years that followed, 1945–1952, I directed 57 two-reel comedies, including 25 with the Stooges.

The enduring popularity of the Stooge two-reelers continues to amaze me. We made many other films with many other comedians, and they are described, accurately and with affection, in this book. We who made them thought that many of our non–Stooge efforts were good; they *were* good, and preview audiences agreed with us. The two-reelers starring Buster Keaton, Harry Langdon, Andy Clyde, Charley Chase, Hugh Herbert, Schilling and Lane and Harry Von Zell deserve a showing on TV. Many of them previewed on a par with the best of our Stooge shorts. If they were given TV exposure, as the Stooge films are, perhaps they would gain the recognition they deserve.

But then again, they might not. It now seems probable that the Stooge shorts have some intangible quality that even those of us who made the films were not aware of. How else can we explain the fanatical devotion of successive generations of fans? The Stooge two-reelers are not—decidedly not—all masterpieces. Some of them are embarrassingly crude, violent and incoherent. But true Stooge fans love them all!

I take a certain ungenerous satisfaction in the popularity of our two-reelers today. To understand my feelings, you have to know how we, the short

1

subjects people, were ignored by the Columbia hierarchy. We were even separated from the main lot, housed in a shabby old building. When I first started working for producer Hugh McCollum, he said to me, "I wouldn't mind if the people over there bawled me out for making a bad picture, if just once in a while they'd say, 'Mac, that was a pretty good one.' " The lack of recognition bothered McCollum, and after a while it bothered me too. We'd make some films; perhaps we'd hit a hot streak where each preview topped the one before. We knew the shows were good, but the Columbia bosses never bothered to look at our stuff, and when we shipped the films to New York, they disappeared into a silent void.

For a number of years, our two-reelers have been shown on television all over the country. They may well continue to be shown for years to come. I wish my good friend Hugh McCollum were alive to see how well our poor little neglected two-reelers are doing.

—Edward Bernds

A Historical Overview

Located at Sunset and Gower ("Gower Gulch"), Columbia Pictures, founded in 1924 by Harry Cohn, started out as a Poverty Row studio. As with all Poverty Row denizens, Columbia was sneered at by the major studios; industry wags dubbed it "Columbia, the *germ* of the ocean." Ultimately, it was Harry Cohn who would have the last laugh. By the 1930s, the irascible Cohn—with the considerable aid of a young director named Frank Capra—had built Columbia into a studio to be reckoned with. True, there was still a tremendous amount of low-grade fodder being churned out ("Some were so bad they've yet to play television," says Ed Bernds), but there was now a goodly share of prestige pictures as well, among them *The Bitter Tea of General Yen* (1933), *Lady for a Day* (1933), *One Night of Love* (1934) and *It Happened One Night* (1934).

As Columbia's standing in the industry grew, so did the studio itself. In the early 1930s, before a short subjects department had officially been established, the studio handled the distribution of Walt Disney's *Mickey Mouse* and *Silly Symphonies* cartoons, along with the less popular Charles Mintz *Krazy Kat* and *Scrappy* cartoons. The rest of the lineup was quite a mixed bag. *Monkeyshines* featured an all-simian cast, with overdubbed dialogue. *Travelaughs ("Laughing with Medbury")*, produced by Walter Futter, were one-reel comic travelogues with comic commentaries by John P. Medbury. Entries included *Laughing with Medbury in Abyssinia,* . . . *in Death Valley,* . . . *in Mandalay*, and . . . *on Voodoo Island. Buzzell Specialties* were one-reelers billed as "Radio Bedtime Stories" and featured comedian (later director) Eddie Buzzell. Shot silent, Buzzell would simply supply the voices for the characters in the story. Buzzell had previously been a Broadway musical comedy star and was, in the words of an associate, "an All-American No-Talent." Edward Bernds relates how this series came about: "Harry Cohn had a Tin Pan Alley background as a songplugger. If he had a weakness, call it a liking if you will, it was for musically inclined people. Buzzell came to Columbia as a sort of 'yes man' and court jester. Cohn gave him this series as a pat on the head."

Foreshadowing things to come, the studio also released a series of two-reel comedies made by the Lambs Club, a fraternity of professional actors. Billed in the trade journals as *Sunrise Comedies*, they featured such

3

comedians as Leon Errol *(Poor Fish)*, Will Mahoney *(The Entertainer)*, Ken Murray *(Preferred List, Brother Could You Spare a Million?)* and Smith and Dale *(Hot Daze, Love in Tents, Fifty Million Dollars Can't Be Wrong)*. There were burlesques of "old time meller-dramas" with titles like *The Curse of a Broken Heart* and *The Strange Case of Poison Ivy*. The remainder of the short subjects releases consisted of a handful of *Mickey McGuire* comedies starring Joe Yule, Jr. (soon to gain fame and fortune as Mickey Rooney) and the usual quota of *Sports Thrills* and *Screen Snapshots*.

But Cohn had bigger plans. Rather than merely release shorts made by independent units, he wanted his studio to have its own short subjects department that would produce two-reel comedies. One day, while at Grauman's Chinese Theatre, Cohn happened to see one of MGM's *Pete Smith* shorts directed by Jules White. Cohn was with his agent, who was also White's agent, and remarked, "I'd like to have *that* guy make shorts like that for me."

Jules White started in the business as a child actor, appearing in such milestone pictures as *The Spoilers* (1914) and *The Birth of a Nation* (1915). At the age of twenty, Jules joined his older brother Jack at Educational Pictures, where Jack was in charge of his own comedy unit. At Educational, Jules went from assistant film editor to full-fledged director within a short span of five years. In addition to his work at Educational, Jules directed comedies at Fox and helped to organize the MGM shorts department in 1929. During his MGM stint, White directed several of the early *Pete Smith* shorts and, with director Zion Myers (brother of silent screen star Carmel Myers), created the *Dogville* comedies (or "barkies," as White refers to them), canine spoofs of then-current movies. Taffy on the dogs' tongues made their mouths move repeatedly, allowing Jules to dub in human voices later. The series spawned such entries as *The Dogway Melody, All Quiet on the Canine Front, Trader Hound* and *The Big Dog House*.

While serving as associate director on the Paramount feature *King of the Jungle* (1933), White was contacted by Columbia. He recalls:

> My dear friend Norman Taurog, whom I worked with at Educational, told Sam Briskin, Columbia's production chief, I was available, so he sent for me. He informed me that the studio wanted to form a comedy shorts department; after a long discussion with Briskin, he said, "I think you're a good man for this spot. Let's go in and talk to Harry (Cohn) about it."

His first encounter with Columbia's legendary tyrant amounted to a verbal jousting match:

> I walked into Cohn's office and the first thing he said was "Can you make the best comedy shorts in the world?" I snapped back, "Can you make the best feature pictures in the world? No, wait — don't bother to answer that. I've seen them! Believe me, you need me more than I need you!"

The man who started it all: a 1937 portrait of writer-producer-director Jules White,
who organized Columbia's comedy shorts department.

> Cohn looked perturbed, so I said, "You sent for me, Mr. Cohn, I
> didn't come to you asking for a job," and with that, I headed for the
> door. He said. "Wait—where are you going?" "You still want to talk
> to me?" I asked. "Sure, why not?" he said. "We may not make the best
> pictures in the world, but they're good enough and we try our best."
> "Well, I try my best," I told him, "and *mine* have been good
> enough."

Cohn respected anyone who stood his ground and fought back; White's
forthrightness prompted Cohn to hire him on the spot.

White began organizing the department in 1933, a department that concerned itself only with the two-reel comedies produced at Columbia's
Hollywood studio. He had no connection with the two-reel musical shorts produced in New York by Ben K. Blake. Serials, *Screen Snapshots* ("I had that
turkey for a while, but I got rid of it in a hurry," says Jules), travelogues, sports

reels, newsreels and sing-alongs were also out of White's jurisdiction.

After only a month, White left the studio. "I didn't make a single picture. I just couldn't get started right. I had some discussions with Sam Briskin and then I just left." After his departure, Zion Myers accepted Cohn's offer to assume the position vacated by White. Myers was Jules' partner and an old friend. As a neighbor of the White family in Edendale, he and the White children grew up together; whenever Zion would want to stay over for dinner, Mrs. White would say, "That's all right, we'll just add a little more water to the soup."

Myers' first act as producer was to hire Archie Gottler. A show producer, director and songwriter, Gottler was responsible for the first "official" Columbia comedy shorts, *Musical Novelties* a series of musical comedies with the dialogue delivered in rhyme.

At Myers' request, White returned to the unit in 1934 and quickly sprang into action, hiring an impressive roster of comedy talents. As two-reel comedy programs were being phased out by other studios, the department became a haven for veterans who had difficulty securing work elsewhere. Most had roots in silent screen comedy. Gag writers Felix Adler, Arthur Ripley, Al Giebler and Johnnie Grey had all worked for Mack Sennett in the 1920s. Harry Edwards had also worked for Sennett, directing several of Harry Langdon's silent comedies. White learned that Del Lord, at one time the highest paid director on the Sennett lot, was selling used cars in Studio City and immediately signed him up. Writer-director Clyde Bruckman had worked with Buster Keaton, Harry Langdon, Laurel and Hardy, Harold Lloyd and W.C. Fields prior to his stint at Columbia. Raymond McCarey, brother of Leo McCarey, directed a number of the shorts, as did Educational Pictures alumnus Charles Lamont. Jules' brother Jack White directed under the pseudonym Preston Black; another brother, Sam White, directed two shorts. Jules hired a young writer named Elwood Ullman, who established himself as one of the department's finest gag men and story constructionists. Ray Hunt, a propman and infrequent director at Sennett's became the unit's ace propman.

And there were the comedians. Andy Clyde, Leon Errol, Charley Chase, Monte Collins, Tom Kennedy, George Sidney, Charlie Murray, Walter Catlett and El Brendel had their own series. At a time when they were virtually unemployable, silent screen greats Harry Langdon and Buster Keaton found refuge at Columbia. The Three Stooges (Moe Howard, Larry Fine, Jerry "Curly" Howard) were signed to a contract after their split with mentor Ted Healy; soon, they became the unit's top attraction, starring in comedy shorts that are now hailed as classics.

Realizing the importance of a dependable stock company of supporting players, White rounded up some of the finest in the business. No mention of the department would be complete without acknowledging the immeasurable contributions of Vernon Dent and Bud Jamison, two gifted secondary players who added much zest to the films. Symona Boniface, Ann Doran,

Columbia comedians ponder global affairs in this rare 1942 publicity still. Pictured l. to r.: Larry Fine, Monte Collins, Harry Langdon, Moe Howard, Curly Howard.

Dorothy Appleby, Bess Flowers, Dorothy Granger and June Gittelson were among the ladies who courageously took their lumps with the best of them. Al Thompson and Johnny Kascier not only appeared in small roles but doubled for many of the stars as well, executing hazardous stunts for the grand slapstick tradition. Other valuable performers who enlivened these pictures include Fred Kelsey, Gino Corrado, William Irving, Arthur Housman, Stanley Blystone, Esther Howard, Emmett Lynn, Eddie Laughton, Lynton Brent, John Tyrrell, James C. Morton, Cy Schindell, Bob McKenzie, Eva McKenzie, Harry Semels, Dick Curtis, Dudley Dickerson, Jack "Tiny" Lipson, Ted Lorch, Richard Fiske, Jack Norton, Victor Travers, Charles "Heine" Conklin, Robert "Bobby" Burns, Lew Kelly, Marjorie Deanne, Vivien Oakland, Mary Ainslee, Lew Davis, John T. Murray, Lucille Lund, Ethelreda Leopold, Hilda Title, Beatrice Blinn, Bert Young and Bobby Barber.

Silent screen actresses Mae Busch, Betty Compson, Betty Blythe and Clara Kimball Young turned up in these films, as did comedy veterans Snub

Pollard, Chester Conklin, Charlie Hall, Billy West, Charles Dorety and Spec O'Donnell.

In time, other talented secondary players were added to the roster. Christine McIntyre developed into a first-rate comedienne, exuding poise and femininity in the midst of the most absurd situations. Emil Sitka's smooth versatility enabled him to portray a wide variety of lovable eccentrics. Kenneth MacDonald brought a wonderfully urbane quality to his roles as comic villains. Dick Wessel had the market cornered on burly oafs who were never able to conceal their hostilities. Phil Van Zandt was adept at playing an assortment of comic foils, ranging from foreign spies to mad scientists. Other expert players added to the lineup include Jean Donahue (later known as Jean Willes), Lynne Lyons, Gene Roth, Harold Brauer, Barbara Slater, Nanette Bordeaux, Frank Sully, Brian O'Hara, Judy Malcolm, Rebel Randall, Joe Palma, Claire Carleton, Frank Lackteen, Dee Green, Phil Arnold, Benny Rubin, Minerva Urecal, Marion Martin, Arthur Q. Bryan, Charles Middleton, Matt Willis, Duke York, Matt McHugh, Margie Liszt, Maxine Gates, John Merton and Henry Kulky.

Several up-and-coming actors were seen in supporting roles in the two-reelers. Says Sam White, "Columbia had a great many contract players whom everyone used in features, but there were some who worked in short subjects as well in order to get experience and grooming." Betty Grable and Lois January were featured in a few of the early *Musical Novelties*. Lucille Ball, then an unknown contract player, was spotted by Leon Errol, who cast her in a bit part as a secretary in *Perfectly Mismated* (1934); she also appeared with the Three Stooges in *Three Little Pigskins* (1934). Says Lucy today, "Working with Leon Errol and the Three Stooges was my first training in slapstick and real physical comedy. And I very much appreciated training with some real greats." Lorna Gray, who later changed her name to Adrian Booth and starred in a succession of "B" Westerns and serials, says of her work for the unit, "It was great fun making pictures with the madcap Three Stooges, the funny Charley Chase and the brilliant Buster Keaton." Louise Currie, another veteran of westerns, appeared in three shorts, two with Harry Langdon: "Working with Harry was an acting lesson in humor and timing." Bruce Bennett, best known for his roles in *Mildred Pierce* (1945) and *The Treasure of Sierra Madre* (1948), recalls, "The comedians I worked with at Columbia — the Three Stooges, Charley Chase, Andy Clyde, Buster Keaton — were all hardworking, clever performers with great ability that was certainly evident to all." Lloyd Bridges, James Craig, Adele Mara, Yvonne DeCarlo, Noel Neill, Dan Blocker, Linda Winters (Dorothy Comingore), Rita Rio (Dona Drake), Adele Pearce (Pamela Blake), Walter Brennan, Don Beddoe, Jimmy Dodd and Jacques O'Mahoney (Jock Mahoney) were also among the players who popped up in these films at early stages in their careers.

Running the department gave White precious little time to pursue his true passion — directing — so in 1937, Hugh McCollum, a former secretary to Harry Cohn and the business manager for the short subjects department since

Phyllis Crane, Lucille Ball and Gertie Green eavesdrop as the Three Stooges go into a huddle in *Three Little Pigskins* (1934). Jack White recalls, "Lucy was just a contract player in those days. Harry Cohn didn't want to bother with her; would you believe he didn't think she had any talent?"

1934, began sharing production chores. Both men ran their own separate units within the department. Elwood Ullman comments, "McCollum was basically a businessman. Jules White was more active in the writing and directing of the shorts."

"The short subjects department had a separate building across the street from the rest of the studio," recalls Emil Sitka. Edward Bernds adds:

> We were across Beachwood Drive, isolated to some extent from the lofty 'A' productions in a building so old and rickety that McCollum used to say that only the termites held it together. Strangely, the two-reeler operation was never banished to "Columbia Sunset," where the Columbia 'B' picture unit was sort of segregated. It was a couple of miles from the main studio. We sometimes used their sound stages, but only when the main lot was busy.

By the late 1930s, the department was at the height of its powers, turning out the best two-reel comedies in the industry, many of which were more technically and artistically proficient than the studio's feature product. The shorts were previewed to gauge audience reaction; their response decided what was deleted, retained or padded.

"We averaged twenty-five shorts a year," says Jules White. "The front

Adele Mara (left) and Lloyd Bridges (center) were among the contract players who appeared in two-reelers before landing prominent roles in feature films. In this scene from the El Brendel short *A Rookie's Cookie* (1943), both look on as Brendel takes a spill.

office dictated how many two-reelers we were allowed to produce. If it was a profitable year, then the more shorts we were permitted to make. If things were slow, we had to cut back accordingly. But the Three Stooges shorts were always in demand, regardless of whether profits were up or down." The demand for the Stooge shorts is no exaggeration. Their films were audience favorites, and after a while, Columbia refused to supply exhibitors with Stooge comedies unless they agreed to book some of the studio's lesser 'B' features.

In "What the Picture Did for Me," a regular feature of the industry trade journal *Motion Picture Herald*, one can see just how well-received the Columbia comedy shorts were. In this column, exhibitors from all over the country (mostly from cities with small town patronage) expressed their views of current releases, with a strong slant on audience response:

Back to the Soil (George Sidney and Charlie Murray, 1934): "A side-splitter for laughs and the audience proved they liked it. This team has been making some dandy comedies. Just the type that fits the whole audience." *B.A. McConnell, Emerson Theatre, Hartford, Ark.*

Oh, Duchess! (Polly Moran, 1936): "This is the first one we played of this star, but believe you me, it won't be the last. Play this with some of the weak pictures Columbia has been putting out this season and it might make them forget the feature." *H.M. Gerber, Roxy Theatre, Hazelton, N.D.*

3 Dumb Clucks (The Three Stooges, 1937): "This trio of comedians are the hit of the show. They are nine-tenths of my box office appeal for the kids. You can have your Marx Brothers and your Laurel and Hardy, but give me just one feature-length Stooge picture and I'll be out of the red for a good while. Thank you Curly, Larry and Moe. You are tops with me." *Walter Currell, Gem Theatre, Logan, Utah.*

Half-Way to Hollywood (Tom Kennedy and Johnny Arthur, 1938): "Boy! Columbia knows that they have a comedy team in this pair and therefore these are ace comedians." *R.W. Crickmore, Rainbow Theatre, Newport, Wash.*

The Nightshirt Bandit (Charley Chase, 1938): "Here is one of the funniest two-reel comedies Columbia has ever produced. This comedy had the audience howling. By all means, play this one. Columbia has the best two-reel comedies." *Edelstein Amusement Co., Homer Theatre, Hibbing, Minn.*

All-American Blondes (Andy Clyde, 1939): "Brought this back as second run. Very funny slapstick. Everyone pleased." *Fred C. Allen, Princess Theatre, Piedmont, Ala.*

Andy Clyde Gets Spring Chicken (Andy Clyde, 1939): "A dandy Andy Clyde comedy and house in uproar. In fact, they loved it, young and old." *C.L. Niles, Niles Theatre, Anamosa, Iowa.*

You Nazty Spy! (The Three Stooges, 1940): "These Stooges comedies go over here in a big way. We had a very weak program and this is the only thing that saved it from complete failure." *Peter Kavel, Campau Theatre, Hamtramck, Mich.*

You're Next (Walter Catiett, 1940): "Don't miss booking this. It was excellent." *George S. Caporal, Yale Theatre, Oklahoma City, Okla.*

Money Squawks (Andy Clyde, 1940): "This comedy certainly brought the house down with laughter. No company in the business makes the shorts that this company does. A swell comedy." *A.J. Inks, Crystal Theatre, Ligonier, Ind.*

How High Is Up? (The Three Stooges, 1940): "All I can say is that the patrons almost died laughing at these three nuts. If that's what my patrons want, they shall get it. To the many exhibitors that haven't booked this short, do so at once." *Harry H. Shaw, Dillard Theatre, Wardell, Mo.*

The Spook Speaks (Buster Keaton, 1940): "Buster Keaton in all his glory. Went over big with our audiences. This old timer still means something at the box office and deserves splendid mention in your newspaper ads." *Pearce Parkhurst, Larcom Theatre, Beverly, Mass.*

Cactus Makes Perfect (The Three Stooges, 1942): "Hope Columbia holds on to these boys. They have saved the day for me many a time." *Ed Mansfield, Regent Theatre, Kansas City, Mo.*

Groom and Bored (Johnny Downs, 1942): "Very good. They all roared. Columbia comedies are tops." *J.H. Taylor, Zap Theatre, Zap, N.D.*

A Blitz on the Fritz (Harry Langdon, 1943): "Our patrons love these comedies and actually ask for more in preference to some of the so-called features which we are forced to show them." *Robert E. Floeter, Burton Theatre, Flint, Mich.*

Blonde and Groom (Harry Langdon, 1943): "Good farce comedy and the kind of hokum our patrons like. Columbia makes the best slapstick comedies on the market today." *A.H. Kaufman, Fountain Theatre, Terre Haute, Ind.*

Bachelor Daze (Slim Summerville, 1944): "Here is a scream. Play it by all means. Two reels of real comedy." *Fred Flanagan, Moon Theatre, Stratton, Colo.*

She Snoops to Conquer (Vera Vague, 1944): "The audience laughed from start to finish. Don't miss playing it. They will love it and so will you." *Robert E. McCurdy, Liberty Theatre, Muncie, Ind.*

Booby Dupes (The Three Stooges, 1945): "If your patrons like slapstick, get it by all means. All I have to do is advertise the Three Stooges. It brings them." *S.M. Underhill, Flint Theatre, Gentry, Ark.*

A Hit with a Miss (Shemp Howard, 1945): "One of Columbia's comedies that will put your slapstick fans in the aisles. I played it Friday and Saturday and it went over 100 percent." *F.W. Hamilton, Shelby Theatre, Shelbyville, Mo.*

A Bird in the Head (The Three Stooges, 1946): "Had a weak feature on and this screamer saved the day. Columbia is always a life saver here with short subjects and comedies." *Harold J. Pederson, Gonvick Theatre, Gonvick, Minn.*

Out West (The Three Stooges, 1947): "We had to fasten down all the seats when this was over. These birds are always tops in comedy. Play this by all means." *Frank D. Fowler, Princess Theatre, Mocksville, N.C.*

A trade journal advertisement for the Three Stooges short *Ants in the Pantry* (1936) and other Columbia two-reel comedies. Although Edgar Kennedy is listed among the studio's contract comedians, it was actually Tom Kennedy, Edgar's brother, who appeared in the Columbia shorts. Edgar had his own series at RKO.

Tall, Dark and Gruesome (Hugh Herbert, 1948): "Played this two months ago, midweek, and brought it back for a Friday and Saturday playdate. Advertised it and got repeat customers." *Shirley W. Booth, Booth Theatre, Rich Hill, Mo.*

The Hot Scots (The Three Stooges, 1948): "As usual the Stooges are always well received here. They are my number one short subject. In some instances their presence means as much as the program feature." *Robert H. Perkins, Lynn Theatre, Woodbine, Kentucky.*

Billie Gets Her Man (Billie Burke, 1948): "A very good two-reel comedy full of laughs from beginning to end." *P.B. Williams, Gretna Theatre, Gretna, Va.*

It's worth noting that several of the above mentioned comedies are, contrary to the rapturous testimonials, very weak efforts, hardly exemplary of the department at its best. But through these exhibitors' reports one can gauge the popularity of the pictures. Hungry for escapist fare, audiences embraced these films as nostalgic throwbacks to "good old-fashioned slapstick" despite their weaknesses. This was a major factor of their success: at a time when others were abandoning this type of comedy, Columbia was one of the sole purveyors of the slapstick tradition, embellishing the wild sight gags with inspired sound effects. Film historians have routinely accused the Columbia comedy shorts of bastardizing the art of visual comedy, blatantly disregarding the foundations set by past masters (a curious criticism, since many past masters worked on the films). This accusation is true to varying degrees; however, if the Columbia shorts lacked the originality and ingenuity of their predecessors, they more than compensated for their faults in terms of overall laugh content.

During the 1940s, other comedians were added to the already burgeoning roster: Hugh Herbert, Vera Vague, Shemp Howard, Gus Schilling, Richard Lane, Sterling Holloway, Harry Von Zell, Wally Vernon, Eddie Quillan, Joe DeRita and Joe Besser were among the funsters who had their own starring series. A sound mixer named Edward Bernds was given the opportunity to write and direct two-reelers; before long, he was turning out top-notch comedies.

As production costs escalated, the quality of the shorts began to decline. Liberal use of outdoor photography and elaborate sight gags became a thing of the past, and the films took on an increasingly claustrophobic look. Edward Bernds explains, "On the average, the two-reelers were budgeted at around $35,000. It wasn't that budgets decreased over the years; rather, it was that costs rose sharply and the dollar simply didn't buy as much. So the budgets remained the same, but you just weren't able to stretch them as far as they could in the 1930s."

Still, there were ways to get around these economic limitations. For example, standing sets from *The Bandit of Sherwood Forest* (1946), a feature film, were used for the Three Stooges shorts *Squareheads of the Round Table,*

Producer Hugh McCollum (seated) poses with Moe Howard, Larry Fine, Christine McIntyre and Shemp Howard on the set of *The Hot Scots* (The Three Stooges, 1948).

Fiddlers Three and *The Hot Scots* (all 1948 releases). Remaking earlier shorts and using stock footage from them became a common practice.

By the 1950s Columbia was virtually alone in the two-reel comedy field, although the output had been reduced from twenty-five shorts a year to fifteen; reissues of earlier shorts made up the difference. In 1952 Hugh McCollum was ousted in a power play instigated by Jules White. The situation had been brewing for some time, as the ill will between the two began to escalate. With the reduced output of two-reelers, White was able to convince the studio hierarchy that keeping two short subjects producers on the payroll was unnecessary. As one observer states:

> They had been on each other's nerves for years. Jules could be insensitive, but in all fairness, a good part of it was McCollum's fault; if he had been a little less belligerent and antagonistic, the crisis might not have come to the attention of the front office.
>
> Jules was constantly doing favors for the top brass: organizing picnics, running little errands and the like. So when he decided to oust McCollum, he had no difficulty in getting the bigwigs to side with him.

This raises a question: why didn't Harry Cohn intercede on McCollum's behalf? After all, McCollum had been Cohn's secretary and was doing his job well as a short subjects producer. By all accounts, Cohn left others to sink or swim, to fight their own battles, regardless of his personal feelings. This, plus the fact that Cohn never considered the short subjects department important enough to interfere with any internal machinations, may explain McCollum's ignoble dismissal. With McCollum's departure, White took charge of the entire operation. When Edward Bernds left the unit, out of loyalty to McCollum, the responsibility of directing all of the comedy shorts also fell on White's shoulders.

In the early 1950s, the motion picture industry, faced with overwhelming competition from television, experimented with new ideas in hopes of luring audiences back into the theatres. One revolutionary (albeit short-lived) gimmick was 3-D. Through this process, projectiles that were hurled at the camera by the actors appeared to leap off the screen and out into the audience. White envisioned 3-D as a rebirth: "I thought 3-D would open up a whole new market for two-reel comedies. Well, it didn't take long before I realized it was a big mistake." In 1953 he produced and directed a trio of 3-D shorts: *Spooks* and *Pardon My Backfire*, both starring the Three Stooges, and *Down the Hatch* starring Harry Mimmo (according to White, *Down the Hatch* was only released in 2-D; recently, Columbia has struck up, for the first time, a brand new 3-D print of this title). When seen in their original format, these films were moderately amusing, but the abundance of 3-D effects failed to hide the paucity of material. Filming in 3-D was an arduous procedure; *Down the Hatch* took fourteen and one-half hours overtime to complete. The time-consuming camera setups required for this process, coupled with waning public interest in the novelty, convinced White to cancel his plans for an entire series of 3-D comedy shorts.

Because production costs were skyrocketing, White now made it a standard practice to lift footage from earlier shorts and film new stories to conform with the older scenes. Utilizing identical sets, costumes and, in many instances, the same supporting players, a new two-reeler could be completed in as little time as half a day. For example, it took four hours and fifteen minutes to complete all the new sequences (twenty-two scenes) required for the Wally Vernon–Eddie Quillan short *A-Hunting They Did Go* (1953), which consists largely of footage from an earlier V & Q two-reeler, *Crabbin' in the Cabin* (1948). While filming these crazy-quilt efforts, White had a moviola on the set, making sure the new scenes matched the older footage, right down to the smallest details. Says Emil Sitka, "I remember Jules once wanted to add some new shots of me to a sequence I had appeared in some years before. He wanted me to look exactly like I did in the earlier picture, so he told me to lose ten pounds in a week!"

On a technical level this deception works surprisingly well, although not well enough to save these patchwork affairs from being below-average outings. By this time, the department had become a White family operation: most of the shorts were scripted by Jack White (Jules' brother) and edited by Harold White (Jules' son).

The extensive use of older footage may have gone unnoticed by most viewers, but Edward Bernds was taken aback when he saw one of these:

When I saw *Fling in the Ring* (The Three Stooges, 1955), I couldn't believe what I was watching. Jules had taken *Fright Night* (1947), a Stooge short I directed, and had just added a few new scenes. Now, Columbia had the right to use the old footage, but I felt that I had the right to some credit. It upset me terribly that this much old footage was being passed off as new product. I handed the case over to the Director's Guild, claiming it was a cheat on the exhibitors. The Guild contacted Columbia, who claimed they notified me in advance that they were using these tactics (they never did).

I eventually got some money out of it ($2500), but not as much as I felt I deserved. You see, if I demanded a price that was higher than the cost of splicing in a credit ("Sequences directed by Edward Bernds"), they'd just add the credit and leave it at that. And, as the Guild attorney informed me, that credit would probably just appear in the Los Angeles releases—after all, I couldn't go around the country checking up on every single print. But if I asked for an amount lower than the cost of adding a credit, it would be cheaper—and easier—for Columbia just to pay me off. So I opted for the lower price.

To prevent any further repercussions, subsequent comedies gave credit ("Story by . . .") to Bernds, Clyde Bruckman, Elwood Ullman and others who were involved with earlier productions from which the stock footage was culled.

Commenting on the decline and fall of the two-reel comedy market, Jules White says, "It went downhill a little at a time in the 1950s. Theatres were running double features, and they could no longer afford the money or the time to open up with a short." He completed his last two-reeler, *Flying Saucer Daffy* with the Three Stooges, on December 20, 1957.

White remembers a fateful meeting with Harry Cohn:

I went to Cohn's office and said, "The short subjects business has gone to hell. We're not getting the bookings we used to. It's time to get out. I'm throwing in the towel. I'm going to retire." "Retire?" he says. "You're crazy—you'll go nuts!" "No," I said, "*you'll* go nuts. I have hobbies. I know how to relax. But you, you'll wind up killing yourself if you don't get out of this office. Why don't you get out and do other things?"

He just looked at me and said, "I don't know how to do other things." Two weeks later he was dead.

Cohn died in 1958. Soon after, the short subjects department was shut down and, after twenty-five years of allegiance to the lady with the flaming torch, Jules White left the studio. Due to the considerable amount of footage he shot in 1957, Columbia was able to release new shorts until mid-1959.

That the department had lasted this long was astounding; other studios hadn't produced a two-reel comedy in years. To a great extent, the unit's longevity can be attributed to Jules White's working relationship with the much-feared Harry Cohn. Says White:

The end of an era: Joe Besser, Jules White, Larry Fine and Moe Howard on the set of *Flying Saucer Daffy* (The Three Stooges, 1958), the final Columbia two-reeler produced (though not the last one released). This photograph, taken December 20, 1957, was the last publicity still taken in connection with the studio's short subjects department.

He never bothered me; he didn't consider my department important enough to bother with. He'd say to me, "As long as they keep making money, I don't care what you do. Don't bother me too much about it." And yet his door was always open; I could go in and talk things over any time I wanted. I couldn't do that at MGM, not the way Louie B. Mayer ran the place. But at Columbia it was different.

I always leveled with him. Once I went way over budget with a picture, so I went to his office and explained this situation. "I wanted you to hear it from me first," I said. "I'm glad you came in and told me," he said. "Thanks, Kid." He always called me "Kid" or "Short Subjects."

Cohn fought with everybody. I wasn't afraid of him and that's why he liked me. When we argued, he'd call me a dumb son of a bitch, so I'd call him *two* dumb sons of bitches. I'd always top him. We were both bastards; that's why we got along so well.

In light of all the veteran laughmakers who worked there, the Columbia short subjects department is harshly regarded in some circles as an "elephant's graveyard" of comedy, where has-beens spent the last waking hours of their career. While it is true that some of these veterans were well past their creative prime and plagued by personal demons (alcoholism was, sad to relate, an all-too-familiar problem), the department was still capable of turning out quality product. More importantly, it provided gainful employment for many who had nowhere else to turn. "It put a lot of bread on the table for a lot of people," comments Ed Bernds.

Making these comedy shorts often proved to be a nerve-wracking task. "We were always fighting the budget and the time," says Jules White. "I had a month's pay on the line with every picture, so I had to pinch every penny. That's a hell of a burden to have on your shoulders. I wince when I see some of the comedies now—if only I didn't have to skimp on them." Tight schedules, penny-pinching practices and personality conflicts were but a few of the pressures employees had to contend with. "Del Lord used to say, 'You don't have to be nuts to work here, but it helps,' " recalls Elwood Ullman. "That's a pretty good assessment of our working conditions." In the final analysis, however, everyone connected with the department toiled for a single purpose: to make people laugh. And the care still shows; the department's best work ranks among the finest comedy shorts ever made.

The Comedy Shorts Department: A Close-Up

The comedy shorts were the result of a combined effort on the part of directors, writers, performers and other creative talents connected with the department. The following is a closer look at various aspects of production.

Directors

Throughout the years, a variety of directors worked for the comedy shorts department. Archie Gottler, a show producer and songwriter, created the unit's first "official" series, *Musical Novelties*. Gag writers Clyde Bruckman, Lou Breslow, Al Ray and Al Boasberg directed an occasional two-reeler. Writer-comedian Benny Rubin helmed two of the *Radio Rogues* entries. James W. Horne, Robert McGowan, James Parrott (the brother of comedian Charley Chase) and Raymond McCarey, better known for their work at Hal Roach, directed a handful of Columbia shorts.

Arthur Ripley's Columbia output was sparse, but his contributions were major: it was Ripley who suggested Del Lord and Harry Langdon to Jules White, who hired them immediately.

Sam White, who worked with Ripley at RKO and Columbia, comments:

> I knew Arthur Ripley quite well. I found something deep in this man, a special quality that I hadn't found in very many people. While he was an inventive writer-director and probably created a great many of those visual gags, he liked the human element of a story. He had a great deal to do with Harry Langdon because his style of humor was Chaplinesque, playing the dramatic for comedy.

Sadly, Ripley's Columbia shorts are hardly indicative of the man's talents. His Harry Langdon comedies *Counsel on De Fence* (1934) and *The Leather Necker* (1935) miss the mark far more often than they hit and are marred by too many bizarre and vulgar touches.

Charles Lamont's Columbia shorts are of a generally high calibre — efforts like *Playing the Ponies* (The Three Stooges, 1937), *The Wrong Miss Wright*

(Charley Chase, 1937) and *A Doggone Mixup* (Harry Langdon, 1938) — but he also had a fair share of misfires: *Restless Knights* (The Three Stooges, 1935), *Sailor Maid* (Polly Moran, 1937) and *Calling All Doctors* (Charley Chase, 1937). While Lamont enjoyed working for the unit, his opinion of studio chieftain Harry Cohn was another matter. "I had an intense hatred of Cohn," says Lamont, "so my stay at Columbia was a brief one." Moving on to greener pastures, Lamont eventually found a home at Universal, where he directed several of the Abbott & Costello and *Ma and Pa Kettle* features.

Richard Quine *(The Solid Gold Cadillac, Operation Mad Ball, How to Murder Your Wife)* was being groomed for feature film assignments when he was given the chance to direct two-reelers for the unit. His deliberate, overly-mannered directorial style may have served him well for feature-length pictures, but it was the kiss of death to comedy shorts, as his limited output — *Foy Meets Girl* (Eddie Foy, Jr., 1950), *The Awful Sleuth* (Bert Wheeler, 1951) and *Woo-Woo Blues* (Hugh Herbert, 1951) — exemplifies.

Short subjects producer Hugh McCollum tried his hand at directing when Ed Bernds became busy with feature assignments. McCollum's style has been described as gentle and tasteful (like the man himself), and this is why his comedies never reach their full potential. At times, his direction of *Hula-La-La* (The Three Stooges, 1951) is too restrained and robs several scenes of their comic punch.

But the directors who were responsible for the bulk of the department's output were Del Lord, Preston Black (Jack White), Jules White, Charley Chase, Harry Edwards and Edward Bernds. They, more than any of the others, were the ones who shaped and influenced this body of work.

Del Lord

"Del Lord was the master," says Ed Bernds. "He had a boundless energy that he put into his comedies."

"Del was a godsend," adds Elwood Ullman. "His flair for comedy made my scripts seem that much better."

Other co-workers echo this wholehearted admiration for Lord and his talents. Lord had been the premier director for Mack Sennett in the 1920s, and his strengths as a filmmaker were his imaginative visual style and his uncanny ability to execute brilliantly staged stunt sequences (a position as the driver of the Keystone Kops paddy wagon gave Lord firsthand experience with the intricacies of auto stunts, chases and crashes). His tenure with Sennett also resulted in a near-complete working knowledge of the West Coast terrain, which proved invaluable in making comedy shorts for Columbia. Says Ed Bernds, "The barrel-chasing climax for *Three Little Beers* (The Three Stooges, 1935) was shot in Edendale, close to the old Mack Sennett Studios. Del had remembered the streets and steep hills where, years earlier, he had shot Sennett comedies, so it was no problem obtaining the best locations and camera positions for the Stooges to do their stuff."

On the set of the Columbia feature *Kansas City Kitty* (1944), director Del Lord reviews the script while comedienne Joan Davis peers quizzically over his shoulder.

But as with many veterans whose roots were in silent screen comedy, Lord was never comfortable with dialogue scenes (which always took a back seat to the visual humor in the Columbia shorts). A good sampling of his virtues and weaknesses can be found in *Free Rent* (Collins and Kennedy, 1936). The stunt work involving a house trailer is breathtaking, yet the pace falters whenever the actors open their mouths to speak. For all his filmmaking expertise, Lord was an unlettered man, which may explain, in part, his frequent inability to successfully handle verbal passages. "Del hadn't even finished grammar school," says Ed Bernds. "When I inherited his office when he went on to make features, I found these notes scribbled: *'Mabe'* — instead of *maybe* — 'Andy comes in . . .' Once, while outlining the action for a Three Stooges comedy, Del said, 'Curly comes in and *bunks* his head . . .' Of course, he meant *bumps.*" Fortunately for Lord, the majority of the comedians he worked with — The Three Stooges, Andy Clyde, Charley Chase — were adept at handling dialogue and required no coaching in this area.

Lord's best work for the unit was during the 1930s; his comedies from this period are generally inventive, distinguished by some surprisingly elaborate visual gags. *The Peppery Salt* (Andy Clyde, 1936) contains a spectacular gag involving Andy's oceanside diner getting nailed to the side of a ship; when the ship pulls out, it takes the diner along with it. Lord actually filmed this out on a pier, utilizing a real ship. "Those were the kind of things we could do back then," says Elwood Ullman, "but as time wore on, elaborate gag sequences were pretty much out of the question."

Increasing production costs eventually forced Lord to curtail the use of complex stunt sequences, his specialty. By the mid-1940s, his two-reelers took on a tired, assembly-line quality; the results were alarmingly pedestrian (albeit still competently made) efforts from a man who, under ideal circumstances, was the department's finest director.

Del's best Columbia shorts include *The Peppery Salt* (Andy Clyde, 1936), *The Big Squirt* (Charley Chase, 1937), *Pie a la Maid* (Charley Chase, 1938), *The Heckler* (Charley Chase, 1940), *Cold Turkey* (Harry Langdon, 1940), *Love at First Fright* (El Brendel, 1941), *Groom and Bored* (Johnny Downs, 1942), *One Shivery Night* (Hugh Herbert, 1950), and the Three Stooges comedies *Pop Goes the Easel* (1935), *Uncivil Warriors* (1935), *Hoi Polloi* (1935), *Three Little Beers* (1935), *False Alarms* (1936), *Dizzy Doctors* (1937), *Cash and Carry* (1937), *The Sitter Downers* (1937), *Termites of 1938* (1938), *A-Plumbing We Will Go* (1940), *How High Is Up?* (1940), *No Census, No Feeling* (1940) and *Shivering Sherlocks* (1948).

Preston Black (Jack White)

Jack White, Jules' older brother, was a major influence in motion picture comedy during the 1920s. As the head of Educational Pictures' "Mermaid Comedies," Jack was responsible for a series of Lloyd Hamilton shorts that were as well received by colleagues (the films were revered by Chaplin and Keaton) as they were by the public. In 1935 Jack came to work for Columbia in a varied position: to write, direct and help produce the comedy shorts. At the time, he was experiencing divorce problems; in order to "keep the lawyers from molesting me," he changed his screen name to Preston Black. Under this pseudonym, he directed a number of two-reelers, several with Andy Clyde and the Three Stooges.

His directorial style was a smooth blending of verbal and visual comedy; unlike his silent comedy peers, Jack was able to master the techniques of mixing dialogue routines with sight gags in a coherent fashion. Commenting on his abilities, Jack is quick to give credit to the comedians themselves:

> Andy Clyde took direction very well; he always had something good up his sleeve. As for the Stooges, they had a set way of working and you had to work their way. The three of them would go into a huddle and hold discussions. That was their stuff as far as I was concerned. My brother Jules might have helped them invent some of the things they did, but on the whole, I was glad to just finish the job.

White's modesty downplays the expert guidance he brought to the films. *Disorder in the Court* (1936), *A Pain in the Pullman* (1936), *Slippery Silks* (1936), *Grips, Grunts and Groans* (1937) and *Back to the Woods* (1937) are among the Stooges' (and White's) best comedies.

Jules White

Opinions are sharply divided on Jules White: to some, he was the department's best director; to others, he was the worst. Both schools of thought carry weight, as he was alternately responsible for some of the unit's finest and weakest films. The quality of his work fluctuates during almost any given period: it is not uncommon to find a couple of certifiable gems followed by a few undeniable clinkers. But Jules' best comedies require no apologies or explanations; they rank among the funniest shorts the unit ever made.

White was a former film editor and, possessing a keen visual sense, knew how to make a picture move at a sprightly tempo. Even his worst two-reelers race along at an astonishing pace, unequalled by any other director in the department. Says White, "My theory was to make those pictures move so fast that even if the gags didn't work, the audience wouldn't get bored. Some of my films may have been bad, but they sure weren't dull." His style has been championed in some circles as the model of efficient, compact direction.

One criticism continually leveled at Jules is his reliance on violent sight gags. While it is true that a number of the gags were too sadistic in nature to induce laughter—as in *Pardon My Backfire* (The Three Stooges, 1953) in which a probing wire enters Larry Fine's nostril and exits out through his ear—the simple fact is that many of the Columbia comedy shorts, *including* the non–White-directed efforts, are marred by excessively cruel comic violence and Jules, whose name is synonymous with the department, has received the brunt of the condemnation. Indeed, the single most violent gag in the unit's history—a climbing spike plunged into Moe Howard's eye—is not in a White short at all, but in Del Lord's *They Stooge to Conga* (The Three Stooges, 1943). Due to the nature of the physical humor in these pictures, writers and directors were faced with a number of aesthetic questions as they walked the thin line between comedy and brutality: Is a rap on the head with a hammer more violent than a kick in the stomach? At what point does a sock in the nose cease being funny? As far as White is concerned, all such discussions are pointless; this trademark brand of mayhem, an integral part of these comedies, was too exaggerated to be taken seriously:

> I patterned the characters—the Stooges in particular—as living caricatures. Analyze it and you'll find it's true. They weren't for real, so you couldn't take anything they did seriously, like the eye-poking or head-slapping bits. So how can anyone pick on this stuff and call it violent? I see more genuine violence in a single night of television viewing than in all my years making pictures.
>
> If we removed the knockabout aspect from these comedies, it would have taken away their appeal. Their flavor would be gone. Audiences loved to see this kind of humor and we always aimed to please. It's like with westerns: take away the cowboy's six-shooter and there's no gunplay; without gunplay, it's a lousy western. The same applies to slapstick comedy: no slapstick, no laughs.

On this point many agree, including Emil Sitka, who adds, "Perhaps it was a little too graphic at times, but we didn't mean to be offensive. We were just trying to get laughs."

As director, White exercised total control over every facet of the production: "I always added to the scripts while on the set. I would dictate the final shooting script; I was responsible for at least one-quarter of every script I directed."

One common recollection among White's coworkers focuses on his penchant for showing actors how to play a scene. "He used to act out everyone's part," recalls Richard Lane. "He didn't tell you what he wanted to see, he showed you. It really didn't make it easier for us; I think we humored him more than anything. He just loved to act." Eddie Quillan concurs, "You'd start to rehearse your scene and he'd be saying your lines. It would get to the point where we'd start kidding him good-naturedly, 'What are you sitting there for? Why don't you get up and let us sit there? After all, you're reading all the dialogue.'" Emil Oster, a camera operator during the 1930s and 1940s, remembers, "We used to say that if we turned the camera around and photographed Jules' reactions and instructions, it would be funnier than what was taking place out on the set."

Not everyone found amusement in this didactic manner of direction. "Jules was an abortive ham," comments one observer. "How could anyone have the audacity to show Buster Keaton or Harry Langdon how to do a scene? Imagine!" For all his offscreen histrionics, White expressed no desire to step in front of the camera. Says Richard Lane, "I asked him once why he didn't appear in these things himself and he said, 'Oh, no, not me. I've got a face like a horse and buggy.'"

White supervised every aspect of his films: writing, producing, directing—even the publicity stills. While other directors left the studio

A typically outlandish publicity shot conceived by Jules White. L. to r.: Esther Howard, Andy Clyde, Emmett Lynn; from *Wolf in Thief's Clothing* (1943).

photographers to their own devices, Jules would conduct the photo sessions himself. Emil Sitka recalls, "He dominated those sessions; the photographer just stayed back. Jules was fond of gagging up the photos—he'd say, 'Put *this* on your head, stick *this* in your ear . . .' You can always tell the photos he worked on—they're the ones that are really outlandish."

Despite his overbearing behavior, many found it an absolute joy to work with Jules. "Jules White was wonderful," says Richard Lane. "I loved working with him very much." To others, White's peccadillos were inexcusable. "Jules was a notoriously inefficient director," an associate remarked. "The shooting schedule for a two-reel comedy was four eight-hour days. With Jules it was four twelve-hour days." But there's no denying White's indefatigable dedication to the comic art. "I don't think there's anything about two-reel comedies that Jules doesn't know," says Eddie Quillan. "To do the things he did at Columbia—my gosh! He could do everything!"

White's attitude toward his work is best revealed in this anecdote by Richard Lane: "I once asked him, 'Don't you do anything else besides these little comedies?' I've never forgotten his answer: 'What else is there to do? As far as I'm concerned, every one of these pictures is *Gone with the Wind.*'"

Jules' best Columbia shorts include *The Nightshirt Bandit* (Charley

Chase, 1938), *Andy Clyde Gets Spring Chicken* (Andy Clyde, 1939), *Pardon. My Berth Marks* (Buster Keaton, 1940), *Money Squawks* (Andy Clyde, 1940), *Doctor, Feel My Pulse* (Vera Vague, 1944), *Bachelor Daze* (Slim Summerville, 1944), *A Fool and His Honey* (Vernon and Quillan, 1952), and the Three Stooges comedies *Three Sappy People* (1939), *Nutty But Nice* (1940), *From Nurse to Worse* (1940), *In the Sweet Pie and Pie* (1941), *Dizzy Pilots* (1943), *Hold That Lion* (1947), *Sing a Song of Six Pants* (1947), *I'm a Monkey's Uncle* (1948), *Dunked in the Deep* (1949), *Scrambled Brains* (1951), *Pest Man Wins* (1951), *Gypped in the Penthouse* (1955) and *Blunder Boys* (1955).

Charley Chase

Charley Chase's directorial efforts for the unit frequently suffer from attempts to squeeze overly (and needlessly) complex storylines into a two-reel running time. Even with slim plots, Chase had an annoying habit of dwelling too long on certain scenes, using up valuable time that would have been better spent trying to resolve a number of the plot entanglements. As a result, his films meander to unsatisfactory conclusions, often coming to abrupt halts after two reels have elapsed. Lacking the originality and wondrous comic invention of his earlier work, the Chase-directed Columbia shorts are strictly mechanical affairs (curiously, Chase never directed any of his own starring Columbia comedies). Although the department didn't (and, because of budgetary limitations, couldn't) provide him with the relaxed, impromptu atmosphere he had enjoyed at the Hal Roach Studios, the failure of these films can be largely attributed to Chase himself. The inexplicable haste in which he made these pictures gave them an uninspired, assembly-line look. Says one co-worker:

> The comedy shorts were shot on a schedule of four eight-hour days. With Charley, it was four six- or seven-hour days. I could never fully understand his method; he always seemed to be in a big rush, although no one was pressuring him. He'd shoot many of the scenes in a single take, even though he had the time for another one. Sometimes actors don't get the feel of a scene on the first take, regardless of how many times they've rehearsed, so it's up to the director to decide whether another take is necessary. Because of his rapid manner of direction, when you worked for Charley you knew you'd be going home early, but it was a sloppy way to make a picture.

This is not to imply that his Columbia shorts are completely without merit. Many individual sequences have enormous charm and compare favorably with his best work. His Three Stooges comedies *Tassels in the Air* (1938) and *Mutts to You* (1938) possess moments of subtlety and gentility unlike any other Columbia two-reelers. Chase would also compose an occasional novelty song, such as the delightful "Swingin' the Alphabet" from *Violent Is the Word for Curly* (The Three Stooges, 1938).

Harry Edwards

Harry Edwards holds the unenviable title of the department's worst director. Edwards' past record was impressive: a lengthy career in silent comedy, directing, among others, Ham and Bud (Lloyd Hamilton and Bud Duncan), Augustus Carney, Billy Bevan, Ben Turpin and Harry Langdon. But by the time he began working at Columbia, a bad drinking problem, coupled with an insecurity about his advanced years, resulted in disappointing and frequently disastrous pictures. Under Edwards' plodding guidance even short, simple comic bits like Andy Clyde getting tangled up in a backyard hammock (in *Heather and Yon*, 1944) became protracted and tedious.

Edwards' ineptitude wasn't tolerated by everyone. After only two shorts, *Matri-Phony* (1942) and *Three Little Twerps* (1943), the Three Stooges requested that they never work with him again (they never did). For the same reasons, Vera Vague took an immediate dislike to Edwards and asked to work exclusively with Jules White. Eventually, Edwards was fired; producer Hugh McCollum was dissatisfied with his work ("It's disgusting!" McCollum remarked about an Edwards-directed eating sequence that was deleted from the Harry Langdon–El Brendel short *Pistol Packin' Nitwits*) and, committing the cardinal sin, his pictures ran over budget. "That was the one thing the front office would whip producers for," says Ed Bernds. "They ignored short subjects producers as a rule, but if you went over budget, you'd hear from them."

Edward Bernds

Edward Bernds, Columbia's top sound mixer during the 1930s and early 1940s, began writing and directing comedy shorts in the mid-1940s. Instead of straying from established formulas, Bernds embellished his films with an acute sense of characterization and a more uniform plot structure. Says Bernds:

> I learned my craft from people I consider masters of the film art — people like Frank Capra, Leo McCarey and Howard Hawks. So I like to think that what I was able to learn from them made my pictures that much better.
>
> Both Hugh McCollum and I felt that just because we were making two-reelers that was no reason why we shouldn't give them strong storylines that came to logical conclusions. True, we were doing some crazy things, but you should still have a plot that comes full circle, without leaving any loose ends. Many of the other shorts I saw simply ended after two reels, without bothering to resolve any of the plot complications.
>
> Now when I see some of my pictures on television, the first five minutes are usually lopped off, rendering our stories senseless. Without the introductory scenes, you have no idea who the characters are or what's motivating them.

Another concern was toning down the gratuitous comic violence prevalent in so many of the comedy shorts:

> Now, sensitivity in two-reel comedies may sound ridiculous, but it's not. You could be believable within the context of being unbelievable. You should exercise a certain amount of taste; there are some things that are utterly tasteless. For instance, I never liked the Three Stooges' eye-poking bit and didn't ever use it. Before the very first picture I did with the boys, I talked to Moe about it; I expected an argument but there wasn't any. I think Moe had already come to the conclusion that this was too graphic, too cruel. We used to have a saying, "Nobody ever *really* gets hurt in a Stooge picture." If someone gets hit on the head with a sledge hammer, they'd just say "Ouch!" But the eye-poking bit was just too real and too dangerous. If one kid anywhere injured another kid's eyes because of this routine, I'd feel very badly about it. I guarantee you'll never see that bit in any of the Stooge shorts I directed.

Bernds' on-set directorial conduct was far less autocratic than that of his peers. Whereas Jules White supervised the actors to the *n*th degree, Bernds displayed a willingness to listen to the suggestions of the performers. Says Emil Sitka:

> I'll tell you the difference between Jules White and Ed Bernds. My first movie role was as a drunk in *Hiss and Yell* (1946), a Vera Vague short directed by Jules. When I got the script, it didn't say what kind of a drunk. Well, there's not just one kind of drunk; I figure there's about two dozen types. You may be a brooding drunk, a happy-go-lucky drunk, a talkative drunk, whatever. So, knowing from my stage experience, I started practicing every type of drunk I could think of.
>
> When I came on the set, I said, "Mr. White, I'm going to play the drunk in this picture. You know, there's about twenty-five different kinds of drunks and I've prepared myself . . ." "None of those; just wait for me," he said. Down the tubes went everything I prepared for so carefully. So when the time came for me to shoot my scene, Jules says, "Just do what I tell you." He makes faces, hiccups, shows me how to do a double-take and acts out my role every step of the way. To please him, I did it the way he did and it came out alright.
>
> After that, I got to work with Ed Bernds. I figured it was going to be more of the same. Then Ed asks me, "How are you going to do this part?" I said, "How am I going to do it? Jules White showed me every step!" Ed was very receptive to my suggestions and I was allowed to play my character the way I envisioned it. So every time I worked with them—and remember, I worked with both for years—I knew what to expect. With Jules White, I became like a puppet, prepared to have my strings pulled. With Ed Bernds, I had my idea of how my character should be played and he always liked the way I did it.

Director Edward Bernds (center) confers with Shemp Howard (left) and Tom Kennedy on the set of *Society Mugs* (1946).

Bernds was unique in that he gave actors the freedom to interpret their roles as they saw fit. In the case of the Three Stooges, he conferred with them on storylines. Says Bernds:

> I'm pretty sure I was the only director at the time who had story conferences with the boys. Moe was very helpful. He had a remarkable memory; he'd remember routines from his vaudeville days. He had a good sense of story construction; he knew what would fit into our premise and what wouldn't. Larry was the flaky one. He came up with a lot of ideas we couldn't use — they were so off-the-wall. But now and then he'd contribute something substantial. Curly didn't contribute much, but this may have been because he was quite ill by the time I was directing him. Shemp would reminisce about his early years on stage; once in a while he'd come up with something. But Shemp was more creative when the cameras were rolling; he was a brilliant ad-libber.

In Bernds' opinion, a director must be flexible enough to make the changes he feels will improve the picture, even if it's only a little two-reel short:

> When I was directing, I never stopped making changes in the script. Even on scripts I wrote, I frequently second-guessed myself and cut or changed dialogue or action. Much of a director's serious thinking about shooting a picture is done at night, when he's preparing the following day's work. He's in the swing of production then, has the feel of how the actors perform, and often rewrites or cuts dialogue at that time.
>
> Even two-reelers could be made better and funnier by spending a little more time trying to make a gag work better, shooting some extra angles so you had some editing flexibility. We often let routines run, in the hope of getting unrehearsed, spontaneous ad-lib comedy we could use. Because of this zany method, we confused the hell out of the script clerks, whose job it was to time the actual first cut of footage of the picture.
>
> But I was less inclined to improvise than many of my colleagues. I never understood the method some directors had of improvising gags from a loose shooting script. If you can't devise good material when you're writing the script—in the solitude of your own office—how can you do it while you're on the set, with all the pressures of film production working against you? Many of our gags required a great deal of planning: breakaway props, wire-belt rigging, the use of stunt doubles—all these things involved a lot of advance preparation. With our limited budgets and schedules, it was foolish to throw these sort of things into a picture at the last minute.

Bernds' comedies often eschew the disorganized, chaotic style favored by other directors. His *Scooper Dooper* (Sterling Holloway, 1946) is hardly one of the funniest Columbia shorts, but it miraculously manages to present plausible characters in a plot that moves at a logical progression—all within a two-reel running time. Occasionally, Bernds' attempts at credibility went a step too far. In *Crime on Their Hands* (The Three Stooges, 1949), there's an uncomfortably realistic murder at the beginning of the picture, and the film never recovers from it. And there are some Bernds comedies that spend far too much time on expository plotting, leaving little room for gags. But such miscalculations are few and, on the whole, the Bernds-directed shorts have a high batting average.

Ed's best Columbia shorts include *Wedding Belle* (Schilling and Lane, 1947), *Radio Romeo* (Harry Von Zell, 1947), *Two Nuts in a Rut* (Schilling and Lane, 1948), and the Three Stooges comedies *Micro-Phonies* (1945), *Three Little Pirates* (1946), *Fright Night* (1947), *Out West* (1947), *Brideless Groom* (1947), *Squareheads of the Round Table* (1948), *Who Done It?* (1949), *Fuelin' Around* (1949), *Vagabond Loafers* (1949), *Punchy Cowpunchers* (1950), *A Snitch in Time* (1950), *Three Arabian Nuts* (1951) and *Gents in a Jam* (1952).

Writers

Two-reel comedies, like TV comedy shows, burned up a terrific amount of material in a brief span of time, requiring a reliable staff of writers whose job it was to furnish a steady supply of gags. Columbia staff members included Andrew Bennison, Al Ray, John Grey, Ewart Adamson and Mauri Grashin. Comedian Monty Collins, who appeared in many of the shorts, frequently worked on the scripts, as did Jules White, Jack White, Zion Myers and Harry Edwards. "The short subjects department liked to use the same staff of writers because we were aware of the budgetary limitations," says Elwood Ullman. "Writers from the East would submit scripts, and there would be some good things in them, but they didn't have any conception of what kind of budgets we were working with. So they'd write these elaborate gags that were completely out of the question."

"We had marvelous writers," remarks Jules White. "People like Clyde Bruckman, Felix Adler and my brother Jack. You could give these fellows any subject and they'd come up with some brilliant material."

Clyde Bruckman

Though Clyde Bruckman is revered today, closer examination of his work raises a question as to whether he was ever the great comedy writer many film historians claim he was. Bruckman was fortunate enough to have been a member of Buster Keaton's writing staff in the 1920s; by his own admission, Bruckman's contributions to these films were minimal. Keaton was the driving force behind his pictures, and it was from his mind that most of the brilliant gags sprang; he relied on his writing staff primarily to furnish a story line or basic framework. Bruckman's collaboration with Keaton peaked with *The General* (1926), for which Bruckman served as codirector. It is generally agreed that Keaton directed all of his silent comedies and the others who received directorial credit merely took their cues from Buster. Such is the case with *The General*: at the time, Bruckman was trying to establish himself as a director, so Keaton graciously allowed his old friend to share in the directing credit. Bruckman went on to work with Harold Lloyd, Laurel and Hardy, and W.C. Fields, but the pattern was always the same: he worked with comedians who had a strong sense of their comic characters and they, more or less, directed themselves.

By the time Bruckman came to Columbia, his alcoholism was beginning to take its toll. He was barely able to function at times, and his scripts were chock-full of routines lifted from earlier comedies he had worked on. These routines were often gratuitously inserted into the storylines. "Bruckman's scripts were very sloppy," says Ed Bernds. "I would frequently have to revise his work, as there were so many unconnected pieces. Some of his scripts were totally incomprehensible." Bruckman wrote an Andy Clyde short titled *Andy Plays Hookey* (1946) that was merely a two-reel version of *The Man on the*

Flying Trapeze (1935), a W.C. Fields feature Bruckman had directed. Bruckman lifted a gag sequence, concerning a loosely-basted suit, from Harold Lloyd's *The Freshman* (1925) and reused it in *Three Smart Saps* (1942), a Three Stooges short. The climactic chase sequence he wrote for *Sock-A-Bye Baby* (The Three Stooges, 1942) is largely comprised of gags taken from Harold Lloyd's *Professor Beware* (1938).

And so it went, as Bruckman borrowed freely from earlier films, regardless of whether he had any legal or artistic claim to the material. This practice proved to be his undoing when he dusted off the magician's coat routine from Harold Lloyd's *Movie Crazy* (1932), which Bruckman had directed, and reused it — word for word — in the Three Stooges short *Loco Boy Makes Good* (1942). In 1946 Lloyd sued Columbia, seeking $500,000 in damages; when the court compared the *Movie Crazy* and *Loco Boy Makes Good* scripts, they were identical, and Lloyd won the case.

For all the comedies Bruckman either wrote or directed, there is no definite style or "typical Clyde Bruckman gag" one can point to as an example of his work. Not that he was completely without talent; no one who worked as long as he did could be. But he has been given prestige by association only: having collaborated with so many great comedians, he has basked in the spotlight of reflected glory. Bruckman may have been a competent gagster, but his own writing lacked the qualities that could be considered "great." Because he used the same routines over and over again, he has erroneously been given credit for their conception. The creative credit should instead go to the comedians with whom he collaborated, since they were the ones who devised most of "his" material.

Nonetheless, Bruckman does have a fair share of quality scripts to his credit, as several of his Three Stooges comedies — *Three Little Beers* (1935), *Three Sappy People* (1939), *From Nurse to Worse* (1940), *Dizzy Pilots* (1943), *Three Little Pirates* (1946), *Fright Night* (1947), *Out West* (1947), *Brideless Groom* (1947) — attest. But just how much of this quality can be attributed to Bruckman, as opposed to the contributions of others, is open to conjecture.

Felix Adler

Felix Adler had been a gag writer for Mack Sennett and Hal Roach prior to coming to Columbia. Adler concentrated more on gags and gag sequences than on stories and situations; the plots of Adler scripts are slim, often incoherent premises. But if he lacked finesse as a story constructionist, his gags compensated for the narrative flaws.

Adler's best work bursts with an ebullience that stemmed from the man himself. Says Emil Sitka, "Most of the comedy writers were reserved, laid-back types who rarely cracked a smile. But not Felix; he was always cheerful, always laughing. Sometimes when he was describing a gag sequence, he'd start laughing as he was telling it to you."

Like other veteran comedy writers, Adler frequently borrowed from his earlier work. Adler worked on several Laurel and Hardy pictures, and his later Columbia scripts reused a number of L & H routines, such as the crowded telephone booth sequence from *Our Relations* (1936) which was reworked in *Scrambled Brains* (The Three Stooges, 1951). Adler even took the storyline from *Way Out West* (1937) and rewrote it as a Max Baer–Maxie Rosenbloom short, *Rootin' Tootin' Tenderfeet* (1952).

Many of Adler's gags read much funnier than they played in the finished film. Jules White has the highest praise for Adler's talents: "If I made a bad picture from one of Felix's scripts, it wasn't his fault."

Among Adler's best—and most famous—screenplays are his Three Stooges comedies *Hoi Polloi* (1935), *Disorder in the Court* (1936), *Nutty But Nice* (1940), *Dizzy Detectives* (1942), *Hold That Lion* (1947), *Sing a Song of Six Pants* (1947), *Dunked in the Deep* (1949), *Scrambled Brains* (1951), *Pest Man Wins* (1951) and *Blunder Boys* (1955).

Elwood Ullman

Jules White hired Elwood Ullman in 1936. With a background that included writing humor for newspapers and magazines, Ullman was more story-oriented than most of his contemporaries. "Slapstick for the sake of slapstick isn't funny to me," he explains. "That's why I felt you had to have a solid story and good dialogue to punctuate the visuals."

Ullman's early scripts were written in collaboration with either Searle Kramer or Al Giebler. "Jules liked to team me up with Giebler, who was an old Mack Sennett hand. Al was an unfortunate man. He was a very good hand with visual comedy and dialogue, and had a certain amount of talent, but not enough to hit the big time. He'd been a literary roustabout all his life."

Working with the Columbia coterie helped Elwood to master the difficult art of writing visual comedy. "Charles Lamont, Del Lord, Harry Edwards, Charley Chase and Jules White taught me a lot about writing for two-reelers. And then, of course, there's my long association with Ed Bernds, who's still a very close friend." The Bernds-Ullman collaboration produced some of the unit's finest efforts, as both men brought characterization and story construction to the madcap antics.

On the subject of writing comedy, Elwood comments:

> Many's the time I paced up and down the lot, striving to come up with ideas. Miraculously, I kept coming up with them. I'd walk around the sets that were being built and get ideas about what kind of comedy we could shoot there.
>
> With "scare" comedies you had half the battle won. Just place a comedian in a spooky setting and it was easy to furnish gags for the situation. And they'd always get big laughs.
>
> I'd submit my ideas to Jules White and Hugh McCollum both verbally and written down on paper. If they liked the basic idea, they'd

give me an okay to elaborate and expand upon it. But the director is the one who fills out the gags; it's up to him to decide how they're going to look on film.

Among Elwood's best screenplays are *Cold Turkey* (Harry Langdon, 1940), *Love at First Fright* (El Brendel, 1941), *Wedding Belle* (Schilling and Lane, 1947), and the Three Stooges comedies *Termites of 1938*, *Tassels in the Air* (both 1938), *A-Plumbing We Will Go*, *How High Is Up?* (both 1940), *Shivering Sherlocks*, *The Hot Scots* (both 1948), *Fuelin' Around*, *Vagabond Loafers* (both 1949), *A Snitch in Time* (1950) and *Three Arabian Nuts* (1951).

Edward Bernds

Director Edward Bernds also scripted many of the two-reelers. Like his frequent collaborator Elwood Ullman, Bernds often got ideas from walking around the studio lot:

> I walked in on Stage Seven one day and saw this beautiful castle set they had built for a feature film [*The Bandit of Sherwood Forest*, 1946]. So I dragged Mac [Hugh McCollum] over and asked for an okay to do two scripts. He asked me if I could complete the pictures within a certain number of days; I said yes. When the production office granted permission to use the sets, we were off and running. I wrote one script, *Squareheads of the Round Table*, and Elwood wrote another, *The Hot Scots*. Both films, which I directed, starred the Three Stooges.

In time, all of the writers did remakes or reworkings of earlier Columbia shorts. Thus, *A Pain in the Pullman* (The Three Stooges, 1936) was remade as *Training for Trouble* (Schilling and Lane, 1947), *I'm a Father* (Andy Clyde, 1934) became *Oh, Baby!* (Hugh Herbert, 1944), *The Big Squirt* (Charley Chase, 1937) inspired *The Awful Sleuth* (Bert Wheeler, 1951) and so on. For those critical of this policy, Bernds explains:

> We'd often reuse and rework old material. We did it and we got away with it. No one—exhibitor, Columbia brass, or even viewers—ever called us on it. Our doing so was neither illegal or unethical. Until 1960 Columbia owned everything any writer or director did, in perpetuity. Therefore, old scripts were mine to borrow from if I chose to. McCollum encouraged me to do this. If I was stuck on a story, he'd often recall a routine or story device that would unstick me. A routine is a routine and some date back to the Dark Ages of film. We'd take a routine and rework it or get an idea from it. If you think a cat has nine lives, just take a look at comedy routines! For example, the man who's eating a bowl of oyster stew and an oyster comes up and takes his cracker—I don't know how many times *that* bit has been used.
>
> But you must remember that these pictures were meant to be seen weeks, months, even years apart from one another. You've got to look at it from that perspective. Only through constant television reruns has this repetition become apparent.

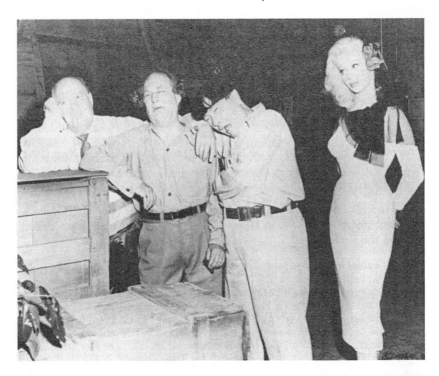

Many of the later Stooge Shorts were remakes of earlier films. The scene above is from *Sappy Bull Fighters* (1959), which was a remake of a 1942 short, *What's the Matador?* L. to r.: Joe Besser, Larry Fine, Moe Howard, Greta Thyssen.

The Shooting Script: Final Draft

For those who think that movie comedians merely stood in front of the cameras and ad-libbed their way through an entire picture, it may come as quite a shock to learn how detailed the shooting scripts actually were. Here's the famous "Maharaja" sequence from the final draft (dated April 4, 1946) of *Three Little Pirates* (Columbia Production No. 4067), a Three Stooges comedy written by Clyde Bruckman and revised by Edward Bernds. (This sequence employs a variation of a routine that was a staple of the Three Stooges' stage act for years. Ed Bernds remembers that Moe Howard dictated the routine to scriptwriter Clyde Bruckman.)

The Stooges, shipwrecked and imprisoned on Dead Man's Island, try to make their escape by posing as wayfarers bearing valuable gifts for the Governor (Vernon Dent). As part of his disguise, Curly is wearing extremely thick-lensed glasses, making it impossible for him to see clearly. Rita (Christine McIntyre), the Governor's unwilling bride-to-be, plans to flee with the boys and helps them with their masquerade.

The Three Stooges (Moe Howard, Curly Howard, Larry Fine) in costume for the "Maharaja" routine from *Three Little Pirates* (1946).

Scene No.
27   *MEDIUM LONG SHOT MAIN ROOM*
As Stooges and Rita cross and pause in front of the Governor.
28   *MED. SHOT GROUP*

RITA: *(she bows to Governor)* Your Excellency, these men bring rare gifts for you. Allow me to present the . . . Maharaja of . . .

MOE: *(interrupting)* Of Canarsie. *(indicates Curly)*

Curly acknowledges the introduction by going through a series of gestures, winding up with a rap under Moe's chin.

RITA: *(indicating Moe)* . . . and this is his interpreter . . .

LARRY: *(interrupting)* The Gin of Rummy.

MOE: *(indicating Larry)* And we mustn't forget our valet, Rudy.

Larry starts a series of gestures, but before he can complete his maneuvers, Moe bops him.

LARRY: *(plaintively)* What was that for?

MOE: Just in case.

GOVERNOR: Can we dispense with the formalities and make with the gifts?

MOE: *(to Curly)* Sit down!

Curly tries to locate a chair, bumps into it, looks down, picks it up, holds it close to his eyes, puts it back on the floor, turns around and sits down on the floor. Moe runs over, helps Curly to his feet and places him on the chair. (Note: next to Curly's chair is a small occasional table and another chair.)

GOVERNOR: *(to Moe)* What priceless gifts does the Rajah bring?

MOE: We shall see.

Moe crosses to Curly, sits down.

MOE: *(to Curly)* Ma hah.

CURLY: Ah hah.

MOE: Razbanyas yatee benee futch ah tinney herongha dot pickle head askee taskee wateecha fertzieek you goddit.

CURLY: Nyothing.

MOE: Nyothing?

CURLY: Tah!

MOE: *(rising)* Oh, boy!

Moe turns to Governor.

MOE: The Ma hah . . .

Curly jumps from his chair facing the opposite direction from where the conversation is coming.

CURLY: Ah hah, yatee benee futch ah . . .

MOE: *(interrupting)* Quiet! *(to Governor)* The Rajah says that he bears, as a gift for you, a rare and beautiful jewel. It is known as the . . .

Moe, fishing for words, looks around at Curly, who has taken a lollypop from his pocket and is just removing the cellophane as he prepares to eat it. The Governor, seeing the lollypop:

GOVERNOR: A ruby — a ruby as large as a turkey's egg.

He steps over and takes the lollypop from Curly's hand and stands admiring it.

MOE: *(thinking fast)* Why yes — a rare gem — the ruby of lollypopski . . .

CURLY: *(interrupting)* Raspberry!

GOVERNOR: What fire! I have many pigeon blood rubies, but never have I been given the raspberry!

The Governor sticks the lollypop in with the rest of the jeweled ornaments on his chest, then turns back to Moe with anticipation.

GOVERNOR: What other rarity does the Rajah have for me?

MOE: He had some bubble gum, but he swallowed it. We shall see what we shall see.

Moe crosses to Curly and sits down next to him.

MOE: Ma hah.

CURLY: Ah hah.

MOE: Razbanyas yatee benee futch ah tinney harongha that frog head askee taskee wateecha fertziok you got it something else you got it buddy.

CURLY: Rasbanyas, etc. I shall see.

Curly takes a fountain pen from his breast pocket with his left hand and then starts fishing in the pocket with his right hand. The Governor suddenly spots the fountain pen held by Curly.

GOVERNOR: Ah, the tusk of a black walrus.

MOE: Guaranteed forever.

The Governor takes the pen from Moe's hand and starts examining it eagerly.

29 *MED. SHOT GROUP*
The Governor places the pen on the table. He rubs his hands with anticipation.

GOVERNOR: *(to Moe)* Ask the Ma hah . . .

Curly jumps up from his seat.

CURLY: *(interrupting)* Ah hah razbanyas, etc.

MOE: *(to Curly)* Sit down!

Moe cuts him short by bopping him, then turns back to the Governor. Curly leans elbow on table—flips. Larry helps him up—bends him over—chair—etc.

GOVERNOR: *(calls Moe close)* Are there fair damsels in the Rajah's domain?

MOE: Aha—damsels. *(he winks at the Governor)* We shall see.

Moe crosses to Curly and sits down.

MOE: Mah hah.

CURLY: Ah hah.

MOE: Razbanyas yatee benee futch ah tinney harongha that ironhead askee taskee wateecha fertziok you got it some slick chicks.

CURLY: Oh, a wolf!

Moe cracks Curly and Curly yells.

CURLY: Oooow!! Razbanyas yatee benee futch ah tinney harongha padee rickman heehah I'd like to see some babes myself.

MOE: Me too—ixnay!

Moe bops him, gets up and crosses to the Governor.

MOE: The Ma hah . . .

Curly jumps up.

CURLY: *(interrupting)* Ah hah yatee benee . . .

MOE: *(interrupting)* Sit down you Flatbush flathead!

Curly sits down and Moe turns back to the Governor.

MOE: *(to Governor)* The Rajah says that in his domain, on the tropical isles of Coney and Long, there are droves of lovely chickadees! If you give us till sundown we'll bring you some samples by sunup.

GOVERNOR: Excellent! Excellent! Be on your way with winged feet.

Moe and Larry start for the archway leading to entrance hall, while Curly heads off in another direction and does a header over a chair. Moe rushes to him.

30 *MED. CLOSE SHOT MOE AND CURLY*
Moe leans over Curly.

CURLY: *(mutters)* Razbanyas yatee benee futch ah I fall down.

Moe yanks Curly to his feet.

MOE: Pick up your winged feet and let's get going!

Moe grabs him by the ear and drags him out of scene, Curly at the same time feeling with his hands like a blind man.

If you're familiar with this sequence as it appears in the completed picture, you'll detect slight differences in the filmed version, although the action still remains remarkably faithful to the final draft. That the action is so carefully mapped out doesn't denigrate the performers; on the contrary, it is to their everlasting credit that they can make this prepared material seem spontaneous.

Editing

To a movie comedy, in which timing is everything, editing is particularly crucial. Takes that are cut too short, allowed to run on too long, or appear at inappropriate moments can undermine even the funniest material. "Every director makes mistakes," says Ed Bernds, "and often they can be corrected in the editing room. You cut for tempo; two-reelers *must* move." The Columbia comedy shorts were handled by staff editors, who generally treated these efforts as just another assignment. The lack of concern is understandable; they were hardly prestige pictures, so why give them preferential treatment? Even so, some of the best Columbia shorts are marred by a startling degree of technical sloppiness.

Jules White supervised the editing of the two-reelers he directed. White, a former film editor, knew how to pace a comedy, right down to a single frame, so it isn't surprising that his efforts contain the best editing techniques. Jules had learned his editing skills from Charles Hochberg, who was an editor for Jack White at Educational Pictures. It turned out to be a case of the student surpassing the teacher, as Hochberg wound up at Columbia during the 1930s and 1940s, editing several of Jules' comedies.

But though most of the editors were competent, they weren't top-notch. An associate rates a few of them:

> Paul Borofsky wasn't a very sharp editor; he hurt a number of good two-reelers. Edwin Bryant and Hank Demond were better; I'd say they were probably the best. Hugh McCollum wasn't as good an editor as he was a producer. Henry Batista was very opinionated; he wanted to do everything by the book, which often led to arguments.

Sound Effects

Sound effects were an integral part of the Columbia comedy shorts, as they helped to soften the potentially painful aspects of the physical humor while adding a properly outrageous touch. Edward Bernds recalls:

> Joe Henrie was our sound effects man. He instinctively knew where to put the sound effects. He was our best audience, particularly where the Three Stooges were concerned. I'd go by his cutting room and hear him laughing. The fact that he was laughing at a scene just by watching it on a moviola shows you how much he loved it.

Henrie loved the Stooge comedies so much that he usually reserved them for himself. However, by the mid-1940s, Henrie became busy with other assignments, and Morrie Opper did all of the two-reelers exclusively.

Jules White's whistling provided the "bird chirps" heard whenever a character was knocked unconscious. White's voice was frequently heard offscreen in several shorts, usually as a radio announcer, as in *Sing a Song of Six Pants* (The Three Stooges, 1947) in which he delivers a commercial for *"No Burp-o-line*, the only gasoline with bicarbonate of soda."

The "eye-poking" sound was two plunks of a ukelele or violin recorded a frame or two apart. The crack of a whip supplied the sound for face slaps. A kettledrum would make a kick in the stomach seem less brutal — and sound much funnier. The "hollow head" effect was made by striking a wooden tempo block. Various ratchets were used when ears or limbs were twisted. Cracking walnuts furnished the sound for knuckles being crunched. The sound of hair getting yanked out was made by tearing a piece of cloth. The "nose honk" was produced by a rubber squeeze-bulb horn, which had an infectious, laugh-provoking effect. The "drinking" sound, used when someone swallowed the entire contents of a glass or pitcher in a single gulp, was accomplished by pouring water out of a one-gallon glass bottle. When a character took a swig of a potent beverage (almost always alcoholic in nature), auto horns, bells, and other resonant noises was heard on the soundtrack.

Many of these sound effects were first recorded for use in the Walter Catlett short *Get Along Little Hubby* (1934). On the rerecording stage, Sam Briskin, the studio's production chief, saw them mixing a reel with these sound effects and stopped the session. Briskin and Jules White then stepped outside and "had a few choice words about each other's ancestors." Jules insisted that the comedies needed the cartoon quality of the sound effects to punctuate the visuals, and said he would abide by whatever reaction they received at the preview. Needless to say, the audience response proved that Jules was right, and from then on the sound effects were a key ingredient.

Stunts . . . and Injuries

Due to the roughhouse nature of these pictures, doubles were required for most contract comedians. Johnny Kascier, who appeared in many two-reelers as a tray-carrying waiter who is invariably knocked down, was a frequent stand-in for Moe Howard and doubled for all of the Stooges from time to time. Al Thompson, also featured in supporting roles, doubled for Andy Clyde. Nevertheless, studio stuntmen were required for some of the more arduous action scenes. Edward Bernds explains:

> The stuntmen loved our department. We weren't allotted the budgets of 'A' pictures naturally, so they'd charge us lower rates. But they always gave their all. In *Punchy Cowpunchers* (The Three Stooges, 1950) Christine McIntyre is cowering at the sight of these burly western villains, only to clobber them, one by one, moments later. There's some wonderful stunt work in those scenes. I should explain that in films with a great deal of rough stuff — in the case of *Flat Feat* (Sterling Holloway, 1948), a four-man free-for-all — we hired actors who did their own fights and stunts. It was impractical to double all the supporting players, so we sometimes sacrificed acting ability for the advantage of having actors who could (and would) do their own rough stuff.

Ex-pugilists Cy Schindell and Wally Rose, usually cast as comic heavies, frequently took their lumps for the sake of laughter. Jacques O'Mahoney, later known as Jock Mahoney, was a skilled stuntman featured in several Three Stooges shorts that required him to execute truly breathtaking pratfalls.

Al Thompson (center) and Johnny Kascier (right) doubled for many of the Columbia comedians and played supporting roles in the two-reelers as well. Here they're seen with Harry Langdon in a scene from *Mopey Dope* (1944).

With Emil Sitka, the unit was blessed with a superb comic actor who could perform his own stunts. Emil recalls:

> In *Honeymoon Blues* (Hugh Herbert, 1946) I did a part where I had no dialogue but I appeared all through the picture. They had a stuntman dressed like me who took a fall down some stairs. Technically, he did everything right, but it wasn't funny. Just slipping on a banana peel isn't always a surefire laugh. If you slip and it looks like you got hurt, the audience gasps instead. When the scene was done, the director, Ed Bernds, couldn't find fault with it, but he wasn't satisfied either. I asked Ed, "Does he have to do that? Couldn't I do it myself?" "You mean you would?" he asked. "Sure," I told him, it's only ten stairs." That started it. I did it—*BANG!*—the crew roared, laughed and gave me a big hand. From that point on, I did my own stunts.

Despite the expertise of the stunt people and the special effects department, there was still a fair share of mishaps that ocurred during production. Noah Beery, Jr., suffered a broken nose during the filming of *Glove Slingers* (1939), a boxing comedy. While crashing through a breakaway door in *Who Done It?* (The Three Stooges, 1949), Moe Howard injured his shin and ankle but insisted on completing the picture on schedule. Moe can be seen limping pronouncedly throughout the final scenes. For *Three Troubledoers* (The Three Stooges, 1946), a bazooka gun backfires and shoots soot into Moe's face. Ed Bernds remembers, "The special effects man used too much air pressure, so some of the soot shot up under Moe's eyelids. They had to pry his eyes open and remove these big chunks of black powder from his eyes. I was terrified; I thought the poor guy had been blinded."

In *Heavenly Daze* (The Three Stooges, 1948), Moe and Larry invent a fountain pen that writes under whipped cream. In one scene, the pen gets dislodged from a cake mixer, sails through the air and impales Larry right in the middle of his forehead. The pen, suspended on a wire, was to land on a small metal washer fastened to Larry's forehead. While preparing for the scene, he asked director Jules White to have the hole in the washer filled with cork to blunt the impact of the pen's sharp point. Larry was assured that such a precaution was unnecessary and that there was nothing to worry about. But when the scene was shot, the pen pierced his skin, and when he removed it, ink and blood came spilling out of the wound. So when you see Larry screaming in pain, he isn't acting.

The Stooges' hair-pulling bit remains one of their trademark gags. Clusters of fake hair strands were combed into an actor's real follicles, but according to Emil Sitka, "They still managed to get some of your real hair regardless of how careful they were."

In *Billie Gets Her Man* (Billie Burke, 1948) the script called for Sitka to be on the receiving end of a breakaway vase. The vase landed squarely on the bridge of his nose, resulting in a broken nose and facial cuts. Emil comments, "I also cracked one of my vertebrae during the filming of that picture and I didn't learn about it until four or five years later! But you must realize that all of us looked upon these injuries as occupational hazards. With the kind of comedy we were doing, you had to expect to get knocked around now and then. Just so long as you made it *look* funny."

As for special effects, Ray Hunt deserves special mention for his contributions. Says Ed Bernds:

> Ray Hunt was the propman who worked on all of the two-reelers. He was a wizard at special effects, supplying us with breakaway props, wire-belt rigging—and he was a great pie thrower. He had his own recipe for pies, which included the use of shaving cream instead of whipped cream because it didn't stain like whipped cream did. Ray was a very valuable man; we were all indebted to him.

Previews

Up until the early 1950s, the Columbia comedy shorts were previewed. "You never know for sure whether a gag is going to go over with an audience," says Ed Bernds. "That's why it was so important to preview the pictures."

The previews took place in and around the Los Angeles area: Glendale, Inglewood, Santa Monica, Compton and Huntington Park. In the early days of sound films, Jack White designed a device that measured audience response at previews; it was this device that Columbia used. A recorder would pick up the audience laughter, while an "off mike" picked up dialogue from the screen. Afterwards, the preview track was run with the picture, and where they didn't get the anticipated laughs, it was recut according to this audience guide track. On occasion, some scenes were even reshot. It was the audience response that decided what was cut, padded or retained.

In one instance, a preview resulted in an *additional* two-reeler. Ed Bernds explains:

> I wrote and directed a Three Stooges short titled *Merry Mavericks* (filmed in 1950, released 1951). There was a dentistry routine in the picture that ran long, but it was previewed that way. Well, that routine got such a great response, Hugh McCollum didn't want to trim any of it. There was no way we could have it in as is, so we just removed it and built another premise around it. It took two days to shoot some additional footage, and the result was another Stooge short, *The Tooth Will Out*. By doing this, we were even able to save a little money.

Theme Songs

The majority of the theme songs used for the opening credits (incidental music was rarely employed) were stock themes, nondescript and interchangeable. "Merrily We Roll Along" was used for most of the contract comedians (Keaton, Langdon, Vera Vague, Schilling and Lane, Vernon and Quillan, etc.). "The Man on the Parallel Bars," a composition sung by Leon Errol in *Perfectly Mismated* (1934), turned up in the credits of a few shorts. "For He's a Jolly Good Fellow" was used to open many of the Charley Chase comedies; when Hugh Herbert began starring in two-reelers for the unit, it was adopted as his theme song. Andy Clyde's most frequent theme song began with strains of "Turkey in the Straw," leading into a lively rendition of "Reuben and Rachel."

The choice of "Three Blind Mice" for the Three Stooges was the unit's most inspired musical selection. Many of the early Stooge shorts opened with the second chorus of "Listen to the Mocking Bird." Then, in 1939, "Three Blind Mice" was chosen, and it quickly became their signature tune.

Casting

Jules White made nearly all the decisions about hiring performers (on rare occasion, the front office would hire comedians — as in the case of Smith and Dale — then assign them to the short subjects department). When Hugh McCollum began sharing production chores, he was consulted in all such matters, but it was White who still had the final word. Emil Sitka recalls his first meeting with White:

I was in *The Viper's Fang*, a play that ran for quite a while all around Southern California. On the very last day, when we were ready to close up the show, someone from Columbia spotted me and wanted me to report to Jules White. I didn't have any other prospects lined up, so I just walked in casually one day and informed the girl at the front desk that I was told to come see Mr. White. When I got to see him, he was busy talking on the phone: "Yeah, I've got to strike that set . . . Who are you? . . . Just a minute, hold on . . ." I'm standing there and he's talking for quite a while, even after the girl let me into his office. He was the busiest guy I ever saw.

Finally he has a minute for me. He puts his cigar down and says, "So you're Emil Sitka, right? Well, you've been referred to me as someone who's very funny. Do something."

"What do you mean 'Do something?' "

"Do something funny. Make me laugh," he said impatiently.

I said, "Mr. White, I'm sorry but I'm not a stand-up comedian. I do a part in a play."

"Okay," he said, "I'll come see it. Tell me when."

I hated to tell him this, but I said, "It's over, it's closed." Boy, everything was wrong.

"Closed? Then tell me when your next play is. You're going to be in another play, aren't you?"

"Yes, but I don't know when. Maybe three months from now."

"Jesus, man . . . well, wait a minute." He went back to answering the phone: "Yeah, Joe, I want that done . . . no, I don't like that at all . . ."

While he's on the phone, he opens his desk drawer and starts looking through some old scripts. He pulls out an old, battered Charley Chase script. It was so badly marked up, I couldn't read it; lines of dialogue were penciled out or written over. He found a scene and added his own pencil marks.

"Look that over for five minutes and then read it to me."

It was hard to figure out at first, but I managed to get the gist of it. After I did the scene for him, he pushed a button and Hugh McCollum came into the office. They both watched me do the scene again and then said, "You'll hear from us." Soon after, I received a call to appear in my first movie, a Vera Vague short titled *Hiss and Yell*. It was the beginning of my long association with the comedy shorts department.

While it may have been a bit rough for Emil, a skilled and versatile per-

Danny Lewis (far right), Jerry's father, couldn't seem to get the hang of the climactic gag sequence in *Three Hams on Rye* (The Three Stooges, 1950). Also pictured (l. to r.): Brian O'Hara, Shemp Howard, Moe Howard, Christine McIntyre, and Larry Fine.

former, to prove his mettle without the benefit of any previous movie credits, others signed by White had no such difficulties. Most, like Buster Keaton, Harry Langdon and Charley Chase, had had long careers in motion pictures prior to their Columbia efforts; White admired their work tremendously and jumped at the chance to hire them.

Now and then, there would be a judgmental error in hiring a performer. In 1950, when Jerry Lewis skyrocketed to fame and fortune with his partner Dean Martin, Jules hired Jerry's father, Danny Lewis, for a supporting role in a Three Stooges short, *Three Hams on Rye*. In the film's climactic sequence, the Stooges, Lewis, and Brian O'Hara are actors performing in a stage play, *The Bride Wore Spurs*. As part of the plot, the men begin to eat a triple-layer cake, unaware that a potholder was accidentally mixed into it; soon they start to cough up feathers. To shoot this sequence, the actors were required to put real feathers in their mouths and then start coughing them up when the camera began rolling. But Jules had trouble getting Lewis to perform the scene properly; instead of coughing up the feathers, he kept swallowing them. It was eventually decided that the elder Lewis, who was also a nightclub entertainer, possessed little of his famous son's timing or talent.

"Those comedies were a delight to do," says Richard Lane. "I don't think anyone ever turned them down when they were offered." Not exactly. While nearly everyone whom Jules approached did consent to work in two-reelers (many were not in a position to refuse, as their careers were at a low ebb), there was one noteworthy exception. In the mid-1940s, White happened to see a new young comedian named Danny Thomas performing at a Los Angeles nightclub. Jules enjoyed Thomas' act and thought he would make a nice addition to the Columbia roster. When he contacted Thomas' manager, White was informed that Danny was being groomed for "bigger things," and those plans didn't include a series of comedy shorts.

In one instance, it was White himself who nixed a potential series. He recalls:

> Henry Armetta specialized in playing comic Italians. He was frequently cast in films as a barber. Well, I knew Armetta when he really was a barber. He was friendly, gregarious and comical and was able to secure movie work as a supporting player.
>
> After he had achieved some measure of success, I met with him in my office one day, with the intention of signing him to a starring series. But the fellow who walked into my office was no longer Henry Armetta, the barber—he was Henry Armetta, *the star*! He looked me straight in the eye and demanded, "I want the right to choose my directors, my writers and my costars." I looked right back at him and said, "Choose your way out." I wanted professionals, not prima donnas.

Pay Scale

Most contract comedians appearing in their own starring series (Vera Vague, Sterling Holloway, Harry Von Zell) were paid the flat sum of $500 per short. However, there were exceptions. When Buster Keaton was signed to a series, it was considered quite a boon to the department, and his salary per short was $1000. Likewise, Harry Langdon started at $1000 per subject, a salary that was later raised to $1250.

The Three Stooges were paid $1000 (for the team) for their first Columbia short, *Woman Haters* (1934). Once their contract had been approved by the studio, the salary was increased to $7500 (divided equally) per short. Yet, despite the growing popularity of the trio, they were never again given a pay hike.

For players who had prominent supporting roles in the films (Christine McIntyre, Vernon Dent, Bud Jamison, Emil Sitka) the pay scale ranged from

$75 to $100 per day. Players who had smaller roles (Cy Schindell, Joe Palma) were paid $55 per day. The two-reelers were shot on a four-day schedule, although the services of these actors weren't always required for all four days.

In the 1930s, extras were paid $8 a day—$22 if they had a line of dialogue. By the mid-1940s, the wages for extras ranged from $16.50 to $35.

As a writer and director, Ed Bernds comments on his salary:

> I never asked for a raise. Mac (Hugh McCollum) saw to it that I got pay increases. My starting wages were around $500 per script and $500 per short I directed. By the time I left Columbia (1952), it was up to $850 per script and $900 for directing.

Behind the Scenes

Recognition is also due the following behind-the-scenes personnel:

Assistant Directors: Jerrold Bernstein, Carter DeHaven, Jr., Gilbert Kay, Irving Moore, Sam Nelson, James Nicholson, Eddie Saeta, Willard Sheldon, Abner Singer.

Directors of Photography: Gert Andersen, Lucien Ballard, Andre Barlatier, Fayte Browne, Ray Cory, Vincent Farrar, Henry Freulich, Glen Gano, Fred Jackman, George Kelly, Benjamin Kline, Irving Lippman, George Meehan, L.W. O'Connell, George Rhein, Allen G. Siegler, John Stumar, Philip Tannura, Rex Wimpy.

Script Girls: Josephine Aleman, Dorothy Cumming, Tessie Wise.

Art Directors: Carl Anderson, Ross Bellah, George Brooks, Charles Clague, Victor Greene, Walter Holscher, Edward Ilou, Cary Odell, Paul Palmentola, Robert Peterson.

To these and other creative talents we have failed to mention, we offer our gratitude for their contributions to these films.

The Series

The Columbia comedy shorts have long been accused of degenerating the art of Mack Sennett. But in truth, they carried on the Sennett tradition of freewheeling, nonstop slapstick — with the same virtues and faults inherent in Sennett's work. To its credit, the Columbia unit rounded up an expert group of comic practitioners, many of whom had worked for Sennett and Hal Roach, and provided them with an atmosphere in which to create pure comedy. On the debit side, the resulting pictures — generally speaking — had a one-dimensional, sledgehammer approach to comedy. Like Sennett's, the comedians at Columbia weren't afforded much opportunity to stray from tried-and-true formulas. Rapid pace and a quick succession of gags had top priority, even if it meant sacrificing characterization and plot structure. When this formula succeeded — and it frequently did — the results could be glorious. This slam-bang, no-frills style was a perfect match for the wacky, uninhibited shenanigans of the Three Stooges, who were responsible for some of the unit's best efforts.

But comedians like Buster Keaton and Harry Langdon, whose humor stemmed from a completely different set of ground rules, were woefully out of place. Their uniqueness worked against them; their distinctive personalities were lost in a myriad of mechanical gags and cardboard storylines. Comics with limited emotional depth were able to adapt better. Hence, it comes as no surprise that Harry Von Zell's Columbia shorts are, on the whole, more entertaining than Buster Keaton's.

The unit repeatedly tried to develop its own comedy team (teams such as the Three Stooges and Smith & Dale were already formed by the time they were signed by Columbia). Among the combinations conceived were Monte Collins & Tom Kennedy, Tom Kennedy & Johnny Arthur, Buster Keaton & Elsie Ames, Harry Langdon & Elsie Ames, Una Merkel & Harry Langdon, El Brendel & Shemp Howard, Harry Langdon & El Brendel, Shemp Howard & Tom Kennedy, Gus Schilling & Richard Lane, Wally Vernon & Eddie Quillan, and Max Baer & Maxie Rosenbloom. The constant shuffling and reshuffling of the roster (at one point, the unit tried teaming Monte Collins with nearly every solo comedian under contract) indicates a cavalier attitude towards the performers, as though individualism didn't matter at all and any pair was interchangeable. Very few of these couplings paid off; most of the resulting comedies were just as contrived as the partnerships (a notable exception was Schilling & Lane, the only one of these teams to rival the Three Stooges in terms of performance, compatibility, and gag content).

And yet, even the worst Columbia shorts served a purpose: upholding the grand tradition of slapstick, especially during those years when other filmmakers had abandoned it. In their day, the comedies were wholeheartedly embraced by moviegoers as nostalgic throwbacks to "good old-fashioned slapstick." So it may be unduly harsh to criticize these two-reelers from a perspective that's three to five decades removed. They filled a need and were successful because they did; that many of them don't hold up today doesn't change what they meant to audiences then.

Below, all series comprised of six or more entries are discussed chronologically, in accordance with the release date of the first entry. Series consisting of two or four entries are covered in "Mini-Series." Solitary efforts are covered in "Single Entries."

Even though many of these films are remakes of earlier comedies produced by Mack Sennett, Hal Roach and others, we have identified as remakes only those which are remakes or reworkings of other Columbia shorts. Since the Columbia shorts reused so many time-honored gags and situations, it would be impossible to compile a comprehensive listing of *all* such credits.

"Musical Novelties"

The first "official" Columbia two-reelers were a series of musical comedy shorts. The series was the brainchild of director-songwriter Archie Gottler, who made eight of the nine shorts produced. Some entries, like *Um-Pa* (1933) and *Woman Haters* (1934), were done completely in rhyming dialogue. Edward Bernds, a sound mixer at the time, remembers the difficulty in recording these films:

> It was a very hard technique, done in low playback. First, we would record the music for a short, then on the set we would play back the music at low volume. The dialogue wasn't sung—instead we called it "patter." It was difficult for a sound man because you had to keep the volume of the playback low, or else the fidelity of the recording wouldn't be reproduced properly on the soundtrack. Then you'd dub the full orchestration onto the track in synch with the recitation.

The shorts showcased the talents of Arthur Jarrett, Frank Albertson, Lou Holtz, The Three Stooges (then known as "Howard, Fine and Howard") and two up-and-coming young starlets, Betty Grable and Lois January. Miss January, who starred in four of these productions, recalls the films with a great deal of fondness:

Lois January and Jack Osterman in *Um-Pa* (1933), the first "official" Columbia comedy short.

> I was under contract to Universal at the time, and they loaned me out to Columbia for these little muscial comedies. I was happy because the shorts gave me the chance to sing in pictures; I had never had the opportunity before. And I liked working for Columbia to begin with. I knew Jules White just slightly, but I grew to know him well. I liked him so much.
>
> We'd shoot about five days on these musical shorts, although a few were shot in three days. Usually a musical took longer because you had to learn the lyrics and the dance steps. It was a challenge to me; I was young, new in the business, and I wanted to sing. The actors—Lou Holtz I adored, Frankie Albertson was a joy. I recall Jules' co-workers, Zion Myers, whom I didn't know too well, and Archie Gottler. I knew Archie particularly because he wrote the songs and I performed some of them. He was a cute little man, just a dear person.

These films were well made and often handsomely mounted, but the format was quickly abandoned; these pictures weren't particularly well received, and the unit decided to devote its energies to producing straight comedy fare.

Of all the musical novelties, only *Woman Haters* (1934), which is part of the Three Stooges TV package, is currently in circulation. Columbia has deemed the other titles too obscure (i.e. no foreseeable profits) to warrant new prints struck up for television and rental markets. So it's open to conjecture as to whether they're curios or minor masterpieces awaiting rediscovery. Either way, they're noteworthy for being the earliest efforts of what would become a most prolific comedy shorts unit.

The "Musical Novelties" Series

The films are listed in order of release (*Um-Pa* was the first short produced, although *Roamin' Thru the Roses* was the first one issued). The director's name (D) follows the release date; the cast listing follows the director's credit.

Roamin' Thru the Roses (11/11/33) D: Archie Gottler. Arthur Jarrett, Margaret Nearing, Neeley Edwards, Carol Wines, Bobby Watson. Musical short showcasing Jarrett and Nearing.

Um-Pa (11/24/33) D: Archie Gottler. Jack Osterman, Lois January, Gloria Shea, Gus Reed. Musical nonsense about a patient (Osterman), his two nurses (January, Shea) and an "um-pa" bird.

School for Romance (1/31/34) D: Archie Gottler. Lou Holtz, Lois January, Billie Seward, Gloria Warner, Carol Tevis. Professor Holtz instructs his pretty pupils on affairs of the heart. Working title: *Lessons in Love*.

Love Detectives (2/28/34) D: Archie Gottler. Frank Albertson, Betty Grable, Gloria Warner, Armand Kaliz, Red Stanley, Tom Dugan. Albertson and Kaliz vie for the affections of Grable.

When Do We Eat? (3/19/34) D: Alf Goulding. Lou Holtz, Bud Jamison, Luis Alberni, Adrian Rosley, Benny Baker, Eddie Fetherstone, Arthur Treacher, Charles Dorety, Julia Griffith, Phil Dunham, William Irving, Dorothy Compson, Ethel Sykes, Florence Dudley, Hal Price, Irene Thompson, Amron Isle, Sue Brighton, Hugh Saxon. When the members of Holtz's theatrical troupe find themselves in financial straits, they open a nudist restaurant. Working title: *Showmanship*.

Woman Haters (5/5/34) D: Archie Gottler. Marjorie White, Jerry "Curley" Howard, Larry Fine, Moe Howard, Bud Jamison, Monte Collins, Jack Norton, Walter Brennan, A.R. Haysel, Don Roberts, Fred "Snowflake" Toones, Stanley "Tiny" Sandford, Dorothy Vernon, Les Goodwin, George Gray, Gilbert C. Emery, Charles Richman. After joining the Woman Haters Club, Larry weds Marjorie and tries to keep it a secret from Curley and Moe.

Margaret Nearing and Arthur Jarrett in *Roamin' Thru the Roses* (1933). Although this was the second Columbia comedy short produced, it was the first one to be released.

Susie's Affairs (6/1/34) D: Archie Gottler. Arthur Jarrett, Betty Grable, Lois January, Red Stanley, Gene Sheldon, Thelma White, Marion Byron, Jay Mills. Susie (Grable) and her pals pretend they're society swells.

Tripping Through the Tropics (7/27/34) D: Archie Gottler. Frank Albertson, Lois January, Billy Gilbert, Sam Lewis, Rosa Ray, Gertie Green, Mario Alverez, Irene Coleman, Al Klein, Sidney D'Albrook, Patricia Caron, Allyn Drake, Lorena Carr, Diane Dahl, Mary Carroll, Jean Ashton, Helen Splane, Chuck Colean, Perry Murdock. Albertson and January find romance on a tropical isle. Working title: *Tropical Madness*.

Hollywood Here We Come (8/29/34) D: Archie Gottler. Arthur Jarrett, Inez Courtney, Joan Gale. Two aspiring actresses plan to take Hollywood by storm. Working title: *Hollywood Cinderella*.

Charlie Murray (left), Charles Dow Clark and George Sidney in *Fishing for Trouble* (1934).

Sidney and Murray

In the 1920s, George Sidney, a popular vaudeville entertainer, and Charlie Murray, a veteran of the Mack Sennett Studios, enjoyed great success when they were teamed in Universal's *The Cohens and the Kellys* series, domestic farces involving two families, one Jewish, the other Irish. The popularity of these feature-length comedies began to wane in the 1930s, as such entries as *The Cohens and Kellys in Hollywood* (1932) and *The Cohens and Kellys in Trouble* (1934) played to dwindling audiences.

In 1934 Columbia signed the pair for a series of comedy shorts, which were heavily influenced by the Cohen and Kelly pictures. There were six Sidney and Murray shorts in all; Murray was featured without Sidney in *His Old Flame* (1935), a two-reeler originally planned for Walter Catlett.

Like the musical novelties, this series is currently unavailable for reappraisal.

The Sidney and Murray Series

Ten Baby Fingers (1/26/34) D: Jules White. Harry Woods, Dorothy Granger, Thomas Francis, Lee Norton Taylor. George and Charlie take care of an abandoned baby. Remade with Andy Clyde as *My Little Feller* (1937), and with the Three Stooges as *Mutts to You* (1938) and *Sock-A-Bye Baby* (1942).

Radio Dough (2/5/34) D: Al Boasberg. Ed Gargan, Jill Dennett, Lillian Elliott, Lester Lee, Donald Haines, Walter Brennan, William Irving. Two clothing store operators aspire to be radio performers.

Stable Mates (4/6/34) D: Jules White. Dewey Robinson, William Kortman, Johnny Kascier, Floyd Criswell. A couple of bankers, victims of the Depression, find work on a Western ranch. Working title: *Banker Buckeroos*.

Fishing for Trouble (5/4/34) D: Sam White. Billy Dooley, Charles Dow Clark, Esther Howard, Walter Brennan, William Simon, Georgia O'Dell, Broderick O'Farrell, Nelson McDowell, Bob McKenzie, Ann Brody, Charles Dunbar, Johnny Kascier, Jack Hill. George and Charlie go fishing one Sunday—with disastrous results. Working title: *Holy Mackerel*.

Plumbing for Gold (6/29/34) D: Charles Lamont. Jack Shutta, Billy Seward. George and Charlie get jobs as plumber's assistants; on their first assignment, they reduce a house to shambles in search of a lost ring. Remade with El Brendel and Shemp Howard as *Pick a Peck of Plumbers* (1944) and with the Three Stooges as *Scheming Schemers* (1956). Partially remade with the Three Stooges as *A-Plumbing We Will Go* (1940) and *Vagabond Loafers* (1949).

Back to the Soil (8/10/34) D: Jules White. Lynton Brent, Eddie Baker, George Ovey, Maidena Armstrong, Al Thompson, Billy Engle, Georgia O'Dell, Don Roberts, Harry Watson, Frank Yaconelli, Nelson McDowell, William Irving, Rita Ross, Lillian West, Jack Rockwell, Bonita Barker, Jack Hill, Johnny Kascier. George and Charlie become prospectors and discover an outlaw's stolen loot. Working title: *Pay Dirt*. Remade with the Three Stooges as *Yes, We Have No Bonanza* (1939), and with Andy Clyde as *Gold Is Where You Lose It* (1944) and *Pleasure Treasure* (1951).

Charlie Murray appeared without George Sidney in the following:

His Old Flame (1/25/35) D: James W. Horne. Geneva Mitchell, Billy Gilbert, Elaine Baker, Lucille Ball, Betty McMahan, Kay Hughes, Eve Reynolds, Doris Davenport, Doris McMahan, Alice Dahl, Carmen Andre, Roger Gray, Charles King, Charles Dorety. Just as Charlie is running for mayor on a purity platform, an old flame threatens to show his torrid love letters to his wife if he doesn't withdraw from the campaign.

Marion Martin and Walter Catlett pose for *Blondes and Blunders* (1940).

Walter Catlett

Throughout the 1930s, bespectacled and befuddled Walter Catlett appeared in innumerable feature films and short subjects for a variety of studios; his Columbia shorts represent just a minute sampling of his prolific movie work. From 1934 to 1940, Catlett starred in a sporadic series of two-reel comedies that were equally sporadic in quality.

His initial efforts, *Elmer Steps Out* and *Get Along Little Hubby* (both 1934 releases), are unremarkable and uninspired. In fact, *Get Along Little Hubby* resembles a typical Leon Errol comedy: Walter is a henpecked husband at the mercy of a nagging wife (Vivien Oakland) and insufferable brother-in-law (Monte Collins). Two years passed before Catlett starred in another picture for the unit: *Fibbing Fibbers* (1936), which ranks as one of the all-time worst Columbia shorts. Walter absentmindedly makes a date with his girlfriend (Billie Bellport) on the same evening he's supposed to accompany his boss to a boxing match; to extricate himself from the conflicting engagements, Walter pretends to have been in a serious auto accident. The film is completely devoid of humor, ending on a downbeat note as Walter is about to be arrested for hit-and-run driving!

Three more years elapsed, and Catlett returned to the unit for his final group of two-reelers. *Static in the Attic* (1939) was directed by Charley Chase, though it's hard to believe that a major comic talent like Chase had anything to do with this flaccid effort. *You're Next* (1940) is a standard but lively "scare" comedy that teams Catlett with Monty Collins and Dudley Dickerson. *Blondes and Blunders* (1940) is a collection of frenetic gags centering around Walter's innocent involvement with jewel smuggler Marion Martin; the laughs are few and far between.

Catlett never remained with the department long enough at any one time for his series to sustain momentum, but it's just as well; his feature film appearances are far more rewarding than these erratic, halfhearted endeavors.

The Walter Catlett Series

Elmer Steps Out (2/28/34) D: Jules White. Anita Garvin, Arthur Housman, Greta Meyer, Gloria Warner, Betty Grable, James P. Burtis, Marion Lord, Jack Hill, Bert Young, Robert "Bobby" Burns. To avoid getting a speeding ticket, Walter poses as an expectant father rushing to see his wife; when the cop follows him, he's forced to come up with a wife and child. Working title: *Playful Husbands*. Remade with Alan Mowbray as *Three Blonde Mice* (1942).

Get Along Little Hubby (6/15/34) D: Raymond McCarey. Vivien Oakland, Monte Collins, Billy Gilbert, Charles "Heine" Conklin. When Walter's wife receives a telegram notifying her that she's inherited $50,000, Walter quits his job and assumes he can now take life easy, but his wife makes him do all the housework.

Fibbing Fibbers (10/19/36) D: Preston Black. Clarence Muse, Billie Bellport, Bud Jamison. Walter pretends to have been in an auto accident in order to get out of two conflicting engagements. Remade with Vera Vague as *Calling All Fibbers* (1945).

Static in the Attic (9/22/39) D: Charley Chase. Ann Doran, Charles Williams, Tommy Bond, Eddie Laughton, Bud Jamison, Beatrice Blinn. Walter is gifted with a "ham" radio on his birthday.

You're Next (5/3/40) D: Del Lord. Monty Collins, Dudley Dickerson, Roscoe Ates, John T. Murray, Chester Conklin. Monty and Walter, as Pruitt and Slocum of the Eagle Eye Detective Agency, go to the aid of a millionaire who has been abducted by a mad scientist. Reworked with Schilling and Lane as *Pardon My Terror* (1946), and with the Three Stooges as *Who Done It?* (1949) and *For Crimin' Out Loud* (1956).

Blondes and Blunders (11/29/40) D: Del Lord. Ann Doran, Marion Martin, Matt McHugh, Richard Fiske, Bud Jamison, Vernon Dent, Eddie Laughton, Stanley Brown, John Tyrrell. A beautiful blonde plants a stolen diamond necklace on an unsuspecting Walter. Remade with Hugh Herbert as *A Pinch in Time* (1948).

The Three Stooges

Many scholarly studies of motion picture comedy have overlooked the Three Stooges entirely—and not without valid reasoning. Aesthetically, the Stooges violated every rule that constitutes "good" comedic style. Their characters lacked the emotional depth of Charlie Chaplin and Harry Langdon; they were never as witty or subtle as Buster Keaton. They weren't disciplined enough to sustain lengthy comic sequences; far too often, they were willing to suspend what little narrative structure their pictures possessed in order to insert a number of gratuitous jokes. Nearly every premise they've employed (spoofs of westerns, horror films, costume melodramas) has been done to better effect by other comedians. And yet, in spite of the overwhelming artistic odds against them, they were responsible for some of the finest comedies ever made. Their humor was the most undistilled form of low comedy; they weren't great innovators, but as quick laugh practitioners, they place second to none. "They were very funny, no doubt about it," says Jack White. "They were also short-changed; they should have gotten recognition long before they died. The critics ignored them, so they never received their proper due." But if public taste is any criterion, the Stooges have been reigning kings of comedy for over fifty years.

When Moe Howard (the one with the sugar-bowl haircut), Larry Fine (with the frizzy hair and blank expression) and Jerry "Curly" Howard (the cherub with the clean-shaven head) were signed by Columbia, they had just split from their mentor, Ted Healy; together, they had comprised an act called "Ted Healy and His Stooges." Up until this time, their screen personalities were indistinct, primarily because they had never been permitted to overshadow Healy, who dominated the act. Once on their own, however, the Stooges quickly began to evolve from abstract grotesques into likable buffoons.

The Stooges, or "Howard, Fine and Howard," as they were then known, were initially signed for a single two-reeler, with an option for more—an option that was, obviously, exercised. They joined the unit at a time when director-songwriter Archie Gottler was making the "Musical Novelties" series so their first Columbia short, *Woman Haters* (1934), was one of these pictures. The format of this series, rhyming dialogue set to music, didn't suit the team at all; it was apparent that the unit was unsure of how to handle them. In *Woman Haters* their characters aren't clearly drawn, although Moe had already assumed the role of the martinet leader who kept his companions in line by slapping them around (Moe once commented, "I took over Healy's

Larry, Moe and Curly in *Three Little Pigskins* (1934), one of the team's earliest Columbia shorts.

role. I was no fool!"). Larry has more footage than his teammates; in fact, the entire plot revolves around him and a top-billed Marjorie White, a vivacious comedienne who was killed in an auto accident the following year. Curly (spelled "Curley" in the credits until 1936) is on the receiving end of much of Moe's abuse. Curly's engaging mannerisms hadn't surfaced yet, so he does little else but stand there and take it.

Punch Drunks (1934), their second short, was a decided improvement and ranks as one of their best early efforts. Moe is a down-on-his-luck fight manager who observes that a mild-mannered waiter (Curly) goes on a rampage every time an itinerant musician (Larry) plays "Pop Goes the Weasel" on his violin. The three join forces, grooming Curly as a championship boxer. The Stooges received story credit in the film ("Story by Howard, Fine and Howard"), as they did when it was remade with Shemp Howard as *A Hit with a Miss* (1945). *Punch Drunks* marked the first time the comedians were billed as "The Three Stooges."

Men in Black (1934), their third short, secured the team's position with Columbia. Jules White recalls, "*Men in Black* opened at the Cathay Circle Theatre in Los Angeles. The audience response was tremendous; I never knew people could laugh so hard. The film was even nominated for an Academy Award. *Men in Black* erased any doubts the studio had as to whether the boys were worth hanging on to." All this acclaim is puzzling in retrospect. The film is a spoof of *Men in White*, a 1934 MGM feature starring Clark Gable, based on Sidney Kingsley's Pulitzer Prize–winning play. The short is merely a shapeless pastiche of frenetic hospital gags, with none of the polish that marked their later work.

It wasn't long before the Stooges hit their stride. In 1935 director Del Lord, a veteran of the Mack Sennett Studios, stepped into the picture. Edward Bernds states, "Del is the man who got the Stooges on the right track. He brought to them a special comedic sense that made them so successful for such a long time." The first Lord-directed Stooge short, *Pop Goes the Easel* (1935), set a high standard that their comedies would maintain for the next several years. Along with Lord, Preston Black (Jack White), Charles Lamont, Jules White and Charley Chase shared directorial responsibilities, with generally pleasing results.

The Stooge shorts created an immediate sensation. Says Jules White, "Fan mail came pouring in from all over the world. We couldn't believe the overwhelming response the boys had generated." So great did the demand for their films become that Columbia eventually refused to supply exhibitors with Stooge comedies unless they also agreed to book some of the studio's lesser 'B' features.

And yet, throughout their years with Columbia, the Stooges were never fully aware of their own drawing power (despite the fact that their series received the Exhibitor's Laurel Awards for being the top two-reel moneymakers for 1950, 1951, 1952, 1953 and 1954). Their contract included an open option that had to be renewed each year. When option time rolled around, the front office painted a bleak picture for the future ("The market for comedy shorts is dying out, fellas"), cruelly making the boys sweat it out, only to come through with a last-minute reprieve. This deception kept the team ignorant of their true worth and, therefore, gave them second thoughts about asking for a raise or an altogether better contract. These scare tactics worked for twenty-four years; during all that time, the insecure Stooges never asked for—nor were they given—an increase in salary. It wasn't until after they stopped making the two-reelers that Moe Howard learned what a valuable commodity they had been to the studio.

The two-reelers made from 1935 to 1941 show the Stooges at the height of their powers. *Hoi Polloi* (1935) employs the classic premise of a professor attempting to transform the uncultured trio into refined gentlemen. In *Three Little Beers* (1935) the Stooges are brewery workers who run amuck on a golf course. The climax—the boys are chased by beer barrels rolling down a steep hill—was shot in Edendale, close to the old Sennett Studios; it was director Del Lord's former stomping grounds. *Disorder in the Court* (1936) is a quintessential Stooge comedy: the boys, star witnesses in a murder trial ("Who Killed Kirk Robbin?"), nearly destroy the judicial system. *Violent Is the Word for Curly* (1938) is very enjoyable, highlighted by a splendid musical interlude, "Swingin' the Alphabet." Other outstanding entries include *Un-*

civil Warriors (1935), *A Pain in the Pullman* (1936), *False Alarms* (1936), *Grips, Grunts and Groans* (1937), *Dizzy Doctors* (1937), *Cash and Carry* (1937), *The Sitter Downers* (1937), *Termites of 1938* (1938), *Tassels in the Air* (1938), *Three Sappy People* (1939), *A-Plumbing We Will Go* (1940), *Nutty but Nice* (1940), *How High Is Up?* (1940), *No Census, No Feeling* (1940), *An Ache in Every Stake* (1941) and *In the Sweet Pie and Pie* (1941).

By the late 1930s, their screen characters had grown considerably. Curly easily became the most popular Stooge. Few comics have come close to equaling the pure energy and genuine sense of fun Curly was able to project. He was merriment personified, a creature of frantic action whose only concern was to satisfy his immediate cravings. Allowing his emotions to dominate, and making no attempt whatsoever to hide his true feelings, he'd chuckle self-indulgently at his own cleverness. When confronted with a problem, he'd grunt, slap his face, and tackle the obstacle with all the tenacity of a six-year old child. His catch-phrases "woo woo woo," "n'yuk, n'yuk, n'yuk," and "I'm a victim of circumstance!" are now legendary, and his gift for improvisation has been hailed by many coworkers. Jules White remarks, "If we wrote a scene and needed a little something extra, I'd say to Curly, 'Look, we've got to fill this in with a 'woo woo' or some other bit of business.' And he never disappointed us."

Moe was still the gruff bully who seemed more preoccupied with getting even than getting ahead, although he was now on the receiving end of much of the physical abuse. Though often regarded as nothing more than a "straight man" for his cohorts, Moe was actually a fine comedian whose inborn sense of comic structure, characterization and timing gave the team a sturdy foundation. He was the glue that held the act together. Larry was the affable middleman who came up with sound ideas but was totally useless when trying to execute them.

In recent years, the Stooges have been the recipients of well-deserved and long-overdue critical recognition, but this latter-day acclaim has almost always praised Curly, at the expense of his teammates. In all fairness, Moe and Larry were immensely gifted performers; though less flamboyant than Curly, they were by no means less talented. Curly was brilliant, but he could also be irritating and exhausting without Moe and Larry around to provide a counterbalance. It's doubtful that Curly would have achieved the same degree of success without his skilled partners.

The Stooge comedies from the 1942–44 period aren't bad, but most— *Loco Boy Makes Good* (1942), *What's the Matador?* (1942), *Sock-A-Bye Baby* (1942), *I Can Hardly Wait* (1943), *A Gem of a Jam* (1943), *Crash Goes the Hash* (1944)—can't hold a candle to the earlier efforts. Rising production costs resulted in a reduced number of elaborate gags and outdoor sequences. *Three Smart Saps* (1942) is one of the better shorts, highlighted by a neat reworking of a routine from Harold Lloyd's *The Freshman* (1925), in which Curly's loosely basted suit begins to come apart at the seams while he's on the dance floor. *Matri-Phony* (1943) starts out nicely (the Stooges are pottery makers in

The Stooges beg for table scraps as Vernon Dent blithely devours a meal in *Half-Shot Shooters* **(1936).**

ancient Rome) then degenerates and arrives at an unfortunately abrupt ending (a fatal flaw in a great many Columbia comedy shorts). *Spook Louder* (1943), a remake of Mack Sennett's *The Great Pie Mystery* (1930), was their worst picture in some time; the tale of a phantom pie-thrower is a repetitious one-joke affair devoid of laughs.

Their wartime shorts poking fun at the Axis powers are decidedly substandard. *You Nazty Spy!* (1940) and its sequel *I'll Never Heil Again* (1941) burlesqued the Hitler gang as Moe played Moe Hailstone, dictator of Moronica. Though revered by many Stooge aficionados, these efforts indulged in a deliberately formless, non sequitur style of verbal humor that simply wasn't their forte; any laughs furnished are due to the team's comic expertise. *They Stooge to Conga* (1943), *Higher Than a Kite* (1943) and *Back from the Front* (1943) have their moments, but with *Gents Without Cents* (1944) and *The Yoke's on Me* (1944) their films sank to a new low. *No Dough Boys* (1944) is the best of these wartime farces. The Stooges, made up as Japanese soldiers for a photo session, are mistaken for genuine saboteurs by a Nazi ringleader (Vernon Dent). In the funniest sequence, the boys perform nonsensical gymnastics (the real spies are renown acrobats) for a skeptical group of enemy agents.

What was far more distressing than the dwindling quality of the shorts was Curly's physical decline. A heavy drinker and all-around merrymaker, Curly's offscreen excesses began to take their toll in 1943. His performances were still energetic, but lines now began to crease his smooth baby face. By 1945 Curly had lost so much weight that Moe and Larry often look heavier by comparison. Gone too was Curly's marvelous panache; his physical movements were sluggish and his voice sounded tired and strained.

Edward Bernds began directing Stooge shorts in 1945. If Curly's actions have an overly rehearsed look to them, Bernds explains, "Curly had a difficult time remembering even the simplest gestures. Moe would take him aside and drill him on a routine, as one would a child. When Curly had it down pat, we'd go ahead and film it. I never would have made it without Moe's help." In addition to the physical gestures, dialogue also became a problem. Says Bernds, "I'd feed Curly a line at a time, film his delivery in closeup, and then intercut the shot on the master take. We didn't have to simplify his lines on the set because if you wrote for Curly, you wrote it simple anyway."

Bernds' first Stooge comedy, *A Bird in the Head*, was pretty limp. At first glance, the poor quality might seem due to the inexperience of a neophyte director. But, in truth, the problems stemmed from the task of directing an ailing Curly. Bernds comments:

> I was the sound man on many of the Stooges' earlier shorts, so I knew the boys personally and they were very cooperative. Curly was sensational in the earlier comedies, but by the time I started directing them, it was apparent that something was seriously wrong. In the first scene we shot, the boys are wallpapering a room. Curly couldn't coordinate his movements; his timing was gone.
>
> I had seen too many directors in my time come into a day's work without being adequately prepared and try to make things up as they went along. So I was prepared—I had a game plan all worked out in detail and even provided for contingencies. But when Curly couldn't carry through with a little 40- or 50-second scene, my plans were shot to hell and I had to improvise. Now, you can be stubborn and keep trying to do it, but when a scene keeps getting worse, you have to bow to reality and do what is known as "break it up"—in other words, shoot closeups. When I started to do that, my carefully laid plans were ruined, and it resulted in what is called *waste motion*. For instance, when I tried to continue and that scene broke down, I would then have to shoot closeups to cover the mistakes; I'd find myself, maybe after an hour's work, doing essentially the same set-up. Production crews hate waste motion of that kind, and I don't blame them. But most of the crew were friends of mine and they realized that Curly was the problem.
>
> We were on a four-day schedule. On the last day I kept making one mistake after another. It so happened that President Roosevelt died on this same day (April 12, 1945). The studio sent everyone home and shut down. This gave me some time to think out a lot of the things that went wrong. The next day when we returned to work, things went smoother as I was able to correct mistakes of the previous three days. But it still wasn't a terribly good picture.

Gino Corrado prepares to skewer Curly in *Micro-Phonies* (1945), one of the Stooges' funniest comedies.

When producer Hugh McCollum saw that Bernds' third Stooge effort, *Micro-Phonies*, was an improvement over his first two (*A Bird in the Head* and *Three Troubledoers*), he arranged to have *Micro-Phonies* released first. "Since I was a fledgling director, I would have been judged by my first picture," says Bernds. "McCollum realized this and did me a tremendous favor." In *Micro-Phonies* (1945) Curly passes himself off as a female vocalist, "Senorita Cucaracha," when a wealthy society matron (Symona Boniface) happens to see him mimicking a recording made by an aspiring singer (Christine McIntyre). Christine is given a superb opportunity to display her vocal talents by singing "The Voice of Spring," and Gino Corrado nearly steals the show in a memorable supporting role as an egotistical violinist named Signor Spumoni. *Micro-Phonies* is one of the team's funniest comedies, and it established Bernds as one of the best directors they ever worked with. Of the film and Curly's fluctuating condition, Bernds adds, "I guess I should be thankful that Curly was in one of his 'up' periods because it was strange the way he went up and down. In the order I shot the pictures, not in the order they were released, he was down for *A Bird in the Head* and *Three Troubledoers*, he was up for *Micro-Phonies*, *way down* for *Monkey Businessmen* and then up again, for the last time, in *Three Little Pirates*."

As a group, the 1946 releases were the worst Stooge comedies to date. *Beer Barrel Polecats, A Bird in the Head, Uncivil Warbirds, Three Troubledoers, Monkey Businessmen, Three Loan Wolves, G.I. Wanna Home* and *Rhythm and Weep* represent a low ebb in the team's career. Curly's performances are alarmingly languid; he merely stands there while the comedic responsibilities are thrust upon his teammates' shoulders. In fact, in *Three Loan Wolves* Larry has the pivotal role, the part Curly would have played had the film been made a few years earlier. *Three Little Pirates* was the sole bright spot of the year; the short is quite funny, with the Moe-Curly "Maharaja" (or "Rasbanyas") routine a standout. Curly is livelier than usual, though still a pale shadow of his former self.

Half-Wits Holiday (filmed in 1946, released 1947), a remake of *Hoi Polloi* (1935), turned out to be Curly's final appearance as one of the Stooges. Jules White, who was familiar with Curly's condition, found it was now even more difficult to direct him. While shooting the picture, many of the lines intended for Curly were either reassigned to Larry or jettisoned entirely. Curly had trouble mastering the briefest dialogue exchanges; in one scene that takes place at a society party, the Stooges try to behave like proper gentlemen when introduced to society swells:

LARRY: Delighted.

MOE: Devastated.

CURLY: Dilapidated.

LARRY: Enchanted.

MOE: Enraptured.

CURLY: Embalmed.

"I had a devil of a time getting that scene," says White. "Curly just couldn't get the hang of it. I should have realized then that he was deteriorating even further."

On May 6, 1946, the last day of filming *Half-Wits Holiday*, Curly suffered a stroke between takes. He was to have taken an active part in the pie-fight finale; when it became evident that he would be unable to participate, White divided the action between Moe and Larry, adding reaction shots of other cast members in an effort to get around Curly's conspicuous absence. Emil Sitka, who played the butler in the film, remembers:

The Stooges display their social graces — or rather, lack of them — in *Half-Wits Holiday* (1947). Symona Boniface (left) will soon be on the receiving end of that pie. This short was Curly's last appearance as a member of the trio; he suffered a stroke between takes on the last day of filming.

> After (the stroke) occurred, Curly was just missing all of a sudden. It wasn't announced to the rest of the cast; nobody knew what happened. So, we're approaching the last scene in the picture, a big pie fight. They had a big set and they put a huge canvas all around; it was going to be like a battleground. They're getting all geared up and the script calls for all the Stooges. I see a dry run-through of the scene and there's no Curly. I thought it was just a change in the script. No one — including Moe, Larry and Jules — ever told us how serious his condition was. It was only after the picture had been completed that I found out he took ill.

With Curly disabled, the next planned Stooge comedy, *Pardon My Terror*, was instead filmed with Gus Schilling and Richard Lane (see *Schilling and Lane* series).

Although *Half-Wits Holiday* marked Curly's swan song as a member of the team, he appeared in two later Stooge shorts. In *Hold That Lion* (1947) he's seen briefly as a sleeping train passenger. Jules White recalls:

> It was a spur of the moment idea. Curly was visiting the set; this was sometime after his stroke. Apparently he came in on his own since I didn't see a nurse with him. He was sitting around, reading a newspaper. As I walked in, the newspaper, which he had in front of his face, came down and he waved hello to me. I thought it would be funny to have him do a bit in the picture, and he was happy to do it.

Curly also had a bit part as a chef in *Malice in the Palace* (1949) but the sequence was inexplicably deleted. He had lost a great deal of weight by this time and was barely recognizable behind a handlebar moustache.

Shemp Howard, Moe and Curly's older brother, was chosen to be the new "third Stooge," although Columbia executives argued that he looked too much like Moe. No official statement was issued to the press or exhibitors on Curly's condition or the fact that Shemp was replacing him. The shorts were still popular, but every now and then, letters from the exhibitors would inquire "Whatever happened to the fat guy?"

Shemp was, and remains to a large degree, the most underrated Stooge, summarily dismissed as being inferior to Curly. While he lacked his younger brother's charisma, Shemp was an enormously talented comedian, possessing a tough streetwise manner ("Copped a sneaker, eh?") which was often put to good use. On many occasions his comic prowess buoys the weak material.

Shemp had been a member of the team during their salad days with Ted Healy (ironically, when Shemp left the act in 1932, it was Curly who took his place), so he was quite at home with their knockabout brand of humor. Wisely, he never attempted to imitate Curly. "When Shemp took Curly's place, I don't recall any great restructuring," says Edward Bernds. "Whatever was done was collaborative anyway. The boys and I would talk things over, most of the time discussing what we would do rather than what we wouldn't do. There was pretty much agreement from all of us from the beginning that we wouldn't try to make Shemp be like Curly." The first Stooge short with Shemp, *Fright Night* (1947), was originally written with Curly in mind. Viewing the completed film, it's hard to imagine anyone other than Shemp essaying the role. Bernds comments:

> Shemp replaced Curly in *Fright Night* and the picture turned out all the better because of it. Curly was a genius in his own right, but Shemp's performances had more depth. Shemp was a much better actor and the Stooge comedies I did with him were an improvement over the ones I did with Curly.
>
> Shemp was a delight to work with. He was an instinctive actor, a great improviser. Many times when I was directing him, I would actually delay in cutting a scene just to see what he would do. He used to bowl me over with the things he'd dream up.

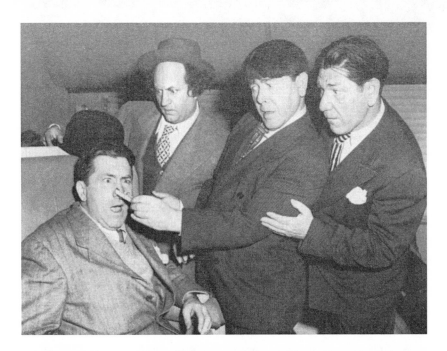

Even after a stroke forced him to leave the Three Stooges in 1946, Curly Howard made cameo appearances in two Stooge shorts. Top: As an innocent train passenger, Curly is beset by the new trio of Stooges in *Hold That Lion* (1947). Bottom: Barely recognizable behind a handlebar mustache, Curly played a disgruntled chef in *Malice in the Palace* (1949); however, for reasons unknown, this sequence is missing from current television prints.

Another plus of the Shemp efforts is that Larry was given a more active role in them. In many Curly shorts, Larry was pushed into the background; his only function seemed to be to remind audiences they were a trio. In the Shemps, he's allotted equal footage, and in a few of the plots, he's the main character. However, there are many who feel that Curly's absence created an irreparable void. "Curly was a great artist," says Jules White. "Don't get me wrong, I loved working with Shemp and thought he was a naturally funny guy, but when Curly left, the Stooge comedies were never the same. We made a few good ones after that, but they were nothing like the Curlys."

Despite budgetary limitations, several Shemp comedies compare favorably to Curly's best efforts. The series breathed new life as the team hit another stride. *Out West* (1947) is an on-target sendup of western films, lampooning the cliches of the genre: the virtuous hero, the pure-hearted heroine, the crooked poker game and the thrilling last-minute rescue by the U.S. Cavalry. *Hold That Lion* (1947) is another top-notch outing. The Stooges hop aboard a train to catch con man Icabod Slipp (Kenneth MacDonald) who swindled them out of their inheritance; hiding in the baggage car, the boys unwittingly unleash a lion, adding to the havoc they've already caused. *Brideless Groom* (1947), a reworking of Buster Keaton's *Seven Chances* (1925), is one of the best comedies the Stooges ever made. Shemp is notified that he must get married within a seven-hour period or lose a half-million-dollar inheritance. After a number of false starts, Shemp finally secures a mate, but the wedding ceremony becomes a free-for-all when his former girlfriends learn of his expected riches and decide to stake their claim. Few entries can match *Brideless Groom* for pacing, performance and sheer energy.

In *Squareheads of the Round Table* (1948) the Stooges play wandering troubadours in the days of King Arthur. The highlight of the film is a musical parody of the "Sextet from Lucia": their version, titled "Oh, Elaine," is sung by the Stooges to the fair Princess Elaine (Christine McIntyre) on behalf of her true love, Cedric the blacksmith (Jacques O'Mahoney, later known as Jock Mahoney). In *I'm a Monkey's Uncle* (1948), one of the best-remembered Shemps, the boys are cavemen; in a riotous scene, they go courting three Stone Age sweeties, Aggie, Maggie and Baggie (Virginia Hunter, Nancy Saunders, Dee Green). Gene Roth steals the show in *Dunked in the Deep* (1949), playing a foreign spy named Mr. Bortch who dupes the Stooges into helping him smuggle microfilms of valuable government documents, concealed inside watermelons, out of the country. *Pest Man Wins* (1951) is a remake of *Ants in the Pantry* (1936) and in many ways it improves upon the original. The tale of three pest exterminators who decide to drum up a little business by unleashing moths, mice and ants at a society party is climaxed by a magnificent pie-fight sequence, augmented with footage from *In the Sweet Pie and Pie* (1941) and *Half-Wits Holiday* (1947). *Gents in a Jam* (1952) is one of the last outstanding Stooge shorts, with Emil Sitka giving a hilarious performance as Shemp's wealthy Uncle Phineas. Other first-rate efforts include *Sing a Song of Six Pants* (1947), *All Gummed Up* (1947), *Shivering Sherlocks* (1948), *The*

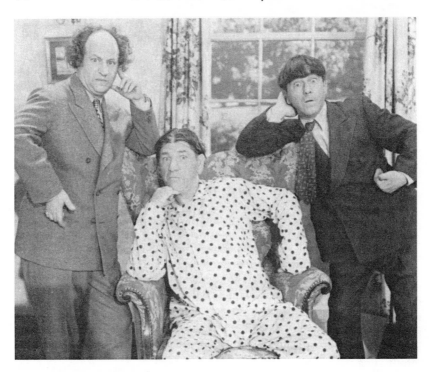

Larry, Shemp and Moe strike a dignified pose in this publicity shot for *Pardon My Clutch* (1948).

Hot Scots (1948), *Mummy's Dummies* (1948), *Who Done It?* (1949), *Fuelin' Around* (1949), *Punchy Cowpunchers* (1950), *A Snitch in Time* (1950), *Three Arabian Nuts* (1951) and *Scrambled Brains* (1951).

There were also a number of misfires. Experimenting with offbeat ideas brought mixed results. In *Self-Made Maids* (1950) the Stooges play all the roles in the film; it's an intriguing concept that doesn't quite come off. The marital farce *He Cooked His Goose* (1952) plays them against one another and is one of their worst comedies. The same holds true for *Cuckoo on a Choo Choo* (1952), notable only for Larry's portrayal of a Marlon Brando-ish lout (à la *A Streetcar Named Desire*). *Three Dark Horses* (1952) aims for political satire, though the humor is blunted by graceless slapstick.

In 1952 Hugh McCollum, a short subjects producer since 1937, was fired from Columbia, and Jules White became the sole head of the comedy shorts department. With McCollum's dismissal, Edward Bernds left voluntarily, leaving White to direct, as well as produce, all of the films himself. Although there would still be some funny Stooge comedies made, the overall quality plummeted drastically. Typical efforts from this period are *Income Tax Sappy* (1954), loaded with inferior reworkings of staple routines, and *Shot in the Frontier* (1954), a flat spoof of *High Noon* (1952). A short-lived venture into the novelty of 3-D produced two mediocre Stooge shorts, *Spooks* (1953) and *Pardon My Backfire* (1953).

To cope with skyrocketing production costs, White grew dependent on lifting footage from earlier shorts, then filming a handful of new sequences to comply with the older scenes, using identical sets and as many of the original cast members as possible. Some of these "remakes" are so identical to the original versions that they're virtually the same film, as in the case of *Sing a Song of Six Pants* (1947) and its remake, *Rip, Sew and Stitch* (1953). Others refashion the stock footage to conform to new stories: in *Stone Age Romeos* (1955), the Stooges are archaeologists screening movies of their expedition for museum curator Emil Sitka. Sequences from *I'm a Monkey's Uncle* (1948), depicting them as cavemen, are then cut in. The most curious of these patchwork shorts is *Pals and Gals* (1954), which not only incorporates sequences from *Goofs and Saddles* (1937) and *Out West* (1947) but goes so far as to have the Stooges murder one supporting character (Norman Willes) in order to bridge the old footage with the new.

Shemp died in 1955, during their shooting schedule (Stooge shorts were filmed months in advance, completing eight two-reelers within a forty-week period). The last four Shemp comedies, all 1956 releases, were made after his death. Joe Palma, a supporting player in many Columbia shorts, doubled for Shemp in the new sequences, which resulted in some awkward transitions. In *Rumpus in the Harem*, Moe and Larry arise to find a note on Shemp's pillow informing them that he'll meet them later at the cafe where they work. When he finally does appear, it's either via stock footage from *Malice in the Palace* (1949) or, when Palma is onscreen, shown from the rear. In *Hot Stuff*, Palma is seen only from the back and leaves a scene quickly when Moe instructs him to follow a pretty girl. Palma then flails his arms and imitates Shemp's trademark cry "Heep-heep-heep." They're plumbers in *Scheming Schemers*, a reworking of *Vagabond Loafers* (1949), and when Palma is shown, he's carrying so many pipes that his face is completely obscured. To top it all off, the soundtrack of an earlier Shemp short, *The Ghost Talks* (1949), is dubbed in for his one "new" line of dialogue ("Hold your horses, will ya?"). *Commotion on the Ocean* liberally uses footage from *Dunked in the Deep* (1949). During one scene (a medium shot bridging the stock footage) Palma is seen standing between Moe and Larry, clumsily covering his face with his arm. Later Moe wonders aloud where Shemp disappeared to. "You know he went up on deck to scout for some food," Larry says matter-of-factly, explaining away Shemp's absence during the next few scenes. That they were able to complete four two-reelers in this manipulative fashion is nothing short of amazing, although the deception doesn't go by undetected.

Joe Besser, a veteran vaudeville comic also starring in a series of comedy shorts for Columbia, was selected to join the Stooges in 1956 and completed the remaining two-reelers. The final sixteen Stooge shorts are undoubtably their worst pictures. Besser was a very funny comedian (his work on "The Abbott and Costello Show" supports this opinion) but his whining mannerisms

Joe Besser (left), seen here in *Oil's Well That Ends Well* (1958), joined the Stooges (Moe, center, and Larry) for the final sixteen Stooge two-reelers.

("Not so hard!") didn't jell with the team's roughhouse antics. But to place the blame for their abysmal quality solely on Besser is an injustice: the scripts were tiresome rehashes and Moe and Larry's performances lacked sparkle.

Besser suggested that Moe and Larry forsake their usual hair styles and comb their hair back in order to give them a more refined appearance. Although the effect was certainly novel, it served to accentuate their ages and weaken the impact of their established personalities. Emil Sitka recalls, "I'm surprised that they consented to do it. Those haircuts were their trademarks; Moe in particular was fussy about their appearance." Jules White remarks, "We were trying out something different, but we couldn't use those new hair styles all the time because they didn't match the older footage."

Several of the Bessers relied heavily on footage from the Curly and Shemp shorts, with new scenes completed in as little time as one day. There aren't many good moments in the Bessers; *A Merry Mix-Up* (1957), *Rusty Romeos*

(1957) and *Oil's Well That Ends Well* (1958) are amusing, and the musical short *Sweet and Hot* (1958) deserves credit for straying from the norm. *Muscle Up a Little Closer* (1957) is perhaps the best of this indifferent group.

The Stooges' contract expired in December, 1957, and it was not renewed. However, since their final two-reelers had been completed so rapidly, the studio continued to release new Stooge comedies until June, 1959. They had outlasted every performer in the department; their twenty-four-year stay at Columbia set a record that has yet to be challenged. (Joe Besser left the team in 1958; Joe DeRita, an exburlesque comic, took his place as "third Stooge." DeRita starred with Moe and Larry in a few feature-length films, including *Have Rocket, Will Travel* [1959], *The Three Stooges Meet Hercules* [1962], *The Three Stooges in Orbit* [1962] and *The Outlaws Is Coming!* [1965].

If the Columbia comedy shorts department is remembered for anything, it's for the Three Stooges comedies. The Stooges had the longest-running and, not surprisingly, most successful short subjects series at the studio. The team also appeared in a variety of other films, but it was these little two-reelers that gave them their greatest fame. Even today, these pictures remain extremely popular in television and theatrical markets, delighting their old fans and winning a new legion of fervent admirers. It's quite a tribute to these talented, hard-working comedians—and the creative people who guided them—that the films are still wonderfully funny.

The Three Stooges Series

With Moe Howard, Larry Fine and Curly Howard

Woman Haters (5/5/34) D: Archie Gottler. Marjorie White, Bud Jamison, Monte Collins, Jack Norton, Walter Brennan, A.R. Haysel, Don Roberts, Fred "Snowflake" Toones, Stanley "Tiny" Sandford, June Gittelson, Dorothy Vernon, George Gray, Les Goodwin, Gilbert C. Emery, Charles Richman. After joining the Woman Haters Club, Larry weds Marjorie and tries to keep the marriage a secret from Curly and Moe.

Punch Drunks (7/13/34) D: Lou Breslow. Dorothy Granger, Arthur Housman, William Irving, Chuck Callahan, Jack "Tiny" Lipson, Billy Bletcher, Al Hill, Larry McCrath. Curly, a mild-mannered waiter, goes berserk whenever he hears the tune "Pop Goes the Weasel"; Moe, a fight manager, decides to build him into a championship boxer. Working titles: *Symphony of Punches* and *A Symphony of Punches*. Remade with Shemp Howard as *A Hit with a Miss* (1945).

Men in Black (9/28/34) D: Raymond McCarey. Dell Henderson, Jeanie Roberts, Ruth Hiatt, Billy Gilbert, Bud Jamison, Bobby Callahan, Little Billy, Hank Mann, Phyllis Crane, Joe Mills, Arthur West, Irene Coleman, Carmen Andre, Helen Splane, Kay Hughes, Eve Reynolds, Lucile Watson, Eve

Kimberly, Billie Stockton, Betty Andre, Arthur Rankin, Neal Burns, Joe Fine, Charles Dorety, Charles King. Doctors Howard, Fine and Howard, interns at the Los Arms Hospital, give their all "for duty and humanity." Nominated for an Academy Award.

Three Little Pigskins (12/8/34) D: Raymond McCarey. Lucille Ball, Gertie Green, Phyllis Crane, Walter Long, Joseph Young, Harry Bowen, William Irving, Lynton Brent, Robert "Bobby" Burns, Jimmie Phillips, Milton Douglas, Johnny Kascier. A gangster's moll mistakes the Stooges for the Three Horsemen of Boulder Dam, collegiate football players.

Horses' Collars (1/10/35) D: Clyde Bruckman. Dorothy Kent, Fred Kohler, Fred Kelsey, Leo Willis, Slim Whittaker, Nelson McDowell, Allyn Drake, Hilda Title, June Gittelson, Alice Dahl, Nancy Caswell, Bobby Callahan, Milton Douglas. The Stooges, three ace detectives, travel West to aid a young woman who was swindled out of the deed to her ranch.

Restless Knights (2/20/35) D: Charles Lamont. Geneva Mitchell, Walter Brennan, George Baxter, Chris Franke, James Howard, Bud O'Neill, Stanley Blystone, Jack Duffy, Billy Franey, Ernie Young, Robert "Bobby" Burns, Lynton Brent, William Irving, Al Thompson, Joe Perry, Bert Young, George Speer, Dutch Hendrian, Marie Wells, Eadie Adams, Corinne Williams, Dorothy King, Patty Price. The Stooges become the Queen's royal bodyguards—and she's promptly abducted!

Pop Goes the Easel (3/29/35) D: Del Lord. Robert "Bobby" Burns, Phyllis Crane, William Irving, Elinor Vandivere, Al Thompson, Jack Duffy, Leo White, Lew Davis. The boys are let loose in an art school.

Uncivil Warriors (4/26/35) D: Del Lord. Ted Lorch, Bud Jamison, Phyllis Crane, Celeste Edwards, Jennifer Gray, James C. Morton, Lew Davis, Marvin Loback, Billy Engle, Ford West, Lou Archer, Si Jenks, Charles Dorety, Charles "Heine" Conklin, Jack Kenny, Charles Cross, George Gray, Hubert Diltz, Harry Keaton, Jack Rand, Wes Warner. During the Civil War, the Stooges are Union spies sent South to masquerade as three Confederate officers— Lieutenant Duck, Captain Dodge and Major Hyde. Working titles: *Operators 12, 14 and 15* and *Operators 13, 14 and 15*.

Pardon My Scotch (8/1/35) D: Del Lord. Nat Carr, James C. Morton, Billy Gilbert, Grace Goodall, Barlowe Borland, Scotty Dunsmuir, Gladys Gale, Wilson Benge, Al Thompson, Symona Boniface, Pauline High, Alec Craig, William Irving, Billy Bletcher, Ettore Compana, Nena Compana, George Gray. The Stooges, mistaken for bootleggers, are hired to pose as genuine distillers.

Between takes of *Hoi Polloi* (The Three Stooges, 1935) an unidentified man mends Curly Howard's trousers as Moe Howard inspects the handiwork. Also pictured (l. to r.): Shemp Howard (kneeling), who was visiting that day; director of photography Benjamin Kline; assistant cameraman Mr. Dawson; grip Walter Meins (with hands on hips); and assistant director George Rhein (peeking from underneath Meins' arm).

Hoi Polloi (8/29/35) D: Del Lord. Harry Holmes, Robert Graves, Kathryn Kitty McHugh, Geneva Mitchell, Bud Jamison, Phyllis Crane, Grace Goodall, Betty McMahan, William Irving, James C. Morton, Robert McKenzie, Arthur Rankin, Celeste Edwards, Mary Dees, Harriett DeBussman, Blanche Payson, Gail Arnold, Gino Corrado, George B. French, Don Roberts, Billy Mann. A professor wagers that he can transform the Stooges into refined gentlemen. Remade as *Half-Wits Holiday* (1947) and *Pies and Guys* (1958).

Three Little Beers (11/28/35) D: Del Lord. Bud Jamison, Harry Semels, Jack "Tiny" Lipson, Eddie Laughton, Frank Terry, Nanette Crawford, Eve Reynolds, George Gray, Stanley Blystone, Charles Dorety, Lew Davis, Frank Mills. The Stooges set out to win a golf tournament sponsored by their employer, the Panther Brewery Company.

Ants in the Pantry (2/6/36) D: Preston Black. Clara Kimball Young, Harrison Greene, Bud Jamison, Isabelle LeMal, Vesey O'Davoren, Douglas Gerrard, Anne O'Neal, James C. Morton, Phyllis Crane, Arthur Rowlands, Al Thompson, Helen Martinez, Hilda Title, Charles Dorety, Bert Young, Lew Davis, Ron Wilson, Robert "Bobby" Burns, Lynton Brent, Arthur Thalasso, Elaine Waters, Althea Henly, Idalyn Dupre, Stella LeSaint, Flo Promise, Gay Waters. The Stooges, exterminators employed by the Lightning Pest Control Company, decide to drum up a little business by unleashing moths, mice and ants at a society party. Working title: *Pardon My Ants*. Remade as *Pest Man Wins* (1951).

Movie Maniacs (2/20/36) D: Del Lord. Bud Jamison, Lois Lindsey, Althea Henly, Kenneth Harlan, Mildred Harris, Harry Semels, Antrim Short, Jack Kenny, Charles Dorety, Elaine Waters, Eve Reynolds, Hilda Title, Bert Young, Eddie Laughton. A case of mistaken identity results in the Stooges taking control of the Carnation Pictures Studio ("Home of Contented Actors"). Working title: *G-A-G Men*.

Half-Shot Shooters (4/30/36) D: Preston Black. Stanley Blystone, Vernon Dent, Harry Semels, Johnny Kascier, Lynton Brent, Lew Davis, Eddie Laughton, Charles "Heine" Conklin, Bert Young. After their discharge from the army, the Stooges accidentally reenlist and are placed under the command of their old top sergeant.

Disorder in the Court (5/30/36) D: Preston Black. Susan Karaan, Bud Jamison, Harry Semels, James C. Morton, Edward LeSaint, Eddie Laughton, Dan Brady, Tiny Jones, Al Thompson, Hank Bell, Nick Baskovitch, Arthur Thalasso, Bill O'Brien, Ed Mull. At a murder trial, the Stooges are called in as star witnesses to answer the question "Who Killed Kirk Robbin?" Working title: *Disorder in the Courtroom*.

A Pain in the Pullman (6/27/36) D: Preston Black. Bud Jamison, James C. Morton, Eddie Laughton, Robert "Bobby" Burns, Hilda Title, Ray Turner, Phyllis Crane, Loretta Andrews, Ethelreda Leopold, Gale Arnold, Mary Lou Dix. Traveling by train, three performers and their pet monkey make things miserable for the other members of their vaudeville troupe. Remade with Schilling and Lane as *Training for Trouble* (1947).

False Alarms (8/16/36) D: Del Lord. Stanley Blystone, June Gittelson. Even

The Stooges and their pet monkey, Joe, are about to create havoc aboard a train in *A Pain in the Pullman* (1936). James C. Morton, Mary Lou Dix and Bud Jamison look on apprehensively.

though their jobs as firemen are in jeopardy, the boys plan to sneak out of the firehouse to attend a birthday party.

Whoops, I'm an Indian! (9/11/36) D: Del Lord. Bud Jamison, Bob McKenzie, Al Thompson, William Irving, Blackie Whiteford, Eddie Laughton, Lew Davis, Elaine Waters, Beatrice Blinn. The Stooges, con artists on the lam, masquerade as Indians. Working title: *Frontier Daze.*

Slippery Silks (12/27/36) D: Preston Black. Vernon Dent, Symona Boniface, Eddie Laughton, William Irving, Jack "Tiny" Lipson, June Gittelson, Hilda Title, Lew Davis, Elinor Vandivere, Blackie Whiteford, Bert Young, Elaine Waters, Beatrice Blinn, Martha Tibbetts, Beatrice Curtis, Mary Lou Dix, Gale Arnold, Loretta Andrews, Gertrude Messenger. Three carpenters inherit a dress salon and design garments that resemble furniture.

Grips, Grunts and Groans (1/15/37) D: Preston Black. Harrison Greene, Casey Colombo, Herb Stagman, Chuck Callahan, Blackie Whiteford, Cy Schindell, Elaine Waters, Tony Chavez, Bud Fine, Sam Lufkin, William

Irving, Everett Sullivan, Harry Wilson. When Bustoff, a world championship wrestler, gets knocked unconscious just prior to an important bout, Curly is recruited to take his place.

Dizzy Doctors (3/19/37) D: Del Lord. Vernon Dent, Bud Jamison, June Gittelson, Eva Murray, Ione Leslie, Louise Carver, Ella McKenzie, Cy Schindell, Wilfred Lucas, Eric Bunn, William Irving, Al Thompson, Charles Dorety, Frank Mills, James C. Morton, Harlene Wood, A.R. Haysel, Betty McMahan. At their wives' insistence, the Stooges go out and look for jobs, and become salesmen for "Brighto," a new miracle medicine.

3 Dumb Clucks (4/17/37) D: Del Lord. Lucille Lund, Eddie Laughton, Frank Mills, Frank Austin, Lynton Brent, Al Thompson, Cy Schindell, Charles Dorety. The boys try to prevent their father from marrying a gold-digging blonde. Remade as *Up in Daisy's Penthouse* (1953).

Back to the Woods (5/14/37) D: Preston Black. Vernon Dent, Bud Jamison, Harlene Wood, Ethelreda Leopold, Cy Schindell, Bert Young, Charles Dorety, Ted Lorch. Three pilgrims do battle with savage Indians. Uses stock footage from *Whoops, I'm an Indian!* (1936).

Goofs and Saddles (7/2/37) D: Del Lord. Stanley Blystone, Ted Lorch, Sam Lufkin, Hank Mann, Hank Bell, Ethan Laidlaw, George Gray, Lew Davis. Undercover agents Wild Bill Hiccup, Buffalo Billious and Just Plain Bill— Moe, Curly and Larry, respectively—take on a gang of cattle rustlers.

Cash and Carry (9/3/37) D: Del Lord. Harlene Wood, Sonny Bupp, Eddie Laughton, Cy Schindell, Al Richardson, Lester Dorr, Lew Davis, John Ince. The Stooges dig for buried treasure, so they can pay for a crippled boy's operation. Working title: *Golddigging in the Treasury*. Remade with Andy Clyde as *A Miner Affair* (1945) and *Two April Fools* (1954).

Playing the Ponies (10/15/37) D: Charles Lamont. Lew Davis, William Irving, Jack "Tiny" Lipson, Billy Bletcher, Charles Dorety. The Stooges swap their failing restaurant for a racehorse named Thunderbolt.

The Sitter Downers (11/26/37) D: Del Lord. Betty Mack, June Gittelson, Marcia Healy, James C. Morton, Robert McKenzie, Jack Long, Bert Young. The Stooges stage a sitdown strike when their fiancees' father refuses to allow his daughters to marry them.

Termites of 1938 (1/7/38) D: Del Lord. Bess Flowers, Bud Jamison, Dorothy Granger, John Ince, Symona Boniface, Beatrice Blinn. Three pest exterminators are mistaken for professional escorts. Remade with Shemp Howard and Tom Kennedy as *Society Mugs* (1946).

Wee Wee Monsieur (2/18/38) D: Del Lord. Vernon Dent, William Irving, Bud Jamison, Harry Semels, John Lester Johnson, Ethelreda Leopold. Three Foreign Legionnaires are ordered to rescue their abducted commanding officer. Working titles: *We We Monsieur* and *The Foreign Legioneers*.

Tassels in the Air (4/1/38) D: Charley Chase. Bess Flowers, Bud Jamison, Vernon Dent, Victor Travers. Moe is mistaken for Omay, a famous interior decorator.

Flat Foot Stooges (5/13/38) D: Charley Chase. Dick Curtis, Chester Conklin, Lola Jensen, Charles "Heine" Conklin, Al Thompson. The Stooges are firemen who still rely on an old horse-drawn fire engine.

Healthy, Wealthy and Dumb (5/20/38) D: Del Lord. Lucille Lund, Jean Carmen, Erlene Heath, James C. Morton, Bud Jamison, Robert "Bobby" Burns. When Curly wins $50,000 in a radio contest, the Stooges immediately check into the ritzy Hotel Costa Plente. Working title: *Cuckoo Over Contests*. Remade as *A Missed Fortune* (1952).

Violent Is the Word for Curly (7/2/38) D: Charley Chase. Gladys Gale, Marjorie Deanne, Bud Jamison, Eddie Fetherstone, Al Thompson, Pat Gleason. The Stooges are mistaken for eminent professors by the dean of a girls' college.

Three Missing Links (7/29/38) D: Jules White. Monte Collins, Jane Hamilton, James C. Morton, Naba. Curly lands a role as a gorilla in a movie to be filmed in Africa.

Mutts to You (10/14/38) D: Charley Chase. Bess Flowers, Lane Chandler, Bud Jamison, Vernon Dent, Cy Schindell. Three professional dogwashers take in an abandoned baby. Working title: *Muts to You*. A remake of Sidney and Murray's *Ten Baby Fingers* (1934) and Andy Clyde's *My Little Feller* (1937). Remade as *Sock-A-Bye Baby* (1942).

Three Little Sew and Sews (1/6/39) D: Del Lord. Phyllis Barry, Harry Semels, James C. Morton, Bud Jamison, Vernon Dent. Three sailors become involved with German spies plotting to steal the Navy's newest submarine. Working titles: *Three Goofy Gobs* and *Submarine Behave!*

We Want Our Mummy (2/24/39) D: Del Lord. Bud Jamison, James C. Morton, Dick Curtis, Robert Williams, Ted Lorch, Eddie Laughton. The Museum of Ancient History hires the Stooges, three private investigators, to find a missing archaeologist; their search leads them to Egypt and the tomb of King Rutentuten.

A-Ducking They Did Go (4/7/39) D: Del Lord. Lynton Brent, Bud Jamison, Cy Schindell, Vernon Dent, Victor Travers. The Stooges sell memberships to the Canvas Back Duck Club, a hunting organization, unaware that it's a crooked operation. Working title: *Never Duck a Duck*. Uses stock footage from *A Pain in the Pullman* (1936).

Yes, We Have No Bonanza (5/19/39) D: Del Lord. Dick Curtis, Lynton Brent, Suzanne Kaaren, Jean Carmen, Lola Jensen, Vernon Dent. The Stooges go prospecting for gold and uncover some stolen bank loot. Working title: *Yes, We Have No Bonanzas*. A remake of Sidney and Murray's *Back to the Soil* (1934). Remade with Andy Clyde as *Gold Is Where You Lose It* (1944) and *Pleasure Treasure* (1951).

Saved by the Belle (6/30/39) D: Charley Chase. Carmen LaRoux, Gino Corrado, LeRoy Mason, Vernon Dent, Al Thompson. Three garment salesmen, peddling earthquake shock absorbers (pillows with straps) in the South American country of Valeska, are mistaken for political assassins.

Calling All Curs (8/25/39) D: Jules White. Lynton Brent, Cy Schindell, Beatrice Curtis, Beatrice Blinn, Dorothy Moore, Robin Raymond, Ethelreda Leopold. Garcon, a prize canine, is stolen from a dog hospital run by the Stooges. Working titles: *Call a Doctor* and *Dog Hospital*.

Oily to Bed, Oily to Rise (10/6/39) D: Jules White. Dick Curtis, Eddie Laughton, Eva McKenzie, Linda Winters, Lorna Gray, Dorothy Moore, Richard Fiske, Victor Travers. The Stooges help a kindly old widow and her three beautiful daughters regain the deed to their farmhouse after conmen swindle them out of it. Remade as *Oil's Well That Ends Well* (1958).

Three Sappy People (12/1/39) D: Jules White. Lorna Gray, Don Beddoe, Ann Doran, Bud Jamison, Eddie Laughton, Richard Fiske, Victor Travers, Beatrice Blinn. Mistaken for psychiatrists Ziller, Zeller and Zoller, the Stooges examine a millionaire's giddy young wife. Working title: *Three Sloppy People*.

You Nazty Spy! (1/19/40) D: Jules White. Lorna Gray, Dick Curtis, Don Beddoe, Richard Fiske, Florine Dickson, Little Billy, John Tyrrell, Bert Young, Joe Murphy. The rise and fall of Moe Hailstone, dictator of Moronica. Working title: *Oh, You Nazty Spy!*

Rockin' Thru the Rockies (3/8/40) D: Jules White. Linda Winters, Dorothy Appleby, Lorna Gray, Kathryn Sheldon, Dick Curtis, Bert Young. En route to San Francisco, the Stooges and a group of chorus girls are attacked by Indians. Working title: *Nell's Belles*.

A-Plumbing We Will Go (4/19/40) D: Del Lord. Bess Flowers, Bud Jamison,

Dudley Dickerson, John Tyrrell, Eddie Laughton, Monty Collins, Symona Boniface, Al Thompson. Running from the police, the Stooges pass themselves off as plumbers and wind up wrecking a society mansion. A reworking of Sidney and Murray's *Plumbing for Gold* (1934). Remade with the Stooges as *Vagabond Loafers* (1949). Reworked with El Brendel and Shemp Howard as *Pick a Peck of Plumbers* (1944) and with the Stooges as *Scheming Schemers* (1956).

Nutty but Nice (6/14/40) D: Jules White. Vernon Dent, John Tyrrell, Cy Schindell, Ned Glass, Lynton Brent, Eddie Garcia, Bert Young, Ethelreda Leopold, Lew Davis, Charles Dorety, Johnny Kascier. Three entertainers search for a little girl's kidnapped father.

How High Is Up? (7/26/40) D: Del Lord. Vernon Dent, Bruce Bennett, Edmund Cobb, Bert Young, Cy Schindell. The Stooges are hired as riveters for a construction company.

From Nurse to Worse (8/23/40) D: Jules White. Lynton Brent, Vernon Dent, John Tyrrell, Dorothy Appleby, Cy Schindell, Marjorie "Babe" Kane, Joe Palma, Dudley Dickerson, Al Thompson, Blanche Payson, Poppie Wilde, Charlie Phillips, Johnny Kascier, Ned Glass, Charles Dorety. In order to collect on a health insurance policy, Curly acts like a dog to convince the examiner that he's insane. Uses stock footage from *Dizzy Doctors* (1937).

No Census, No Feeling (10/4/40) D: Del Lord. Symona Boniface, Marjorie "Babe" Kane, Max Davidson, Vernon Dent, Elinor Vandivere, Bruce Bennett, John Tyrrell, Bert Young. The boys find work as census takers and promptly crash a society party. Working title: *No Answer, No Feeling.*

Cookoo Cavaliers (11/15/40) D: Jules White. Dorothy Appleby, Lynton Brent, Bob O'Connor, Blanche Payson. The Stooges tell a Mexican real estate agent that they want to buy a saloon ("It's gotta have class and gotta have beauty") and wind up with a beauty salon. Working title: *Beauty à la Mud.*

Boobs in Arms (12/27/40) D: Jules White. Richard Fiske, Evelyn Young, Lynton Brent, Eddie Laughton, Charles Dorety, Johnny Kascier, John Tyrrell, Cy Schindell. Three greeting-card salesmen enlist in the army to escape the wrath of a jealous husband, only to discover he's their sergeant. Working title: *All This and Bullets Too.*

So Long, Mr. Chumps (2/7/41) D: Jules White. Vernon Dent, Eddie Laughton, Dorothy Appleby, John Tyrrell, Robert Williams, Bruce Bennett, Bert Young, Lew Davis. A millionaire hires three street cleaners to find an honest man. Working title: *So Long, Mr. Chump.*

Dutiful but Dumb (3/21/41) D: Del Lord. Vernon Dent, Bud Jamison, Fred Kelsey, Eddie Laughton, Chester Conklin, Marjorie Deanne, Stanley Brown, Bruce Bennett, Harry Semels, Bert Young. Photographers Click, Clack and Cluck are sent to Vulgaria, a country where cameras are prohibited under penalty of death.

All the World's a Stooge (5/16/41) D: Del Lord. Lelah Tyler, Emory Parnell, Bud Jamison, Symona Boniface, Richard Fiske, Olaf Hytten, John Tyrrell, Gwen Seager, Ethelreda Leopold, Poppie Wilde. Three window washers are hired to masquerade as refugee children.

I'll Never Heil Again (7/11/41) D: Jules White. Mary Ainslee, Vernon Dent, Bud Jamison, Johnny Kascier, Jack "Tiny" Lipson, Duncan Renaldo, Lynton Brent, Cy Schindell, Don Barclay, Bert Young, Robert "Bobby" Burns. In Moronica, a plot is hatched to overthrow the dictatorship of Moe Hailstone. A sequel to *You Nazty Spy!* (1940).

An Ache in Every Stake (8/22/41) D: Del Lord. Vernon Dent, Bess Flowers, Symona Boniface, Bud Jamison, Gino Corrado, Blanche Payson, Victor Travers. Three icemen help a housewife prepare a birthday dinner for her husband. Partially remade as *Listen, Judge* (1952).

In the Sweet Pie and Pie (10/16/41) D: Jules White. Dorothy Appleby, Mary Ainslee, Ethelreda Leopold, Richard Fiske, Symona Boniface, Vernon Dent, Geneva Mitchell, Eddie Laughton, Lynton Brent, John Tyrrell, Al Thompson, Bert Young, Victor Travers, Lew Davis. In order to collect a legacy, three society girls marry three Death Row convicts about to be executed; when the boys are pardoned, their new wives try to think of ways to get rid of them. Working title: *Well, I'll Be Hanged*. Uses stock footage from *Hoi Polloi* (1935).

Some More of Samoa (12/4/41) D: Del Lord. Symona Boniface, Mary Ainslee, Louise Carver, Tiny Ward, John Tyrrell. Three tree surgeons journey to the tropical island of Rhum Boogie, in search of a rare puckerless persimmon tree.

Loco Boy Makes Good (1/8/42) D: Jules White. Dorothy Appleby, Vernon Dent, John Tyrrell, Eddie Laughton, Bud Jamison, Robert Williams. The boys help an old widow turn her broken-down hotel into a fancy nightclub. Working title: *Poor but Dishonest*.

Cactus Makes Perfect (2/26/42) D: Del Lord. Monty Collins, Vernon Dent, Ernie Adams. Curly invents a gold detector, so the Stooges head West to strike it rich.

What's the Matador? (4/23/42) D: Jules White. Suzanne Kaaren, Harry Burns, Dorothy Appleby, Eddie Laughton, John Tyrrell, Don Zelaya, Bert Young. The boys take their comedy bullfight act down to Mexico, where they tangle with a señora's jealous husband. Working title: *Run, Bull, Run.* Remade as *Sappy Bull Fighters* (1959).

Matri-Phony (7/2/42) D: Harry Edwards. Vernon Dent, Marjorie Deanne, Monty Collins, Cy Schindell, Al Thompson. In ancient Erysipelas, emperor Octopus Grabus decrees all beautiful redheads to be brought to him so he can choose a bride; three pottery-makers help a young woman escape the emperor's clutches.

Three Smart Saps (7/30/42) D: Jules White. Barbara Slater, Ruth Skinner, Julie Gibson, Julie Duncan, Bud Jamison, John Tyrrell, Sally Cairns, Vernon Dent, Eddie Laughton, Johnny Kascier, Victor Travers, Lew Davis, Frank Coleman, Frank Terry. The Stooges try to get their future father-in-law released from jail. Working title: *Father's in Jail Again.*

Even as I. O. U. (9/18/42) D: Del Lord. Ruth Skinner, Stanley Blystone, Wheaton Chambers, Vernon Dent, Bud Jamison, Charles "Heine" Conklin, Jack Gardner, Billy Bletcher. A ventriloquist cons the boys into buying a "talking" racehorse.

Sock-A-Bye Baby (11/13/42) D: Jules White. Bud Jamison, Julie Gibson, Clarence Straight, Baby Joyce Gardner. The boys care for a baby left on their doorstep. Working title: *Their First Baby.* A remake of *Mutts to You* (1938), Sidney and Murray's *Ten Baby Fingers* (1934) and Andy Clyde's *My Little Feller* (1937).

They Stooge to Conga (1/1/43) D:Del Lord. Vernon Dent, John Tyrrell, Dudley Dickerson, Lloyd Bridges, Stanley Brown. Three repairmen fix a doorbell in a house full of saboteurs. Uses stock footage from *Three Little Sew and Sews* (1939).

Dizzy Detectives (2/5/43) D: Jules White. John Tyrrell, Bud Jamison, Lynton Brent, Dick Jensen. Three policemen are hot on the trail of a mysterious ape-man who has committed a series of burglaries. Working title: *Idiots Deluxe.* Uses stock footage from *Pardon My Scotch* (1935). Remade with Joe Besser as *Fraidy Cat* (1951) and *Hook a Crook* (1955).

Spook Louder (4/2/43) D: Del Lord. Stanley Blystone, Lew Kelly, Symona Boniface, Ted Lorch, Charles Middleton. A private investigator relates the tale of three salesmen, a spooky old house and a phantom pie-thrower.

Back from the Front (5/28/43) D: Jules White. Vernon Dent, Bud Jamison,

Stanley Blystone, Charles "Heine" Conklin, Johnny Kascier, Al Thompson, George Gray. Three merchant mariners wind up on a German cruiser. Working title: *A Sailor's Mess*.

Three Little Twerps (7/9/43) D: Harry Edwards. Chester Conklin, Stanley Blystone, Bud Jamison, Duke York, Charles "Heine" Conklin, Al Thompson. The Stooges get jobs with a circus—as targets for a spear-throwing act!

Higher Than a Kite (7/30/43) D: Del Lord. Dick Curtis, Vernon Dent, Duke York, Johnny Kascier. Hiding inside a blockbuster bomb, three mechanics land behind German lines.

I Can Hardly Wait (8/13/43) D: Jules White. Bud Jamison, Lew Davis, Adele Mara, Al Thompson. After several attempts at home remedy, Curly's toothache forces Moe and Larry to drag him to a dentist. Working title: *Nothing but the Tooth*.

Dizzy Pilots (9/24/43) D: Jules White. Harry Semels, Al Thompson, Richard Fiske, Charles Dorety. The Wrong Brothers prepare their new airplane for a test flight. Working title: *Pest Pilots*. Uses stock footage from *Boobs in Arms* (1940).

Phony Express (11/18/43) D: Del Lord. Bud Jamison, Snub Pollard, Shirley Patterson, Chester Conklin, John Merton, Blackie Whiteford, Bert Young, Joel Friedkin, Sally Cleaves, Gwen Seager, Victor Travers. In the Western town of Peaceful Gulch, three vagrants are mistaken for federal marshals. Remade as *Merry Mavericks* (1951).

A Gem of a Jam (12/30/43) D: Del Lord. Dudley Dickerson, Fred Kelsey, Al Hill, John Tyrrell, Al Thompson. The Stooges are janitors mistaken for doctors by three armed gunmen.

Crash Goes the Hash (2/5/44) D: Jules White. Dick Curtis, Symona Boniface, Vernon Dent, John Tyrrell, Johnny Kascier, Wally Rose, Judy Malcolm, Victor Travers, Beatrice Blinn, Ida Mae Johnson, Elise Grover. Mistaken for reporters by a newspaper editor, the Stooges pose as servants to gain entry to a party celebrating the engagement of socialite widow Mrs. Van Bustle to Prince Shaam of Ubeedarn. A remake of Collins and Kennedy's *New News* (1937).

Busy Buddies (3/18/44) D: Del Lord. Fred Kelsey, Vernon Dent, Eddie Gribbon, John Tyrrell, Eddie Laughton, Victor Travers, Johnny Kascier. The bills keep mounting at the Stooges' short-order restaurant, The Jive Cafe, so they enter Curly in the County Fair's cow-milking contest, hoping to win first prize.

The Yoke's on Me (5/26/44) D: Jules White. Bob McKenzie, Emmett Lynn. Labeled 4-F by the draft board, the patriotic Stooges become farmers to aid the war effort. Working title: *Fouled by a Fowl.*

Idle Roomers (7/16/44) D: Del Lord. Christine McIntyre, Vernon Dent, Duke York, Eddie Laughton, Joanne Frank, Esther Howard. A wolfman is on the loose at a hotel where the Stooges work as bellhops.

Gents Without Cents (9/22/44) D: Jules White. Lindsay Bourquin, Laverne Thompson, Betty Phares, John Tyrrell, Lynton Brent, Judy Malcolm, Eddie Borden. The Stooges team up with three girl dancers and stage a benefit show for the war effort. Working title: *Tenderized Hams.*

No Dough Boys (11/24/44) D: Jules White. Vernon Dent, Christine McIntyre, Kelly Flint, Judy Malcolm, John Tyrrell, Brian O'Hara. Posing as Japanese soldiers for a photo layout, the Stooges are mistaken for genuine saboteurs. Working title: *The New World Odor.*

Three Pests in a Mess (1/19/45) D: Del Lord. Christine McIntyre, Vernon Dent, Brian O'Hara, Snub Pollard, Robert Williams, Charles "Heine" Conklin, Victor Travers, Johnny Kascier. Curly believes he's killed a man (it's a mannequin), so the boys sneak into a pet cemetery to dispose of the corpus delicti. A remake of El Brendel's *Ready, Willing but Unable* (1941).

Booby Dupes (3/17/45) D: Del Lord. Rebel Randall, Vernon Dent, John Tyrrell, Dorothy Vernon, Snub Pollard, Wanda Perry, Geene Courtney, Lola Gogan. Three fish peddlers decide to increase profits by purchasing a boat and catching their own fish.

Idiots Deluxe (7/20/45) D: Jules White. Vernon Dent, Paul Kruger, Eddie Laughton. Moe's nerves are frayed, so Larry and Curly take him on a hunting trip for rest and relaxation. Working title: *The Malady Lingers On.* A reworking of Collins and Kennedy's *Oh, My Nerves!* (1935). Remade as *Guns A-Poppin'* (1957).

If a Body Meets a Body (8/30/45) D: Jules White. Fred Kelsey, Ted Lorch, Joe Palma, Victor Travers, Al Thompson, John Tyrrell, Judy Malcolm. When Curly's rich uncle dies, the boys go to a spooky old mansion to collect the inheritance. Working title: *Nearly in the Dough.*

Micro-Phonies (11/15/45) D: Edward Bernds. Christine McIntyre, Gino Corrado, Symona Boniface, Fred Kelsey, Sam Flint, Chester Conklin, Lynton Brent, Bess Flowers, Charles "Heine" Conklin, Ted Lorch, Judy Malcolm. When Curly mimes a recording at a radio station, a wealthy society matron mistakes him for a female vocalist.

Beer Barrel Polecats (1/10/46) D: Jules White. Vernon Dent, Eddie Laughton, Robert Williams, Bruce Bennett, Joe Palma, Al Thompson, Blackie Whiteford. Three would-be bootleggers are sent to prison. Working title: *Three Duds in the Suds*. Uses stock footage from *So Long, Mr. Chumps* (1941) and *In the Sweet Pie and Pie* (1941).

A Bird in the Head (2/28/46) D: Edward Bernds. Vernon Dent, Robert Williams, Frank Lackteen, Art Miles. A mad doctor schemes to put Curly's minuscule brain into the head of a gorilla.

Uncivil Warbirds (3/29/46) D: Jules White. Faye Williams, Eleanor Counts, Marilyn Johnson, Robert Williams, Ted Lorch, John Tyrrell, Maury Dexter, Cy Schindell, Joe Palma, Blackie Whiteford, Lew Davis, Johnny Kascier, Victor Travers, Al Rosen. At the outbreak of the Civil War, Moe and Larry enlist in the Union army while Curly joins the Confederacy. Working title: *Three Southern Dumbbells*. A remake, with stock footage, of Buster Keaton's *Mooching Through Georgia* (1939).

Three Troubledoers (4/25/46) D: Edward Bernds. Christine McIntyre, Dick Curtis, Blackie Whiteford, Ethan Laidlaw, Hank Bell, Budd Fine, Steve Clarke, Joe Garcia. Curly is made sheriff of Dead Man's Gulch and helps save Nell from the clutches of Badlands Blackie.

Monkey Businessmen (6/20/46) D: Edward Bernds. Kenneth MacDonald, Fred Kelsey, Snub Pollard, Jean Donahue, Cy Schindell, Rocky Woods, Wade Crosby. The Stooges check into Dr. Mallard's Rest Home, a crooked sanitarium. Working titles: *Sanitarium Stooge* and *Monkey Business*. A remake of Smith and Dale's *Mutiny on the Body* (1939).

Three Loan Wolves (7/4/46) D: Jules White. Beverly Warren, Harold Brauer, Wally Rose, Joe Palma, Jackie Jackson. The daily routine at the Stooges' hock shop is disrupted when a gangster's girlfriend leaves a baby in Larry's care. Working title: *In Hock*.

G.I. Wanna Home (9/5/46) D: Jules White. Judy Malcolm, Ethelreda Leopold, Doris Houck, Symona Boniface, Al Thompson. After their discharge from the army, the Stooges learn that their fiancees have been dispossessed.

Rhythm and Weep (10/3/46) D: Jules White. Jack Norton, Gloria Patrice, Ruth Godfrey, Nita Bieber. The Stooges and three girl dancers are cast in a Broadway musical backed by an eccentric millionaire. Working title: *Acting Up*.

Three Little Pirates (12/5/46) D: Edward Bernds. Christine McIntyre, Vernon

Dent, Robert Stevens, Dorothy DeHaven, Ethan Laidlaw, Joe Palma, Jack Parker, Larry McGrath, Al Thompson. Shipwrecked on Dead Man's Island, the Stooges run afoul with Black Louie, a notorious pirate.

Half-Wits Holiday (1/9/47) D: Jules White. Vernon Dent, Barbara Slater, Ted Lorch, Emil Sitka, Symona Boniface, Al Thompson, Johnny Kascier, Helen Dickson, Victor Travers. A professor wagers a colleague that he can transform the Stooges into refined gentlemen. Working title *No Gents—No Cents*. A remake of *Hoi Polloi* (1935). Remade as *Pies and Guys* (1958).

With Moe Howard, Larry Fine and Shemp Howard:

Fright Night (3/6/47) D: Edward Bernds. Dick Wessel, Claire Carleton, Harold Brauer, Cy Schindell, Sammy Stein, Tommy Kingston, Dave Harper, Stanley Blystone, Charles "Heine" Conklin. A mobster warns three fight managers that their boxer had better lose an upcoming bout—if they know what's good for them. Remade as *Fling in the Ring* (1955).

Out West (4/24/47) D: Edward Bernds. Christine McIntyre, Jacques O'Mahoney, Jack Norman, Stanley Blystone, Vernon Dent, George Chesebro, Frank Ellis, Charles "Heine" Conklin, Blackie Whiteford. The Stooges journey West, where they subdue the infamous Doc Barker and his gang. A reworking of Langdon and Brendel's *Pistol Packin' Nitwits* (1945). Remade as *Pals and Gals* (1954).

Hold That Lion (7/17/47) D: Jules White. Kenneth MacDonald, Emil Sitka, Dudley Dickerson, Charles "Heine" Conklin, Blackie Whiteford, Curly Howard. The Stooges board a train to catch a con man who swindled them out of their inheritance. Working title: *The Lion and the Louse*. Remade as *Booty and the Beast* (1953).

Brideless Groom (9/11/47) D: Edward Bernds. Dee Green, Christine McIntyre, Emil Sitka, Doris Colleen, Nancy Saunders, Johnny Kascier. If Shemp doesn't marry within a seven-hour period, he'll lose a half-million-dollar inheritance. Working title: *Love and Learn*. Remade as *Husbands Beware* (1956).

Sing a Song of Six Pants (10/30/47) D: Jules White. Virginia Hunter, Harold Brauer, Vernon Dent, Phil Arnold, Cy Schindell. A bank robber hides out in the Pip Boys' tailoring shop—and loses his coat and pants. Working title: *Where the Vest Begins*. Remade as *Rip, Sew and Stitch* (1953).

All Gummed Up (12/18/47) D: Jules White. Christine McIntyre, Emil Sitka, Cy Schindell, Victor Travers, Al Thompson, Symona Boniface, Judy Malcolm.

The Stooges are drugstore operators who invent a youth serum. Working title: *Sweet Vita-Mine*. Remade as *Bubble Trouble* (1953).

Shivering Sherlocks (1/8/48) D: Del Lord. Christine McIntyre, Kenneth Mac-Donald, Frank Lackteen, Duke York, Vernon Dent, Stanley Blystone, Cy Schindell, Joe Palma. The Stooges work at the Elite Cafe; when the owner inherits an old mansion, the boys accompany her to the property site. Remade as *Of Cash and Hash* (1955).

Pardon My Clutch (2/26/48) D: Edward Bernds. Matt McHugh, Alyn Lockwood, Doris Revier, Wanda Perry, Emil Sitka, Stanley Blystone, George Lloyd. Shemp needs rest and relaxation, so the boys buy a car and plan a camping trip. Remade as *Wham Bam Slam* (1955).

Squareheads of the Round Table (3/4/48) D: Edward Bernds. Christine McIntyre, Jacques O'Mahoney, Vernon Dent, Phil Van Zandt, Harold Brauer, Joe Palma, Douglas Coppin, Joe Garcia. In the days of King Arthur, three wandering troubadours help advance a romance between a blacksmith and the king's daughter. Remade as *Knutzy Knights* (1954).

Fiddlers Three (5/6/48) D: Jules White. Vernon Dent, Phil Van Zandt, Virginia Hunter, Joe Palma, Sherry O'Neil, Cy Schindell, Al Thompson. Old King Cole's trusty fiddlers rescue the princess from an evil magician. Remade as *Musty Musketeers* (1954).

The Hot Scots (7/8/48) D: Edward Bernds. Herbert Evans, Christine McIntyre, Ted Lorch, Charles Knight. The Stooges, aspiring Scotland Yard sleuths, spend a night in spooky Glenheather Castle. Working title: *Scotland Yardbirds*. Remade as *Scotched in Scotland* (1954).

Heavenly Daze (9/2/48) D: Jules White. Vernon Dent, Sam McDaniel, Symona Boniface, Victor Travers, Marti Shelton, Judy Malcolm. Shemp dies, but isn't allowed into Heaven unless he returns to Earth and reforms Moe and Larry of their wayward habits. Working title: *Heaven's Above*. Remade as *Bedlam in Paradise* (1955).

I'm a Monkey's Uncle (10/7/48) D: Jules White. Dee Green, Virginia Hunter, Nancy Saunders, Cy Schindell, Joe Palma, Charles "Heine" Conklin. Three zany cavemen go courting for brides. Remade as *Stone Age Romeos* (1955).

Mummy's Dummies (11/4/48) D: Edward Bernds. Vernon Dent, Ralph Dunn, Phil Van Zandt, Dee Green, Jean Spangler, Virginia Ellsworth, Suzanne Ridgeway, Cy Malis, Vivian Mason. In ancient Egypt, three used-chariot dealers are arrested for selling defective vehicles.

Crime on Their Hands (12/9/48) D: Edward Bernds. Kenneth MacDonald, Christine McIntyre, Charles C. Wilson, Lester Allen, Cy Schindell, Frank Lackteen. A gangster's moll hides the stolen Punjab Diamond in a bowl of candy, and Shemp inadvertently swallows it. A remake of Andy Clyde's *All Work and No Pay* (1942). Remade as *Hot Ice* (1955).

The Ghost Talks (2/3/49) D: Jules White. Nancy Saunders. The Stooges are moving furniture out of creepy old Smorgasbord Castle when they encounter a suit of armor inhabited by the ghost of Peeping Tom. Working title: *That's the Spirit*. Remade as *Creeps* (1956).

Who Done It? (3/3/49) D: Edward Bernds. Christine McIntyre, Emil Sitka, Ralph Dunn, Duke York, Charles Knight, Dudley Dickerson. After receiving a death threat, a millionaire hires three private detectives for protection. A remake of Schilling and Lane's *Pardon My Terror* (1946); a reworking of Walter Catlett's *You're Next* (1940). Remade as *For Crimin' Out Loud* (1956).

Hokus Pokus (5/5/49) D: Jules White. Mary Ainslee, David Bond, Vernon Dent, Jimmy Lloyd, Ned Glass. The Great Svengarlic hypnotizes the Stooges and has them perform a death-defying stunt. Working title: *Three Blind Mice*. Remade as *Flagpole Jitters* (1956).

Fuelin' Around (7/7/49) D: Edward Bernds. Christine McIntyre, Emil Sitka, Phil Van Zandt, Vernon Dent, Jacques O'Mahoney, Harold Brauer, Andre Pola. Foreign spies mistake Larry for a world-renown scientist. Remade as *Hot Stuff* (1956).

Malice in the Palace (9/1/49) D: Jules White. Vernon Dent, George Lewis, Frank Lackteen, Johnny Kascier. (Curly Howard appeared in a deleted sequence). The Stooges, waiters at the Cafe Cashbahbah, set out to recover the Ruttin' Tuttin Diamond stolen by the Emir of Shmow. Working title: *Here We Go Shmow*. Remade as *Rumpus in the Harem* (1956).

Vagabond Loafers (10/6/49) D: Edward Bernds. Christine McIntyre, Kenneth MacDonald, Emil Sitka, Symona Boniface, Dudley Dickerson, Herbert Evans. Three plumbers foil a plot to steal a valuable painting. A remake, with stock footage, of *A-Plumbing We Will Go* (1940); a reworking of Sidney and Murray's *Plumbing for Gold* (1934). Remade as *Scheming Schemers* (1956).

Dunked in the Deep (11/3/49) D: Jules White. Gene Roth. The Stooges become reluctant stowaways when they unwittingly aid a foreign spy. Stock shot of peeling wallpaper taken from Harry Von Zell's *So's Your Antenna* (1946). Remade as *Commotion on the Ocean* (1956).

Punchy Cowpunchers (1/5/50) D: Edward Bernds. Jacques O'Mahoney, Christine McIntyre, Kenneth MacDonald, Emil Sitka, Dick Wessel, George Chesebro, Bob Cason, Vernon Dent, Ted Mapes. Stanley Price. The Stooges, stableboys for the U.S. Cavalry, go after the Dillon Gang.

Hugs and Mugs (2/2/50) D: Jules White. Christine McIntyre, Nanette Bordeaux, Kathleen O'Malley, Joe Palma, Wally Rose, Pat Moran, Emil Sitka. The Stooges, proprietors of the Shangri-La Upholstery Shop, purchase a chair with a pearl necklace hidden inside.

Dopey Dicks (3/2/50) D: Edward Bernds. Christine McIntyre, Phil Van Zandt, Stanley Price. The boys encounter a mad scientist seeking a human head for his mechanical man. A remake of El Brendel's *Boobs in the Night* (1943).

Love at First Bite (5/4/50) D: Jules White. Christine McIntyre, Yvette Reynard, Marie Montiel, Al Thompson. Awaiting the arrival of their European sweethearts, the boys reminisce about how their romances began. Working title: *New Grooms Sweep Clean*. Reworked as *Fifi Blows Her Top* (1958).

Self-Made Maids (7/6/50) D: Jules White. A tale of three artists and their girlfriends; the Stooges portray all roles in the film.

Three Hams on Rye (9/7/50) D: Jules White. Emil Sitka, Christine McIntyre, Nanette Bordeaux, Mildred Olsen, Judy Malcolm, Brian O'Hara, Danny Lewis, Ned Glass, Blackie Whiteford. The Stooges, theatrical propmen aspiring to be actors, prepare for the premiere of a new play. Working title: *How Hammy Was My Hamlet*.

Studio Stoops (10/5/50) D: Edward Bernds. Kenneth MacDonald, Christine McIntyre, Vernon Dent, Charles Jordan, Joe Palma, Stanley Price. Three termite exterminators become publicity agents and rescue a kidnapped movie starlet.

Slaphappy Sleuths (11/9/50) D: Jules White. Stanley Blystone, Nanette Bordeaux, Emil Sitka, Gene Roth, Joe Palma, Blackie Whiteford. To foil a robbery, three private investigators pose as gas station attendants.

A Snitch in Time (12/7/50) D: Edward Bernds. Jean Willes, John Merton, Henry Kulky. The Stooges, owners of the Ye Olde Furniture Shoppe, tangle with a pair of crooks.

Three Arabian Nuts (1/4/51) D: Edward Bernds. Vernon Dent, Phil Van Zandt, Dick Curtis, Wesley Bly. Shemp falls into possession of Aladdin's lamp and conjures up a genie. Working titles: *Genie with the Light Brown Hair* and *Genie Was a Meanie*.

Baby Sitter Jitters (2/1/51) D: Jules White. Lynn Davis, David Windsor, Myron Healy, Margie Liszt. A child is abducted when three professional babysitters fall asleep on the job.

Don't Throw That Knife (5/3/51) D: Jules White. Jean Willes, Dick Curtis. Three census takers run afoul with a knife-throwing magician. Working title: *Noncensus Takers*.

Scrambled Brains (7/7/51) D: Jules White. Babe London, Emil Sitka, Vernon Dent, Royce Milne, Johnny Kascier. Moe and Larry try to cure Shemp, who's suffering from hallucinations. Working title: *Impatient Patient*.

Merry Mavericks (9/6/51) D: Edward Bernds. Marion Martin, Don Harvey, Paul Campbell, Emil Sitka, Blackie Whiteford, Victor Travers. In the Western town of Peaceful Gulch, Red Morgan and his gang mistake three vagrants for famous lawmen. A remake, with stock footage, of *Phony Express* (1943).

The Tooth Will Out (10/4/51) D: Edward Bernds. Margie Liszt, Vernon Dent, Dick Curtis, Emil Sitka, Slim Gaut. The Stooges, recent dental school graduates, open up an office in the wild and woolly West. Working title: *A Yank at the Dentist*.

Hula-La-La (11/1/51) D: Hugh McCollum. Jean Willes, Kenneth MacDonald, Emil Sitka, Maxine Doviat, Lei Aloha, Joy Windsor. A movie studio sends the Stooges, dance instructors, to a South Seas island to teach the natives the terpsichorean art.

Pest Man Wins (12/6/51) D: Jules White. Margie Liszt, Emil Sitka, Nanette Bordeaux, Vernon Dent, Helen Dickson, Symona Boniface, Eddie Laughton, Charles "Heine" Conklin, Ethelreda Leopold, Al Thompson, Victor Travers, Johnny Kascier. Three pest exterminators crash a society party. Working title: *Mousers in the Trousers*. A remake, with stock footage, of *Ants in the Pantry* (1936). Also uses stock footage from *In the Sweet Pie and Pie* (1941) and *Half-Wits Holiday* (1947).

A Missed Fortune (1/3/52) D: Jules White. Nanette Bordeaux, Suzanne Ridgeway, Vivian Mason, Vernon Dent, Stanley Blystone. The Stooges check into a swank hotel immediately after Shemp wins a quiz show jackpot. A remake, with stock footage, of *Healthy, Wealthy and Dumb* (1938).

Listen, Judge (3/6/52) D: Edward Bernds. Kitty McHugh, Vernon Dent, Mary Emory, John Hamilton, Emil Sitka, Gil Perkins, Chick Collins. Three

Emil Sitka struggles to maintain his composure during a Three Stooges onslaught in *Pest Man Wins* (1951).

repairmen help a woman prepare a birthday dinner for her husband. A partial remake of *An Ache in Every Stake* (1941).

Corny Casanovas (5/1/52) D: Jules White. Connie Cezan. Unbeknownst to one another, the Stooges are in love with the same gold-digging blonde. Working title: *One Won*. Remade as *Rusty Romeos* (1957).

He Cooked His Goose (7/3/52) D: Jules White. Mary Ainslee, Angela Stevens, Theila Darin, Johnny Kascier. Larry, a bachelor with a roving eye, makes a play for Moe's wife and Shemp's fiancee. Working title: *Clam Up*. Remade as *Triple Crossed* (1959).

Gents in a Jam (7/4/52) D: Edward Bernds. Emil Sitka, Dany Sue Nolan, Kitty McHugh, Mickey Simpson, Snub Pollard. Just as they're about to be evicted, the Stooges receive a telegram from Shemp's rich Uncle Phineas, who's planning to pay the boys a visit. A remake of Hugh Herbert's *Hot Heir* (1947).

Three Dark Horses (10/16/52) D: Jules White. Kenneth MacDonald, Ben

Welden. A corrupt campaign manager makes the Stooges convention delegates for an upcoming election. Working title: *Small Delegates at Large*.

Cuckoo on a Choo Choo (12/4/52) D: Jules White. Patricia Wright, Victoria Horne, Reggie Dvorack. Larry steals a railroad car and is tracked down by Moe, a detective for the railroad company. Working title: *A Train Called Schmow*.

Up in Daisy's Penthouse (2/5/53) D: Jules White. Connie Cezan, John Merton, Jack Kenny, Suzanne Ridgeway, Blackie Whiteford, Johnny Kascier. The Stooges try to prevent their father from marrying a gold-digging blonde. A remake, with stock footage, of *3 Dumb Clucks* (1937).

Booty and the Beast (3/5/53) D: Jules White. Kenneth MacDonald, Vernon Dent, Charles "Heine" Conklin, Dudley Dickerson, Blackie Whiteford, Curly Howard. The Stooges board a train in order to catch a safecracker. Working title: *Fun for the Money*. A remake, with stock footage, of *Hold That Lion* (1947).

Loose Loot (4/2/53) D: Jules White. Kenneth MacDonald, Tom Kennedy, Emil Sitka, Nanette Bordeaux, Suzanne Ridgeway. The boys go backstage at the Circle Follies Theatre to catch the conman who cheated them out of their inheritance. Working title: *Filthy Lucre*. Uses stock footage from *Hold That Lion* (1947).

Tricky Dicks (5/7/53) D: Jules White. Ferris Taylor, Murray Alper, Benny Rubin, Connie Cezan, Phil Arnold, Suzanne Ridgeway. Three police detectives are given twenty-four hours to apprehend a killer. Working title: *Cop and Bull Story*. Uses stock footage from *Hold That Lion* (1947).

Spooks (6/15/53) D: Jules White. Norma Randall, Phil Van Zandt, Tom Kennedy, Frank Mitchell. Three sleuths enter a haunted house while searching for a missing girl. Filmed in 3-D.

Pardon My Backfire (8/15/53) D: Jules White. Benny Rubin, Frank Sully, Barbara Bartay, Phil Arnold, Ruth Godfrey, Angela Stevens, Theila Darin, Fred Kelsey. Three garage mechanics tangle with a gang of crooks. Filmed in 3-D.

Rip, Sew and Stitch (9/3/53) D: Jules White. Vernon Dent, Harold Brauer, Cy Schindell, Phil Arnold. Three tailors go after an escaped criminal. Working title: *A Pressing Affair*. A remake, with stock footage, of *Sing a Song of Six Pants* (1947).

Suzanne Ridgeway catches three pairs of roving eyes in this posed shot for *Loose Loot* (1953).

Bubble Trouble (10/8/53) D: Jules White. Christine McIntyre, Emil Sitka, Victor Travers. Three druggists concoct a youth serum. Working title: *Drugstore Dubs*. A remake, with stock footage, of *All Gummed Up* (1947).

Goof on the Roof (12/3/53) D: Jules White. Frank Mitchell, Maxine Gates. To help out a friend, the boys install a new television antenna. A remake of Vernon and Quillan's *Let Down Your Aerial* (1949).

Income Tax Sappy (2/4/54) D: Jules White. Benny Rubin, Marjorie Liszt, Nanette Bordeaux, Vernon Dent, Joe Palma. The Stooges make a fortune as dishonest tax consultants. Working title: *Tax Saps*.

Pardon My Backfire (1953) was one of two Stooge comedies filmed in 3-D. Pictured (l. to r.): Shemp, Frank Sully, Moe, Barbara Bartay, Larry, and Benny Rubin.

Musty Musketeers (5/13/54) D: Jules White. Vernon Dent, Phil Van Zandt, Virginia Hunter, Sherry O'Neil, Charles "Heine" Conklin, Wanda Perry, Theila Darin, Norma Randall, Joe Palma. A evil magician's scheme to marry the princess is thwarted by the Stooges. A remake, with stock footage, of *Fiddlers Three* (1948).

Pals and Gals (6/3/54) D: Jules White. Christine McIntyre, George Chesebro, Norman Willes, Vernon Dent, Charles "Heine" Conklin, Norma Randall, Ruth Godfrey, Frank Ellis, Stanley Blystone, Joe Palma, Blackie Whiteford. The Stooges journey West and save three lovelies from the clutches of the Barker Gang. Working title: *Cuckoo Westerners*. A remake, with stock footage, of *Out West* (1947). Also uses stock footage from *Goofs and Saddles* (1937).

Knutzy Knights (9/2/54) D: Jules White. Christine McIntyre, Jacques O'Mahoney, Vernon Dent, Phil Van Zandt, Harold Brauer, Joe Palma, Ruth Godfrey, Joe Garcia, Douglas Coppin. Three troubadours try their best to cheer up Princess Elaine. A remake, with stock footage, of *Squareheads of the Round Table* (1948).

Shot in the Frontier (10/7/54) D: Jules White. Emil Sitka, Kenneth Mac-Donald, Emmett Lynn, Ruth Godfrey, Theila Darin, Vivian Mason. The Stooges prepare for a shootout with the Noonan Brothers at high noon. Working title: *Low Afternoon.*

Scotched in Scotland (11/4/54) D: Jules White. Christine McIntyre, Herbert Evans, Phil Van Zandt, Charles Knight, Ted Lorch, George Pembroke. Three detective school graduates are sent to Scotland to guard the priceless treasures in Glenheather Castle. Working title: *Hassle in the Castle.* A remake, with stock footage, of *The Hot Scots* (1948).

Fling in the Ring (1/6/55) D: Jules White. Dick Wessel, Claire Carleton, Frank Sully, Harold Brauer, Cy Schindell, Tommy Kingston, Sammy Stein, Joe Palma, Charles "Heine" Conklin. A mobster wants a fighter, managed by the Stooges, to throw an upcoming bout. A remake, with stock footage, of *Fright Night* (1947).

Of Cash and Hash (2/3/55) D: Jules White. Christine McIntyre, Kenneth MacDonald, Frank Lackteen, Vernon Dent, Duke York, Cy Schindell. Three restaurant employees solve the mystery behind an armored car robbery. Working title: *Crook Crackers.* A remake, with stock footage, of *Shivering Sherlocks* (1948).

Gypped in the Penthouse (3/10/55) D: Jules White. Jean Willes, Emil Sitka, Al Thompson. Shemp and Larry meet at the Woman Haters Club and discuss their mutual experiences with the opposite sex. Working title: *Blundering Bachelors.*

Bedlam in Paradise (4/14/55) D: Jules White. Phil Van Zandt, Vernon Dent, Symona Boniface, Victor Travers, Marti Shelton, Judy Malcolm, Sylvia Lewis. Shemp dies, but can't get into Heaven unless he reforms Moe and Larry. Working title: *Gruesome Threesome.* A remake, with stock footage, of *Heavenly Daze* (1948).

Stone Age Romeos (6/2/55) D: Jules White. Emil Sitka, Dee Green, Virginia Hunter, Nancy Saunders, Cy Schindell, Joe Palma, Bill Wallace, Barbara Bartay. A museum curator screens a movie about cavemen, filmed by the Stooges. Working title: *Caved in Cavemen.* A reworking, with stock footage, of *I'm a Monkey's Uncle* (1948).

Wham Bam Slam (9/1/55) D: Jules White. Matt McHugh, Alyn Lockwood, Doris Revier, Wanda Perry. Moe and Larry plan to take Shemp, who's suffering from a case of bad nerves, on a camping trip. Working title: *Enjoying Poor Health.* A remake, with stock footage, of *Pardon My Clutch* (1948).

Hot Ice (10/6/55) D: Jules White. Christine McIntyre, Kenneth MacDonald, Charles C. Wilson, Cy Schindell, Lester Allen, Barbara Bartay, Bud Fine, Blackie Whiteford. Three Scotland Yard gardeners try to recover a stolen gem. A remake, with stock footage, of *Crime on Their Hands* (1948). Also uses stock footage from *The Hot Scots* (1948).

Blunder Boys (11/3/55) D: Jules White. Benny Rubin, Angela Stevens, Kenneth MacDonald, Barbara Bartay, Bonnie Menjum, Marjorie Jackson, Barbara Donaldson, June Lebow, Frank Sully, Al Thompson. In this spoof of *Dragnet*, three hardboiled detectives recount their career, from their army days up to their first — and last — case. Working title: *Cuckoo Cops*.

Husbands Beware (1/5/56) D: Jules White. Dee Green, Christine McIntyre, Emil Sitka, Lu Leonard, Maxine Gates, Doris Colleen, Nancy Saunders, Johnny Kascier. After marrying Shemp's battle-axe sisters, Larry and Moe vow they'll get even with him. Working title: *Eat, Drink and Be Married*. A remake, with stock footage, of *Brideless Groom* (1947).

Creeps (2/2/56) D: Jules White. The Stooges tell their children a bedtime story about their exploits in an eerie old castle. Working title: *Three Brave Cowards*. A remake, with stock footage, of *The Ghost Talks* (1949).

Flagpole Jitters (4/5/56) D: Jules White. David Bond, Mary Ainslee, Vernon Dent, Frank Sully, Don Harvey, Ned Glass, Barbara Bartay, Beverly Thomas, Bonnie Menjum, Dick Alexander. The Great Svengarlic plots a robbery and hypnotizes the Stooges in order to create a diversion. A remake, with stock footage, of *Hokus Pokus* (1949).

For Crimin' Out Loud (5/3/56) D: Jules White. Emil Sitka, Christine McIntyre, Ralph Dunn, Charles Knight, Duke York, Barbara Bartay. Three detectives are hired to protect a councilman who's been receiving death threats from racketeers. Working title: *Nutty Newshounds*. A remake, with stock footage, of *Who Done It?* (1949).

Rumpus in the Harlem (6/21/56) D: Jules White. Vernon Dent, George Lewis, Hariette Tarler, Diana Darrin, Ruth Godfrey White, Helen Jay, Suzanne Ridgeway, Johnny Kascier, Joe Palma. Unless the Stooges find a way to raise some money quick, their girlfriends will be sold to the Sultan of Pish Posh. Working title: *Diamond Daffy*. A remake, with stock footage, of *Malice in the Palace* (1949).

Hot Stuff (9/6/56) D: Jules White. Christine McIntyre, Emil Sitka, Phil Van Zandt, Vernon Dent, Gene Roth, Connie Cezan, Evelyn Lovequist, Jacques O'Mahoney, Andre Pola, Harold Brauer, Joe Palma. Foreign spies mistake Larry for the inventor of a top secret rocket fuel, so they kidnap the Stooges to gain access to the formula. Working title: *They Gassed Wrong*. A remake, with stock footage, of *Fuelin' Around* (1949).

Scheming Schemers (10/4/56) D: Jules White. Christine McIntyre, Kenneth MacDonald, Emil Sitka, Symona Boniface, Dudley Dickerson, Herbert Evans, Al Thompson, Victor Travers, Joe Palma. While searching for a lost diamond ring, three plumbers clash with art thieves. Working title: *Pixilated Plumbers*. A remake of *Vagabond Loafers* (1949) and a reworking of *A-Plumbing We Will Go* (1940), using stock footage from both; based on Sidney and Murray's *Plumbing for Gold* (1934). Uses stock footage from *Half-Wits Holiday* (1947).

Commotion on the Ocean (11/8/56) D: Jules White. Gene Roth, Emil Sitka, Harriette Tarler, Joe Palma. Three aspiring reporters inadvertently become stowaways. Working title: *Salt Water Daffy*. A remake, with stock footage, of *Dunked in the Deep* (1949). Also uses stock footage from *Crime on Their Hands* (1948). Stock shot of wallpaper peeling taken from Harry Von Zell's *So's Your Antenna* (1946).

With Moe Howard, Larry Fine and Joe Besser:

Hoofs and Goofs (1/31/57) D: Jules White. Benny Rubin, Harriette Tarler, Tony the Wonder Horse. The Stooges' sister, Birdie, is reincarnated as a horse—and the boys bring her to their apartment. Working titles: *Galloping Bride* and *Horsing Around*.

Muscle Up a Little Closer (2/28/57) D: Jules White. Maxine Gates, Ruth Godfrey White, Harriette Tarler, Matt Murphy. A diamond ring belonging to Joe's girlfriend is stolen. Working title: *Builder Uppers*.

A Merry Mix-Up (3/28/57) D: Jules White. Frank Sully, Diana Darrin, Ruth Godfrey White, Jeanne Carmen, Suzanne Ridgeway, Harriette Tarler, Nanette Bordeaux. Three sets of triplets cause confusion at a nightclub. Working title: *A Merry Marriage Mix-Up*.

Space Ship Sappy (4/18/57) D: Jules White. Benny Rubin, Doreen Woodbury, Lorraine Crawford, Harriette Tarler, Marilyn Hanold, Emil Sitka. The Stooges meet cannibal women on the planet Sunev (Venus spelled backwards). Working title: *Rocket and Roll It*.

Guns A-Poppin' (6/13/57) D: Jules White. Vernon Dent, Frank Sully, Joe Palma, Johnny Kascier. Moe, on trial for assaulting Larry and Joe, relates his side of the story. Working title: *Nerveless Wreck*. A remake, with stock footage, of *Idiots Deluxe* (1945). A reworking of Collins and Kennedy's *Oh, My Nerves!* (1935).

Horsing Around (9/12/57) D: Jules White. Emil Sitka, Harriette Tarler, Tony the Wonder Horse. The Stooges' sister, Birdie, reincarnated as a horse, wants to be reunited with a circus horse named Schnapps. Working titles: *Just Horsing Around* and *Just Fooling Around*. A sequel to *Hoofs and Goofs* (1957).

Rusty Romeos (10/17/57) D: Jules White. Connie Cezan. Unbeknownst to each other, the Stooges fall in love with the same gold-digging blonde. Working title: *Sappy Lovers*. A remake, with stock footage, of *Corny Casanovas* (1952).

Outer Space Jitters (12/5/57) D: Jules White. Emil Sitka, Gene Roth, Phil Van Zandt, Joe Palma, Dan Blocker, Diana Darrin, Harriette Tarler, Arline Hunter. On the planet Zunev, the Grand Zilch plans to turn the Stooges, three intrepid space travelers, into zombies. Working title: *Outer Space Daze*.

Quiz Whizz (2/13/58) D: Jules White. Gene Roth, Greta Thyssen, Milton Frome, Bill Brauer, Emil Sitka. Joe is swindled out of his TV contest winnings.

Fifi Blows Her Top (4/10/58) D: Jules White. Vanda Dupre, Phil Van Zandt, Christine McIntyre, Yvette Reynard, Harriette Tarler, Suzanne Ridgeway, Wanda D'Ottoni, Al Thompson, Charles "Heine" Conklin, Joe Palma. Joe's former sweetheart, Fifi, moves into his apartment building. Working title: *Rancid Romance*. A reworking, with stock footage, of *Love at First Bite* (1950).

Pies and Guys (6/12/58) D: Jules White. Gene Roth, Milton Frome, Greta Thyssen, Emil Sitka, Symona Boniface, Helen Dickson, Harriette Tarler, Al Thompson, Johnny Kascier. A professor wagers a colleague that he can transform the Stooges into refined gentlemen within a sixty-day period. Working title: *Easy Come, Easy Go*. A remake, with stock footage, of *Half-Wits Holiday* (1947); based on *Hoi Polloi* (1935).

Sweet and Hot (9/4/58) D: Jules White. Muriel Landers. Tiny, Joe's sister, possesses a fine singing voice but is deathly afraid of performing in front of an audience. Stock shot of quacking duck taken from *I'm a Monkey's Uncle* (1948). Stock shot of hound dog with upright ears taken from Joe Besser's *G.I. Dood It* (1955).

Flying Saucer Daffy (10/9/58) D: Jules White. Gail Bonney, Emil Sitka, Bek Nelson, Harriette Tarler, Diana Darrin, Joe Palma. Joe snaps a photo of a flying saucer, but it's Larry and Moe who take credit for it. Working title: *Pardon My Flying Saucer*. Stock shot of dirty dishes in sink taken from Vernon and Quillan's *He Flew the Shrew* (1951).

Oil's Well That Ends Well (12/4/58) D: Jules White. The Stooges go prospecting for uranium—and strike oil instead! A reworking, with stock footage, of *Oily to Bed, Oily to Rise* (1939).

Triple Crossed (2/2/59) D: Jules White. Angela Stevens, Mary Ainslee, Diana Darrin, Connie Cezan. Bachelor Larry makes a play for Moe's wife and Joe's fiancee. Working title: *Chiseling Chiseler.* A remake, with stock footage, of *He Cooked His Goose* (1952).

Sappy Bull Fighters (6/4/59) D: Jules White. Greta Thyssen, George Lewis, Joe Palma. The Stooges perform their comedy bullfight act in Mexico, where they tangle with a gorgeous blonde's jealous husband. Working title: *That's Bully.* A remake, with stock footage, of *What's the Matador?* (1942).

Andy Clyde

Andy Clyde had one of the longest-running series at Columbia, second only to the Three Stooges. A seasoned pro, Andy was well-versed in the art of physical comedy and brought a welcome dimension of subtlety to the broad slapstick antics. With the mere raising of his eyebrows and a plaintive "My, oh my, oh my!" he could convulse an audience. His "old man" characterization, replete with walrus mustache and bifocals, was developed during his tenure with Mack Sennett, and it served him well for over thirty-five years. Since it was a character of advanced years, his physical constitution seemed to change very little as he grew older. Although his humor wasn't dependent upon a youthful-looking persona, he was always lively.

At Columbia there was a significant alteration in Andy's appearance: In nearly all of his shorts for the unit, Andy was sans the stubble of beard that had been an integral part of his makeup during his Sennett days. It was Jules White's idea to give him a clean-shaven look, and it paid off beautifully. With the unsightly stubble gone, Andy's marvelously expressive face was shown off to greater advantage, and he was now able to assume a wider variety of comic roles; he could now play, with a degree of plausibility, doctors, millionaires, political candidates, etc.

Because he projected a folksy, down-to-earth image, Andy was equally at home in both urban and rural locales. Of the latter, Andy made a number of memorable small-town comedies—*Love Comes to Mooneyville* (1936), *Stuck in the Sticks* (1937), *Wolf in Thief's Clothing* (1943)—usually revolving around the premise of Andy and a rival (either portly, crackle-voiced Bob McKenzie or Emmett Lynn, the definitive grizzled old codger) vying for the hand of the local widow (Esther Howard, one of Andy's perennial leading ladies). Whether playing a country doctor, sheriff or locomotive engineer, Andy's character harkened back to a simpler, less complicated era. But no matter what the setting or type of role, he was a humble, sincere everyman figure with whom audiences could readily identify.

Left: A 1934 portrait of Andy Clyde sans makeup. Right: Andy's trademark "old man" character. From *Caught in the Act* (1936).

As a group, Andy's best Columbia shorts are the pre–1941 entries. *Old Sawbones* (1935) is one of the finest Columbia shorts from any period. Andy is a small town medico who, along with rival Dr. Oak E. Doak (James C. Morton) is under consideration for the position of county physician. The town council decides that it will award the post to the one who treats the most patients within a seven-day period. As the competition draws to a close, both are tied at 104 patients each; when the news breaks that a woman in a neighboring county is about to give birth, they race to her home (Doak by automobile, Andy by horse and buggy) in hopes of breaking the stalemate. This final chase sequence, staged by director Del Lord, is a rollicking gem (it was so good, in fact, it was reused for the 1940 Clyde short *Money Squawks*).

In *Hot Paprika* (1935) Andy is told, incorrectly, that he only has three months to live; upon hearing this, he becomes a new man, vowing to live life to the fullest. He winds up in the Republic of Paprika and—shades of Harold Lloyd's *Why Worry?* (1923)—helps to quell a revolution. *Caught in the Act* (1936) has Andy mistaken for Jack the Kisser (John T. Murray), the infamous public "smoocher." A wild motorcycle chase caps this first-rate two-reeler.

The Peppery Salt (1936) is one of the top Clyde comedies. Andy works in a shipyard, relating tall tales about his days as a roving seadog. When he

Andy protects Mary Lou Dix from a gang of kidnappers in *The Peppery Salt* (1936), one of the best Clyde comedies. Also pictured (l. to r.): Harry Keaton (with mustache), Bert Young, and Blackie Whiteford.

receives a telegram notifying him that he's inherited the "Admiral Dewey," he quits his job and prepares for a new seafaring life (complete with flashy nautical garb). But his inheritance turns out to be an oceanside lunch counter; here, Andy becomes involved with a plot to kidnap a shipping magnate's daughter (Mary Lou Dix) and eventually saves the day. The gags are imaginative throughout, aided by a solid budget and an exciting musical score (*any* background music was a rarity in Columbia shorts). The film also contains the most spectacular sight gag the unit ever devised. Andy nails a sign to the wall of his diner, which is situated at the end of a pier. Unbeknownst to Andy and his patrons, the nails are hammered through the wall and into the side of a ship docked alongside the diner. When the vessel lifts anchor and pulls away, it takes the lunch counter with it; moments later, Andy, his customers and the whole establishment go plunging into the briny drink. Director Del Lord shot this sequence on location at a pier, using a real ship; the authenticity helps to make the gag a knockout.

In *Andy Clyde Gets Spring Chicken* (1939), Andy plays an exuberant millionaire who refuses to act his age. He pursues several young showgirls, all of whom deem his behavior eccentric. But when the women learn of his great wealth, they suddenly find him irresistible; before he knows what's happening, Andy is engaged to a bevy of beauties. Though it meanders and arrives at an inconclusive finish, *Andy Clyde Gets Spring Chicken* is sufficiently novel enough to be one of his best efforts. *Money Squawks* (1940) is highly enjoyable thanks to Shemp Howard, who is teamed with Andy. Andy's low-key delivery compliments Shemp's blustery style perfectly, as this routine story is bolstered by Shemp's hilarious stream-of-consciousness ad-libbing.

After this early winning streak, the overall quality of the Clyde shorts declined. There would still be a fair share of worthwhile entries, but the spirit and flavor of these initial efforts was never recaptured. *Host to a Ghost* (1941) contains a truly funny first half, with Andy and Dudley Dickerson (a talented black comedian who was teamed with Clyde in a number of comedies) running a construction — and later, demolition — company. The second half places them in a haunted house setting, with tiresome and tasteless gags abounding. *Lovable Trouble* (1941) has Andy coaching an all-girls baseball team (comprised entirely of showgirls) with amusing, if heavy-handed, results. *Sappy Birthday* (1942) features Andy as a browbeaten husband preparing to go on a fishing trip with his loutish brother-in-law (Matt McHugh). Once again, a potentially funny idea is stretched way beyond its comedic value.

By the mid–1940s, budgetary belts had been tightened, and the Clyde comedies became pedestrian affairs. Efforts like *Gold Is Where You Lose It* (1944), *A Miner Affair* (1945), *The Blonde Stayed On* (1945), *Two Jills and a Jack* (1947), *Wife to Spare* (1947) and *Go Chase Yourself* (1948) aren't bad at all, but they lack the creativity and technical sparkle of his shorts from the 1930s and early 1940s. A typical outing from this period is *Andy Plays Hookey* (1946). A remake of W.C. Fields' *The Man on the Flying Trapeze* (1935), the film suffers when seen today, since most comedy aficionados are familiar with the Fields picture, inviting the inevitable comparisons. Andy, a henpecked husband saddled with a domineering wife (Geneva Mitchell) and boorish in-laws (Minerva Urecal, Dick Wessel), plans to sneak out and attend a prizefight. In order to get the day off from work, he tells his boss that his mother-in-law has passed away. The scheme goes hopelessly awry; Andy never does get to see the fight and, in addition, funeral wreaths and letters of condolence start pouring into the Clyde household, to the surprise and outrage of his relatives. *Andy Plays Hookey* is far from being one of his best shorts, though it's pleasant and well done; one has to marvel at how smoothly the Fields story has been condensed down to two reels.

Andy's series continued throughout most of the 1950s. By this time, the quality of the shorts had sunk to an all-time low. Rising production costs necessitated the practice of lifting footage from earlier two-reelers in order to comply with budgetary limitations. *A Blunderful Time* (1950), *Blonde Atom Bomb* (1951), *Pleasure Treasure* (1951), *A Blissful Blunder* (1952), *Hooked and Rooked* (1952), *Love's A-Poppin'* (1953), *Oh Say Can You Sue* (1953), *Tooting Tooters* (1954), *Two April Fools* (1954), *One Spooky Night* (1955),

Andy Goes Wild (1956) and *Pardon My Nightshirt* (1956) consist largely of older footage. But no other Columbia short utilized more stock footage than *Marinated Mariner* (1950): Footage from *The Peppery Salt* (1936) comprises ninety-five percent of *Marinated Mariner*, which has only a smattering of new scenes.

The series came to an end in 1956, and though the later films were strictly formula affairs, Andy's best efforts rank among the finest the department ever produced. "Andy was a real trouper," says Edward Bernds. "He could perform a scene that could take three or four separate takes in one shot. The way he could follow through a routine, he didn't need closeups for inserts to pepper up a camera take. He was solid all the way."

The Andy Clyde Series

It's the Cats (10/11/34) D: Al Ray. Dorothy Granger, Inez Courtney, Kay Hughes, Frances Morris, Ceil Duncan, Mary Foy, William Irving, Raymond Brown. Andy prepares to speak at a cat-fanciers organization.

In the Dog House (12/1/34) D: Arthur Ripley. Vivien Oakland, Delmar Watson. Andy's new wife has no sympathy for his young son and his pet dog.

I'm a Father (2/7/35) D: James Horne. Lillian Elliott, Geneva Mitchell, Ferdinand Munier, Inez Courtney, Robert Allen, Allyn Drake, Mary Gordon, Grace Goodall, Louise Carver, Phil Dunham, Bess Flowers, Billy Engle, Frank Yaconelli, Charles Dorety, Evelyn Pierce, Phyllis Crane, Sally Tead, Beulah Hutton, Jack Kennedy. Andy, an avowed child-hater, changes his tune when he mistakenly believes his wife is pregnant. Remade with Hugh Herbert as *Oh, Baby!* (1944).

Old Sawbones (4/11/35) D: Del Lord. James C. Morton, Lucille Ward, Wes Warner, Marie Wells, Phyllis Crane, Lou Archer, Ford West, Si Jenks, John Rand, Val Harris, Marvin Loback, Billy Franey, Charles Dorety, Harry Semels, George Ovey, Hubert Diltz, Bud Jamison, Charles "Heine" Conklin, George Gray, Helen Dickson, Eugene Anderson, Rudolf Chavers. Andy and another doctor vie for the position of county physician; the town council decides that whoever treats the most patients in a seven-day period will win the post.

Tramp Tramp Tramp (5/22/35) D: Charles Lamont. Dot Farley, Robert "Bobby" Burns, Charles "Heine" Conklin. When Andy's wife opens their home to derelicts, Andy keeps devising ways to chase them out. Working title: *Helping Handout*.

Alimony Aches (6/29/35) D: Charles Lamont. Vivien Oakland, Jan Duggan, Tommy Bond, Bud Jamison, Bobby Barber, Lon Poff. Andy's ex-wife remarries, but keeps it a secret from him so she can still collect alimony.

It Always Happens (9/15/35) D: Del Lord. Geneva Mitchell, Esther Muir, Esther Howard, Bud Jamison, Arthur Housman, Robert McKenzie, Sam Lufkin. On a business trip, Andy gets into a compromising situation with a client's wife. Remade as *His Tale Is Told* (1944) and with Bert Wheeler as *Innocently Guilty* (1950).

Hot Paprika (12/12/35) D: Preston Black. Helen Martinez, Julian Rivero, Bud Jamison, Ethelreda Leopold, Harry Semels, Bobby Barber, June Gittelson, Johnny Kascier, Ed Brandenburg. Andy quells a revolution in the banana republic of Paprika.

Caught in the Act (3/5/36) D: Del Lord. John T. Murray, Anne O'Neal, Bud Jamison, James C. Morton, Al Thompson, William Irving. Andy is mistaken for Jack the Kisser, a kissing bandit.

Share the Wealth (3/16/36) D: Del Lord. Mary Gordon, Vernon Dent, James C. Morton, Bob Barry, Blackie Whiteford, Tom Dempsey, Fay Holderness, Bobby Barber. Andy is a small-town mayoral candidate running on a "share-the-wealth" platform. The day before the election, he inherits $50,000 and tries to leave town.

The Peppery Salt (5/15/36) D: Del Lord. Mary Lou Dix, Warner Richmond, Bert Young, Harry Keaton, Blackie Whiteford, Tom Dempsey, John Ince, Charlie Phillips, Valerie Hall, Idolyne Dupre, Ethelreda Leopold, Chuck Colean, Antrim Short, Sam Lufkin. Andy, the owner of an oceanside lunch counter, tangles with a gang of kidnappers. Remade as *Marinated Mariner* (1950).

Mister Smarty (7/15/36) D: Preston Black. Leora Thatcher, Henry Hanna, Tommy Bond, Bud Jamison, Frank Mills, Robert McKenzie, Harry Tenbrook, Al Thompson, Bill O'Brien, John Rand, Jack "Tiny" Lipson, Bobby Barber, Billy Engle, Lew Davis, William Irving. Andy believes that he'll be able to clean the house more efficiently than his wife can. Remade as *Sunk in the Sink* (1949).

Am I Having Fun! (9/18/36) D: Preston Black. Arthur Housman, Harry Semels, Gale Arnold, Bud Jamison, Jack "Tiny" Lipson, Helen Martinez, Lew Davis, Bert Young, Al Thompson, William Irving, Bobby Barber, Charles Dorety, Robert "Bobby" Burns, C.L. Sherwood, Sam Lufkin, Johnny Kascier, Ethelreda Leopold. Press agent Housman persuades cab driver Andy to act as a substitute for an uncooperative potentate. Remade with Billy Gilbert as *Crazy Like a Fox* (1944).

Love Comes to Mooneyville (11/14/36) D: Preston Black. Esther Howard, Bob McKenzie. Andy and the local fire chief fall for the same woman.

Knee Action (1/9/37) D: Charles Lamont. Vivien Oakland, Tommy Bond, Lew Kelly, Bob McKenzie, Eva McKenzie, James C. Morton, Bud Jamison, Al Thompson. Andy invents a "knee action" clothes-washer, but his obnoxious stepson ruins the demonstration. Remade with Joe DeRita as *The Good Bad Egg* (1947).

Stuck in the Sticks (3/26/37) D: Preston Black. Esther Howard, Bob McKenzie, Jack Evans, Robert "Bobby" Burns, Tom Dempsey, Eva McKenzie, Jack Hendricks, Bud Jamison, Ethelreda Leopold. Andy's rival has "wanted" posters printed claiming that Andy's sweetheart is a swindler. A sequel to *Love Comes to Mooneyville* (1936).

My Little Feller (5/21/37) D: Charles Lamont. Doodles Weaver, Don Brody, Beatrice Curtis, Cy Schindell, Leora Thatcher, James C. Morton, Robert Rousch. Andy cares for a kidnapped baby. A remake of Sidney and Murray's *Ten Baby Fingers* (1934). Remade with The Three Stooges as *Mutts to You* (1938) and *Sock-A-Bye Baby* (1942).

Lodge Night (6/11/37) D: Preston Black. Joan Woodbury, Nick Copeland, Bonita Weber, Sammy Blum, Doodles Weaver, Penny Parker, Louise Carver, Billy McCall, Antrim Short, Eva McKenzie, Georgia Dell. Andy's lodge meetings put a strain on his marriage.

Gracie at the Bat (10/29/37) D: Del Lord. Louise Stanley, Ann Doran, Leora Thatcher, Bud Jamison, Vernon Dent, Bess Flowers, William Irving, Eddie Fetherstone. Andy manages an all-girl softball team. Working title: *Slide, Nellie, Slide.*

He Done His Duty (12/10/37) D: Charles Lamont. Dorothy Granger, Bob McKenzie. A female con artist tries to fleece Andy and his rival.

The Old Raid Mule (3/4/38) D: Charley Chase. Olin Howland, Ann Doran, Vernon Dent, Bud Jamison, Bob McKenzie, Eddie Laughton. Andy feuds with his hillbilly neighbor.

Jump, Chump, Jump (4/15/38) D: Del Lord. Gertrude Sutton, Bud Jamison, George Ovey, Fred "Snowflake" Toones. Andy foils a gang of crooked politicos.

Ankles Away (5/13/38) D: Charley Chase. Ann Doran, Gene Morgan, Gino Corrado, Grace Goodall, Bess Flowers, Vernon Dent, John T. Murray, Symona Boniface. Andy is duped into thinking his bride-to-be has a wooden leg.

Soul of a Heel (6/4/38) D: Del Lord. Gertrude Sutton, Bud Jamison, Eva

McKenzie, James C. Morton, Cy Schindell, Frank Mann. Andy tries to win the approval of his prospective father-in-law.

Not Guilty Enough (7/30/38) D: Del Lord. Shemp Howard, John Tyrrell, Bud Jamison. Andy is brought to court for assaulting his brother-in-law.

Home on the Rage (12/9/38) D: Del Lord. Lela Bliss, Shemp Howard, Gene Morgan, Vernon Dent. Andy mistakenly believes his wife and brother-in-law are conspiring to murder him.

Swing, You Swingers! (1/29/39) D: Jules White. Bennie Bartlett, Lola Jensen, Elaine Waters, Beatrice Blinn, Blanche Payson, Frederick Spencer, Lynton Brent. Andy, the proprietor of a music store, hates swing music. Remade as *Tooting Tooters* (1954).

Boom Goes the Groom (3/24/39) D: Charley Chase. Vivien Oakland, Monty Collins, Dick Curtis. Just as he's about to be wed, Andy learns that his gold mine is worth a fortune.

Now It Can Be Sold (6/2/39) D: Del Lord. Tommy Bond, Anita Garvin, Dick Curtis. Andy and his junior G-man nephew tangle with bank robbers.

Trouble Finds Andy Clyde (7/28/39) D: Jules White. Ann Doran, Lela Bliss, Beatrice Blinn, Beatrice Curtis, Ethelreda Leopold, Al Thompson, Ned Glass, James Craig, Charles Dorety, Cy Schindell. Andy's twin brother gets Andy in hot water. Working title: *Away with Women*. Remade as *A Blunderful Time* (1950).

All-American Blondes (10/20/39) D: Del Lord. Dick Curtis, Mabel Smaney, Helen Servis. Andy becomes the basketball coach for an all-girls school.

Andy Clyde Gets Spring Chicken (12/15/39) D: Jules White. Beatrice Blinn, Richard Fiske, Dorothy Appleby, Eva McKenzie, Don Beddoe, John Tyrrell, Lorna Gray, Ethelreda Leopold, Kay Vallon. A group of showgirls ignore Andy's romantic overtures—until they discover he's a millionaire. Reworked as *Love's A-Poppin'* (1953).

Mr. Clyde Goes to Broadway (2/2/40) D: Del Lord. Vivien Oakland, John T. Murray, Dorothy Vaughn, Don Beddoe, Vernon Dent. Andy invests in a local theatrical production; when the actors abscond with the money, Andy and his wife are forced to take their places.

Money Squawks (4/5/40) D: Jules White. Shemp Howard, Vernon Dent. Andy and Shemp guard a ten-thousand-dollar payroll. Uses stock footage from *Old Sawbones* (1935).

Dick Curtis (center) has his hands full with Andy (right) and his twin brother (played by Al Thompson, left) in *Trouble Finds Andy Clyde* (1939). Thompson, who doubled for Clyde in many films, was also a supporting player in the Columbia shorts.

Boobs in the Woods (5/31/40) D: Del Lord. Esther Howard, Shemp Howard, Bud Jamison, Bruce Bennett, Jack "Tiny" Lipson. Andy goes on a hunting trip with his wife and brother-in-law.

Fireman, Save My Choo Choo (8/9/40) D: Del Lord. Esther Howard, Roscoe Ates, Richard Fiske, John Tyrrell. Andy races his train against a modern bus; the winner receives a government franchise.

A Bundle of Bliss (11/1/40) D: Jules White. Esther Howard, Dorothy Appleby, Fred Kelsey, Vernon Dent, Bruce Bennett, John Tyrrell, Blanche Payson. Andy mistakenly thinks he's a father. Remade as *A Blissful Blunder* (1952).

The Watchman Takes a Wife (1/10/41) D: Del Lord. Betty Compson, Matt McHugh, Jimmy Dodd, Bob McKenzie, Bud Jamison, Dudley Dickerson, John Tyrrell. Andy, a night watchman, is convinced his wife is unfaithful.

The Ring and the Belle (5/2/41) D: Del Lord. Vivien Oakland, Dudley Dickerson, Vernon Dent, Jack Roper. Andy's dilemma: he's a boxing manager whose fighter has just skipped town.

Yankee Doodle Andy (6/13/41) D: Jules White. Dorothy Appleby, Tom Kennedy, Vernon Dent, Fred Vogeding, Victor Travers, Bud Jamison, Cy Schindell, Al Thompson, Johnny Kascier. Andy, a defense plant worker, thwarts a gang of saboteurs.

Host to a Ghost (8/8/41) D: Del Lord. Dudley Dickerson, Monty Collins, Lew Kelly, Vernon Dent, Bud Jamison, Johnny Kascier. The Clyde Wrecking Company is assigned to demolish a haunted house. Remade as *One Spooky Night* (1955).

Lovable Trouble (10/23/41) D: Del Lord. Ann Doran, Esther Howard, Luana Walters, Blanche Payson, Vernon Dent, John Tyrrell, Eddie Laughton, Stanley Brown. Andy agrees to coach a baseball team, not realizing that the team is comprised of showgirls.

Sappy Birthday (2/5/42) D: Harry Edwards. Matt McHugh, Esther Howard, Vernon Dent, Olin Howland. Andy and his brother-in-law plan a fishing trip but never get beyond the driveway.

How Spry I Am (5/7/42) D: Jules White. Mary Dawn, Nat Bunker, Paul Clayton, Daisy. After an orphanage burns down, hotelkeeper Andy is forced to provide the children with shelter.

All Work and No Pay (7/16/42) D: Del Lord. Frank Lackteen, Duke York, Eddie Laughton, Vernon Dent, Blanche Payson, Bud Jamison, John Tyrrell, Johnny Kascier. Andy boards a ship to recover some stolen gems. Remade with the Three Stooges as *Crime on Their Hands* (1948) and *Hot Ice* (1955).

Sappy Pappy (10/30/42) D: Harry Edwards. Vivien Oakland, Vernon Dent, Barbara Pepper, Marjorie Deanne, Julie Duncan, Bertha Priestly, Lois James, Dorothy O'Kelly. Andy, the owner of a bicycle shop, gets involved with one of his customers.

Wolf in Thief's Clothing (2/12/43) D: Jules White. Emmett Lynn, Esther Howard, Stanley Brown, Spec O'Donnell, Bud Jamison, Vernon Dent. Andy and Emmett try to win the affections of the town widow by presenting her with new whitewall tires.

A Maid Made Mad (3/19/43) D: Del Lord. Barbara Pepper, Gwen Kenyon, Vernon Dent, Mabel Forrest, Blanche Payson. Andy innocently becomes involved with a female customer; his wife jumps to the wrong conclusion and walks out on him. Remade with Joe DeRita as *Slappily Married* (1946).

Farmer for a Day (8/20/43) D: Jules White. Betty Blythe, Shemp Howard, Douglas Leavitt, Adele Mara, Bud Jamison. Patriotic Andy does his bit for the war effort by planting a victory garden.

He Was Only Feudin' (12/3/43) D: Harry Edwards. Bill Henry, Barbara Pepper, Gwen Kenyon, Bobby Barber, Snub Pollard, Bess Flowers. Andy's prospective son-in-law arranges for a pretty girl to flirt with Andy.

His Tale Is Told (3/4/44) D: Harry Edwards. Christine McIntyre, Ann Doran, Vernon Dent, Mabel Forrest, Bud Jamison, Charles "Heine" Conklin, Jack Norton, Snub Pollard. Andy journeys to the big city to sell an invention — followed closely by his suspicious wife. A remake of *It Always Happens* (1935). Remade with Bert Wheeler as *Innocently Guilty* (1950).

You Were Never Uglier (6/2/44) D: Jules White. Emmett Lynn, Esther Howard, Ida Mae Johnson, Buz Buckley, Judy Malcolm. Andy and Emmett, two ex-sailors, discover that married life isn't all it's cracked up to be. A remake of Collins and Kennedy's *Gobs of Trouble* (1935). Remade as *Hooked and Rooked* (1952).

Gold Is Where You Lose It (9/1/44) D: Jules White. Emmett Lynn, Gertrude Sutton, Mel Blanc, Hank Mann, Bud Jamison, Eva McKenzie, James C. Morton, Cy Schindell, Frank Mills. Andy and Emmett go prospecting for gold and uncover stolen bank loot. Working title: *Gold Is Where You Find It*. A remake of Sidney and Murray's *Back to the Soil* (1934) and the Three Stooges' *Yes, We Have No Bonanza* (1939). Remade as *Pleasure Treasure* (1951).

Heather and Yon (12/8/44) D: Harry Edwards. Isabel Withers, Jack Norton, Vernon Dent, Kermit Maynard, Brian O'Hara, Cy Schindell, John Tyrrell, Snub Pollard, Al Thompson, Charles "Heine" Conklin, Johnny Kascier. Andy confesses to a murder so his reporter friend can track down the real killer; complications arise when the reporter is injured and can't continue the investigation.

Two Local Yokels (3/23/45) D: Jules White. Charles Judels, Esther Howard. Andy and Charles fancy themselves as ladies' men — until Andy's wife announces that she wants a divorce. Working title: *Bread and Butler.*

A Miner Affair (11/1/45) D: Jules White. Charles Rogers, Gloria Marlen, Charles Bates, Jack "Tiny" Lipson, Robert Williams, Al Thompson. Clyde and Rogers dig for buried treasure so they can pay for a crippled boy's operation. A remake of the Three Stooges' *Cash and Carry* (1937). Remade as *Two April Fools* (1954).

Spook to Me (12/27/45) D: Harry Edwards. Vie Barlow, Dudley Dickerson, Frank Hagney, Wally Rose, Dick Botiller, Lulu Mae Bohrman. Andy, the scoutmaster of the "Bloodhounds" boys patrol, investigates a reputed "haunted" house. Working title: *Be Prepared.*

The Blonde Stayed On (1/24/46) D: Harry Edwards. Christine McIntyre, Gladys Blake, Vernon Dent, John Tyrrell, Victor Travers. While delivering a fur coat, Andy encounters a jealous husband.

You Can't Fool a Fool (7/11/46) D: Jules White. Fred Kelsey, Esther Howard, Charles "Heine" Conklin, Vernon Dent, Ted Lorch, Joe Palma. Mayoral candidate Andy is examined by a doctor who believes Andy's crazy.

Andy Plays Hookey (12/19/46) D: Edward Bernds. Geneva Mitchell, Minerva Urecal, Dick Wessel, Fred Kelsey, Emil Sitka, Symona Boniface, Charles "Heine" Conklin. In order to take the day off from work and attend a prizefight, Andy tells his boss that his mother-in-law has passed away. Working title: *Wilbur Goes Wild.*

Two Jills and a Jack (4/14/47) D: Jules White. Christine McIntyre, Vernon Dent, Dorothy Granger. Andy thinks that his former sweetheart is now married to an old friend. Remade as *Oh Say Can You Sue* (1953).

Wife to Spare (11/20/47) D: Edward Bernds. Dick Wessel, Christine McIntyre, Lucille Browne, Vera Lewis, Murray Alper, Emil Sitka, Charles "Heine" Conklin. Andy tries to rescue his brother-in-law from the clutches of a blackmailing blonde. Remade as *Blonde Atom Bomb* (1951).

Eight-Ball Andy (3/11/48) D: Edward Bernds. Dick Wessel, Maudie Prickett, Florence Auer, Vernon Dent. Andy's gadget-happy brother-in-law is driving him crazy. Remade as *Andy Goes Wild* (1956).

Go Chase Yourself (10/14/48) D: Jules White. Florence Auer, Dudley Dickerson, Symona Boniface, Al Thompson, Patricia White, Gay Nelson. Professor Clyde is on the lookout for a nightshirt bandit terrorizing the college campus. Working title: *Oh Professor.* A remake, with stock footage, of Charley Chase's *The Nightshirt Bandit* (1938). Remade as *Pardon My Nightshirt* (1956).

Sunk in the Sink (3/10/49) D: Jules White. Margie Liszt, Robert Scott. Andy tries to prove to his wife that he can do the household chores more efficiently than she can. Working title: *What's Cookin'.* A remake, with stock footage, of *Mister Smarty* (1936).

Marinated Mariner (3/30/50) D: Jules White. Jean Willes, John Merton, Blackie Whiteford, Charles "Heine" Conklin, Al Thompson, Johnny Kascier,

Bert Young, Harry Keaton. Andy, the proprietor of an oceanside lunch counter, tangles with a gang of kidnappers. A remake, with stock footage, of *The Peppery Salt* (1936).

A Blunderful Time (9/7/50) D: Jules White. Margie Liszt, Christine McIntyre, Al Thompson. Andy's twin brother creates confusion for Andy and his wife. A remake, with stock footage, of *Trouble Finds Andy Clyde* (1939).

Blonde Atom Bomb (3/8/51) D: Jules White. Jean Willes, Emil Sitka, George Chesebro, Minerva Urecal, Billy Frandes, Clay Anderson. Andy tries to save his nephew from the wiles of a sultry nightclub singer. A remake, with stock footage, of *Wife to Spare* (1947).

Pleasure Treasure (9/6/51) D: Jules White. Emmett Lynn, Margie Liszt, Tom Kennedy, Babe London, Emil Sitka, Johnny Kascier. Andy and Emmett go prospecting for gold. A remake, with stock footage, of *Gold Is Where You Lose It* (1944); based on Sidney and Murray's *Back to the Soil* (1934) and the Three Stooges' *Yes, We Have No Bonanza* (1939).

A Blissful Blunder (5/8/52) D: Jules White. Ruth Godfrey, Esther Howard, Fred Kelsey, Bonnie Bennett, Barbara Lande. When Andy returns home and finds a baby, he mistakenly thinks he's become a father. A remake, with stock footage, of *A Bundle of Bliss* (1940).

Hooked and Rooked (9/11/52) D: Jules White. Emmett Lynn, Margie Liszt, Maxine Gates. Andy and Emmett, two ex-sailors, discover that married life isn't all it's cracked up to be. Working title: *Bridal Wails*. A remake, with stock footage, of *You Were Never Uglier* (1944), and Collins and Kennedy's *Gobs of Trouble* (1935).

Love's A-Poppin' (6/11/53) D: Jules White. Phil Van Zandt, Margia Dean, Dorothy Appleby, Eva McKenzie, Lorna Gray, Suzanne Ridgeway, Ethelreda Leopold, Kay Vallon. An actress believes Andy is wealthy and starts pursuing him. Working title: *Lover Boy*. A reworking, with stock footage, of *Andy Clyde Gets Spring Chicken* (1939).

Oh Say Can You Sue (9/10/53) D: Jules White. Vernon Dent, Christine McIntyre, Dorothy Granger, Gus Schilling. In an attorney's office, Andy explains why he thought his sweetheart married his best friend. A remake, with stock footage, of *Two Jills and a Jack* (1947).

Tooting Tooters (5/13/54) D: Jules White. Bennie Bartlett, Barbara Bartay, Lynton Brent. Andy despises swing music but his nephew loves it. A remake, with stock footage, of *Swing, You Swingers!* (1939).

Two April Fools (6/17/54) D: Jules White. Charles Rogers, Robert Williams, Jack "Tiny" Lipson, Al Thompson. Andy and Charles are suckered into buying a bogus treasure map. A remake, with stock footage, of *A Miner Affair* (1945).

Scratch Scratch Scratch (4/28/55) D: Jules White. Dorothy Granger, Eric Lamond. Andy's nephew's rival resorts to trickery to call off an engagement.

One Spooky Night (9/15/55) D: Jules White. Dorothy Granger, Dudley Dickerson, Monty Collins, Lew Kelly, Joe Palma. Fraidy-cat Andy is assigned to demolish a haunted house. A remake, with stock footage, of *Host to a Ghost* (1941).

Andy Goes Wild (4/26/56) D: Jules White. Dick Wessel, Florence Auer, Maudie Prickett, Vernon Dent. Andy's life is made miserable by his brother-in-law's penchant for crazy inventions. A remake, with stock footage, of *Eight-Ball Andy* (1948).

Pardon My Nightshirt (11/22/56) D: Jules White. Ferris Taylor, Florence Auer, Dudley Dickerson, Joe Palma, Symona Boniface, Gay Nelson, Patricia White, Al Thompson. Professor Clyde is on the lookout for a nightshirt bandit prowling the college campus. A remake of *Go Chase Yourself* (1948) and Charley Chase's *The Nightshirt Bandit* (1938), using stock footage from both.

Harry Langdon

Harry Langdon, the baby-faced, eternal "innocent," experienced such a relatively brief period of stardom that he remains an enigma to film historians today. Was he a talented and creative comedian with too few good films to his credit, or a mediocre vaudevillian fortunate enough to collaborate twice with director Frank Capra? Either assessment has its own partisans. Through a careful examination of his sound films, particularly his Columbia work, the man's real worth as a comedian of any merit is revealed.

That Langdon was a has-been in pictures before the coming of sound is no revelation. Failing as producer, director and star of the Harry Langdon Corporation, with three successive box office flops to his detriment, Langdon secured what odd jobs came his way. Through the courtesy of Arthur Ripley, a Mack Sennett staff writer turned comedy director for Columbia, Harry was introduced to Jules White in the summer of 1934. Under the pretext of a social call, White offered Langdon a contract to star in Columbia shorts.

It was unanimously decided that Ripley, Langdon's former collaborator in the 1920s, accept the director's helm. Therein lies a perplexing problem, seen clearly in Harry's first Columbia release, *Counsel on De Fence* (1934). A takeoff on courtroom melodramas, the short is stodgily paced and heavy-handed, whereas the material it is spoofing had been fast-moving, witty and often tongue-in-cheek. The story, partly Ripley's, is a very good idea. However, the direction, also by Ripley, is hopelessly inept—and this is the work of a man who, years earlier, had been so instrumental in guiding Langdon to stardom! Harry is fine in his pantomimic "turns," but he is literally swallowed up in a two-reeler with enough plot for a feature. The addition of an ill-advised mustache in this short (and the later *A Doggone Mixup*) reveals the filmmakers—or perhaps Langdon himself—groping for a new image when there was nothing wrong with the old icon.

Harry plays Darrow Langdon, a bumbling lawyer who fills in for an injured defense attorney during a sensational murder trial. The climax is a direct spoof of a key sequence in *The Mouthpiece*, a 1932 Warner Brothers feature. In that film, Warren William plays an unscrupulous attorney who swallows a vial of poison—exhibit A—to prove to the jury that his client is innocent of a murder charge. However, the vial actually does contain poison, so after the jury finds his client "Not Guilty," William, who has accounted for the fact that the slow-reacting poison will not take effect until after the jury has reached its decision, nonchalantly strides out of the courtroom and walks across the street to an office where a physician is waiting with a stomach pump. In *Counsel on De Fence*, Langdon gulps down a bottle of poison, believing his assistant has substituted it for a bottle filled with tea. After this dramatic gesture wins the case for him, Harry is informed that the switch never took place and, because of various misunderstandings, he undergoes two stomach pumpings. At the fadeout, he's about to be subjected to yet another "treatment." The satire is intended to be in the contrast of these two sequences: whereas William's scheme is carried out with clockwork precision, Langdon's backfires, making him the recipient of medical attention that isn't necessary (it is implied, in an incredibly tasteless scene, that Harry has vomited the poison during the wild taxicab ride en route to the hospital). Of course, the humor is dependent upon the viewer's knowledge of *The Mouthpiece*—which means that the short's satirical implications, as misfired as they are, will be lost on all but the staunchest film buffs.

Another Ripley-piloted outing, *The Leather Necker* (1935) faithfully recreates the flashback sequence of *All Night Long* (1924), an early Langdon silent written by Ripley and Frank Capra. The situation, revolving around Harry and Wade Boteler as rival marines vying for a pretty señorita in Central America, contains a number of very amusing and characteristic gags, as when Harry, sitting blissfully atop a telegraph pole, contorts himself to avoid a barrage of missiles. But the film's latter-day framework features a poorly motivated car chase that is much less effective than the plotline of the original picture, seriously impairing an otherwise good comedy.

Alf Goulding directed *His Bridal Sweet* (1935), in which Harry and Geneva Mitchell are newlyweds forced to stay in a modern push-button house. As mechanical as the concept sounds, the short works, primarily because the

Harry Langdon (right) and Billy Gilbert in *His Bridal Sweet* (1935).

simple premise gives Harry ample opportunity to display his unique acting skills. Likewise, *I Don't Remember* (1935), directed by Preston Black, harkens back to the early Sennett formula of a put-upon husband (Harry) who's constantly taken in by his good-time buddy (Vernon Dent). The Langdon-Dent chemistry, reminiscent of silent comedy's salad days, supplies the proper feeling for a Harry Langdon vehicle: ingenious plotting, a broad canvas, and some terrific teamwork. Sadly, all three factors are missing from the majority of Langdon's Columbia comedies. Harry still had his talent, but more of the films' running times would be given over to jumbled setups, predictable routines, and an ever-diminishing onscreen relationship with the multifaceted Mr. Dent.

But if Harry's screen persona was suffering from careless neglect, Langdon himself was treated with the utmost courtesy. He was not bound to an iron-clad contract with the department, and was given the freedom to accept any outside offers, with the understanding that he would be welcomed back. In other words, he was pretty much able to come and go as he pleased. After *I Don't Remember*, Harry's output for the unit became erratic, with two-year gaps between some efforts.

A *Doggone Mixup* (1938) shows a clear decline from his earlier Columbia shorts, but contains a few good set pieces. Harry, a compulsive bargain-hunter, buys a St. Bernard dog and a trailer, to the dismay of his no-nonsense spouse (Ann Doran). The short is aided by impressive location filming and stunt work involving the trailer dangling from a cliff. *Sue My Lawyer* (1938), based on Harry's original story "The Ambulance Chaser," has typical Langdon situations (as when he catches his foot in a bucket of water), but cutaway shots to the supposedly more interesting "storyline" reveal where the director's heart is. In his autobiography, Frank Capra, who had had a bitter falling out with Langdon in the 1920s, recounts how he visited the set of *Sue My Lawyer*, watching them shoot a sequence that reworked a gag from *The Strong Man* (1926), a Langdon feature Capra had directed. The scene dealt with Harry's attempts to carry an unconscious woman (in *Sue My Lawyer*, Ann Doran) up a flight of stairs. While Capra does succeed in driving home his point—a great artist like Langdon reduced to appearing in cheap little "fillers"—Capra's recollections are clouded by some woefully inaccurate details (Miss Doran is hardly the "enormous fat lady" he describes).

Coming as late as it does, 1940's *Cold Turkey*, directed by Del Lord and featuring a 56-year-old pixilated Langdon, almost doesn't deserve to be as good as it is. Certainly the best of the Langdon Columbia shorts, it's also one of the finest two-reelers ever produced by the unit. Once again, pure and simple comedy wins out: Harry wins a live turkey in a raffle, brings it home as a pet for his unappreciative wife (Ann Doran) who forcibly orders him to do the bird in. Seeing Harry armed with an axe, his landlord (Monty Collins) gets the idea that Langdon is after *him*—leading to a wild though wholly believable melee through the halls of his apartment building. *Cold Turkey* is a wonderfully paced comedy, neatly inserting Langdon touches, at the same time justifying the film's broader points.

After *Cold Turkey*, Langdon busied himself with assignments elsewhere, returning to Columbia in the early 1940s for his final group of two-reelers. By now Harry looked awful physically, and admitted in print that he was grateful simply to have a job. He was always extremely careless with his money, and the Columbia shorts provided a highly coveted salary of a few thousand dollars a year, regardless of the caliber of the work. Cognizant of his own dilemma, Harry captured his own disenchantment in a 1943 interview with the *Los Angeles Times*: "When I play in what I call the 'O—Ouch—O' comedies, where the comedians run around . . . I am just an animated suit of clothes."

For the casual viewer, these final outings may offer a few diverting moments, but to those who are aware of Langdon's true potential, they're total abortions. *A Blitz on the Fritz* (1943) is a typical effort from this group; the short reworks the climactic chase from Harold Lloyd's 1938 feature *Professor Beware*, but it's all slapstick and no subtlety. *Tireman, Spare My Tires* (1942) is perhaps the best of his later shorts; ironically, it spoofs *It Happened One Night* (1934), the Academy Award winner directed by a former writer for Langdon, Frank Capra.

Particularly disturbing were the repeated attempts by the unit to make

Harry part of a team format; he was paired with, at various times, Elsie Ames, Monty Collins, Una Merkel and El Brendel. *What Makes Lizzy Dizzy?* (1942) is actually a vehicle for raucous comedienne Elsie Ames. Harry is forced to share what little footage he has with Monty Collins, the unit's ubiquitous comic sidekick.

To Heir Is Human (1944), which teamed Langdon with Una Merkel, was, for reasons unknown, given special attention. The film was allotted a bigger budget than most Columbia shorts of the period and benefited from the effective use of background music. But the story of an aspiring private detective (Merkel) who locates a missing heir (Langdon) is overloaded with heavy-handed gag sequences, and the entire enterprise collapses under the weight of them. Harold Godsoe was a curious choice to direct the picture; he had no previous credits with the department and never worked for the unit after that. Godsoe's leaden direction dulls the impact of several potentially funny scenes.

In his last four Columbia shorts, Harry was teamed with El Brendel, another contract comedian whose career was floundering (contrary to previously published reports, Harry *did* receive star billing in these films, although the advertising posters often played up Brendel's participation at Langdon's expense). *Defective Detectives* (1944), *Mopey Dope* (1944), *Snooper Service* (1945) and *Pistol Packin' Nitwits* (1945) reveal Harry as a tired comic with scant regard as to whether or not he's funny. Perhaps encroaching illness accounts for the somber gaze peering out from *Pistol Packin' Nitwits*, his last film. Or perhaps he was sick of the charade his career had become.

Oddly enough, just one year before his death in 1944, the once-famous star made a trenchant comment which reflected not only his battered career but also the livelihood of all the comedians who ever toiled at Columbia:

> A comedian should establish human appeal . . . Such a comedian isn't a machine. I know the limits of my character. I've tried to inject this character into parts offered me, but if the director interfered, the character would be lost. Without character, the comedian is lost.

The Harry Langdon Series

Counsel on De Fence (10/25/34) D: Arthur Ripley. Renee Whitney, Earle Foxe, Marjorie "Babe" Kane, Jack Norton, William Irving, Charles Dorety, Lew Davis, Robert "Bobby" Burns. Harry, a bungling lawyer, chooses an unorthodox method of defending a woman on trial for poisoning her husband. Working title: *The Barrister.*

Shivers (12/24/34) D: Arthur Ripley. Florence Lake, Chester Gan, Louis Vincenot. Mystery writer Harry moves into a haunted house.

A tired Harry Langdon poses with El Brendel and three chorus girls in this publicity shot for *Pistol Packin' Nitwits* (1945), Langdon's last comedy short.

His Bridal Sweet (3/15/35) D: Alf Goulding. Geneva Mitchell, Billy Gilbert, Bud Jamison, Lew Kelly. Due to a quarantine, Harry and his bride are forced to stay in a new model home equipped with crazy gimmicks.

The Leather Necker (5/9/35) D: Arthur Ripley. Wade Boteler, Bud Jamison. Harry and his ex-sergeant recall their rivalry over the same girl.

His Marriage Mixup (10/31/35) D: Preston Black. Dorothy Granger, Vernon Dent, Robert "Bobby" Burns. Harry's bride-to-be is a dead ringer for an escaped axe murderess. Remade with Vera Vague as *A Miss in a Mess* (1949).

I Don't Remember (12/26/35) D: Preston Black. Geneva Mitchell, Mary Carr, Vernon Dent, Robert "Bobby" Burns, Lynton Brent, Harry Semels, Al Thompson, Charles "Heine" Conklin, Bobby Barber. Absentminded Harry is talked into buying an Irish Sweepstakes ticket. Remade with Sterling Holloway as *Moron Than Off* (1946).

A Doggone Mixup (2/4/38) D: Charles Lamont. Ann Doran, Vernon Dent, Bud Jamison, James C. Morton, Eddie Fetherstone, Bess Flowers, Sarah Edwards. Harry, a compulsive bargain-hunter, purchases a St. Bernard dog. Working title: *No Sales Resistance.*

Sue My Lawyer (9/16/38) D: Jules White. Ann Doran, Monty Collins, Bud Jamison, Vernon Dent, Cy Schindell, Don Brody, Charles Dorety, Jack "Tiny" Lipson, Robert "Bobby" Burns. Harry, a struggling attorney, tries to gain recognition by defending a murderer. Original story title: *The Ambulance Chaser.*

Cold Turkey (10/18/40) D: Del Lord. Ann Doran, Monty Collins, Bud Jamison, Vernon Dent, Eddie Laughton. Harry wins a turkey in a raffle.

What Makes Lizzy Dizzy? (3/26/42) D: Jules White. Elsie Ames, Dorothy Appleby, Monty Collins, Lorin Raker, Bud Jamison, Kathryn Sabichi, Kay Vallon. Laundresses Elsie and Dorothy, along with their detective boyfriends Harry and Monty, enter a bowling tournament.

Tireman, Spare My Tires (6/4/42) D: Jules White. Louise Currie, Emmett Lynn, Bud Jamison. Harry, a traveling salesman, befriends Louise, a runaway heiress. Working title: *Honeymoon Blackout.* Sequence with Vernon Dent cut from final version.

Carry Harry (9/3/42) D: Harry Edwards. Elsie Ames, Barbara Pepper, Stanley Blystone, Marjorie Deanne, Dave O'Brien. Harry uses the fire escape to enter a friend's apartment but inadvertently climbs through the wrong window.

Piano Mooner (12/11/42) D: Harry Edwards. Fifi D'Orsay, Gwen Kenyon, Betty Blythe, Chester Conklin, Stanley Blystone. Harry, badly in need of funds, becomes a piano tuner.

A Blitz on the Fritz (1/22/43) D: Jules White. Louise Currie, Douglas Leavitt, Vernon Dent, Bud Jamison, Jack "Tiny" Lipson, Blanche Payson, Charles Berry, Al Hill, Al Thompson, Beatrice Blinn, Joe Palma, Stanley Blystone, Bud Fine, Kit Guard. Patriotic Harry starts a scrap drive and encounters a gang of Nazi spies. Working title: *Swat That Spy.*

Blonde and Groom (4/16/43) D: Harry Edwards. Gwen Kenyon, Barbara Pepper, Eddy Chandler, Stanley Blystone. When Harry's buddy brings his fiancee over for a visit, Mrs. Langdon gets the mistaken impression that hubby is being unfaithful.

Here Comes Mr. Zerk (7/23/43) D: Jules White. Shirley Patterson, John T. Murray, Fred Kelsey, Bob McKenzie, Dudley Dickerson, Hank Mann, Vernon

Harry's embrace with Marjorie Deanne is interrupted by Stanley Blystone in this posed shot for *Carry Harry* (1942).

Dent, Charles "Heine" Conklin, Eva McKenzie, Blanche Payson. A newspaper article carries the wrong caption under bridegroom Harry's photo, identifying him as an escaped lunatic. Working title: *Sue You Later*.

To Heir Is Human (1/14/44) D: Harold Godsoe. Una Merkel, Christine McIntyre, Lew Kelly, Eddie Gribbon, John Tyrrell, Vernon Dent. Una, an aspiring private detective, locates Harry, a missing heir, and accompanies him to a forbidding mansion where he is to collect the inheritance.

Defective Detectives (4/3/44) D: Harry Edwards. El Brendel, Christine McIntyre, Vernon Dent, John Tyrrell, Eddie Laughton, Snub Pollard, Dick Botiller. Private detectives Harry and El are hired to keep on the trail of a mobster who has been threatening injury to a banker and his wife.

Mopey Dope (6/16/44) D: Del Lord. El Brendel, Christine McIntyre, Arthur Q. Bryan, Al Thompson, Johnny Kascier. Absentminded Harry has difficulty remembering his wedding anniversary. A remake of Charley Chase's *The Mind Needer* (1938).

Snooper Service (2/2/45) D: Harry Edwards. El Brendel, Rebel Randall, Dick Curtis, Vernon Dent, Fred Kelsey, Buddy Yarus. Harry and El, private sleuths, are hired to follow a beautiful showgirl.

Pistol Packin' Nitwits (4/4/45) D: Harry Edwards. El Brendel, Christine McIntyre, Brad King, Dick Curtis, Tex Cooper, Victor Cox, Charles "Heine" Conklin. Harry and El protect a pretty saloonkeeper from a gang of Western thugs. Working title: *Tenderfeet*. Reworked with the Three Stooges as *Out West* (1947). Sequence with Vernon Dent was cut from final version.

Collins and Kennedy

The pairing of Monte (also spelled "Monty") Collins and Tom Kennedy marked the first attempt by the unit to create an *original* comedy team. They contrasted well with one another in terms of appearance and behavior: Collins was the scrawny, hatchet-faced, easily exasperated half of the team, Kennedy his burly, thick-witted companion. Both men were energetic performers with long histories in film. Kennedy had been featured in Mack Sennett's early Keystone Comedies; Collins had starred in a series of one-reel "Cameo Comedies," directed by Jules White, for Educational Pictures in the 1920s. Collins, in fact, also appeared in a number of other Columbia comedy shorts concurrent to this starring series with Kennedy. In addition to the customary expertise of the secondary players, the Collins and Kennedy films are aided and abetted by the technical sparkle common to Columbia two-reelers of the period. But most of the efforts are just as contrived as the partnership itself.

The series managed to get off to a good start with *Gum Shoes* (1935), with Monte and Tom as hotel detectives investigating a string of robberies committed by a trained gorilla. Director Del Lord keeps things moving at a breezy clip; a sizable laugh content compensates for the film's lack of subtlety.

Midnight Blunders (1936) is the best of the Collins and Kennedys, and one of the most offbeat shorts the unit ever produced. A scientist (Wilfred Lucas) creates a half human/half-robot monstrosity (Jack "Tiny" Lipson) and demonstrates it to a wooden-legged Chinaman (Harry Semels), who is planning to use the creation for his own sinister purposes. When the scientist refuses to divulge the secret behind his mechanical being, the Chinaman and his henchmen kidnap him and seize all of his equipment. The scientist's daughter (Phyllis Crane) reports the abduction to a couple of bank guards — who else but Monte and Tom — and the boys are soon in hot pursuit of the wily Oriental. Mixing chills with laughs is usually a surefire combination, and *Midnight Blunders* is no exception. The extraordinarily grim depiction of Chinatown after dark is worthy of a legitimate horror film, and provides the film with a properly eerie mood.

But such noteworthy entries were few for this series. The majority of the

Tom Kennedy and Phyllis Crane are unaware of approaching danger in the form of Jack "Tiny" Lipson (left, wearing mask) as Monte Collins registers surprise. From *Midnight Blunders* (1936).

comedies were on the level of *Free Rent* (1936) which, despite the masterfully executed stunt work involving a house trailer, is strictly standard fare. The Collins and Kennedy shorts never caught the fancy of the exhibitors or the public, and after *Fiddling Around* (1938), a mediocre effort, the series ended. Monte Collins felt that the main reason for the series' failure was that he looked "too Jewish" (although he was Irish) and may have offended audiences who misconstrued the humor as being anti–Semitic. So he had his nose bobbed and continued his association with the department as both performer and writer (he coscripted *Midnight Blunders* and several shorts with Andy Clyde, the Three Stooges and Hugh Herbert). Tom Kennedy also remained a fixture of the unit, as a supporting player for other comedians, occasionally being paired with El Brendel or Shemp Howard.

Undaunted by the failure of this series, the comedy shorts department would continue to devise teams, searching for a winning combination.

The Collins and Kennedy Series

Although officially known as the *Collins and Kennedy* series, Kennedy received top billing in a number of the films.

Gum Shoes (3/1/35) D: Del Lord. James C. Morton, William Irving, Lynton Brent, Al Thompson, Leo Willis. Hotel detectives Monte and Tom investigate a series of robberies being committed by a trained gorilla. Remade with Schilling and Lane as *Hold That Monkey* (1950).

Stage Frights (6/1/35) D: Al Ray. Herman Bing, Eve Southern, Fred "Snowflake" Toones, Renee Whitney, Bud Jamison, Phyllis Crane, Hilda Title, Violet Knight, Charles Dorety, Dorothy Shearer, Jack Kenney, Bob Callahan, Joe Bordeaux, Charles "Heine" Conklin, Bert Starkey, Hubert Diltz, Charles Phillips. Detectives Collins and Kennedy come to the aid of a stage actress who has been receiving threatening letters.

Gobs of Trouble (7/12/35) D: Del Lord. Geneva Mitchell, Lona Andre, Tommy Bond, Bud Jamison, Charles Dorety, Charles Phillips. Two sailors decide to settle down and get married—and live to regret it. Remade with Andy Clyde as *You Were Never Uglier* (1944) and *Hooked and Rooked* (1952).

Oh, My Nerves! (10/17/35) D: Del Lord. June Gittelson, Tommy Bond, Jay Healey, James C. Morton, Sam Lufkin, Dick Allen, Al Thompson, Lew Davis, Elaine Waters, Valerie Hall, Ruth Hiatt, Charles Dorety, Charles Phillips. Monte goes on a fishing trip for rest and relaxation, but brother-in-law Tom and the rest of the family tag along and spoil everything. Reworked with the Three Stooges as *Idiots Deluxe* (1945) and *Guns A-Poppin'* (1957).

Just Speeding (1/23/36) D: Del Lord. Ruth Hiatt, Blanche Payson, Eddie Baker, Elaine Waters, Valerie Hall, Harry Semels, A.R. Haysel, Fred "Snowflake" Toones, Bob Callahan, Fay Holderness, Harry Keaton. To avoid getting a speeding ticket from a motorcycle cop, Tom pretends to be a surgeon rushing Monte to the hospital for an emergency operation. Remade with Schilling and Lane as *High Blood Pleasure* (1945).

Midnight Blunders (4/21/36) D: Del Lord. Harry Semels, Phyllis Crane, Wilfred Lucas, James Leong, Jack "Tiny" Lipson, Val Durran. Two bank guards pursue a wooden-legged Chinaman who has kidnapped a scientist. Reworked with El Brendel as *Sweet Spirits of the Nighter* (1941).

Free Rent (12/20/36) D: Del Lord. Carol Tevis, Betty Mack, Sammy McKim, John Rand, Harry Tenbrook, Elaine Waters, Betty McMahan, Gale Arnold, Lois Lindsey, Bobby Koshay, Viola Cady, Robert "Bobby" Burns. Tom persuades Monte to buy a house trailer so they can "live off the fat of the land."

New News (4/1/37) D: Charles Lamont. Clara Kimball Young, Stanley Blystone, Bud Jamison, Harry Semels, Lynton Brent, Lew Davis, William

In *Bury the Hatchet* (1937), Tom Kennedy contemplates enacting the film's title as Monte Collins reads on.

Irving, Bert Young, Eddie Laughton, Jack "Tiny" Lipson, Symona Boniface, Al Thompson. The engagement of Prince Humbert to the wealthy Mrs. Van Gage is the social announcement of the season, and two delivery-men-turned-reporters try to get photos of the lovebirds. Remade with the Three Stooges as *Crash Goes the Hash* (1944).

Bury the Hatchet (8/6/37) D: Del Lord. June Gittelson, Sammy McKim, Beatrice Curtis, Stanley Blystone. Both the Collinses and the Kennedys claim to be the rightful owners of a house won in a lottery, so the two families live together pending a decision. Remade with Vernon and Quillan as *House About It* (1950) and *Nobody's Home* (1955).

Calling All Curtains (10/1/37) D: Del Lord. Bud Jamison, Vernon Dent, William Irving, Cy Schindell. Monte and Tom go into the laundry business. Their first assignment: cleaning 300 curtains.

Fiddling Around (1/21/38) D: Charles Lamont. Gino Corrado, William Irving, Vernon Dent, Harry Semels, Ann Doran, Bud Jamison, Cy Schindell. Private detectives Collins and Kennedy are assigned to guard a violinist's priceless Stradivarius.

El Brendel

El Brendel's brand of comedy depended largely upon his ability to do a Swedish dialect (in real life, he spoke without any trace of an accent); this served him well enough in vaudeville, where there were no great demands made on a performer to have a wealth of material at his disposal. But when he entered films, his relatively small bag of tricks was used up rapidly. At the mercy of writers and directors, Brendel was, for the most part, wasted in movies. In all fairness, however, he didn't give them much to work with. Brendel was primarily a dialect comedian, and a limited one at that; he used his Swede characterization as a means to do "schtick" and offered no tangible personality for gagwriters to draw upon. El wasn't completely devoid of talent; with the right material he could be very entertaining. But at Columbia, substandard material and his inability to rise above it resulted in one of the unit's weakest series.

Brendel's initial stay at Columbia was brief; he made two mediocre shorts, *Ay Tank Ay Go* (1936) and *The Super Snooper* (1937), then busied himself with feature film work. He returned to the unit four years later for *Yumpin' Yimminy!* (1941), a poor excuse for a comedy that didn't give any reason to look forward to future Brendel endeavors. A brief teaming with Tom Kennedy resulted in a few heavy-handed "scare" comedies; bulging eyes and flailing arms constitute the humor in *Ready, Willing But Unable* (1941) and *Phoney Cronies* (1942). *Sweet Spirits of the Nighter* (1941) is laden with tasteless gags as patrolmen El and Tom encounter a mad scientist conducting life-rejuvenating experiments on dead bodies (the British censors found this material objectionable enough to award the short an adults-only "H" certificate, a rating usually reserved for genuine horror pictures).

The series took a tremendous upswing with *Love at First Fright* (1941), easily the best of the Brendel comedies. As a radio announcer caught in the middle of a hillbilly feud, El was given a solid script (by Harry Edwards and Elwood Ullman) that for once defined his character as an amiable, somewhat resourceful simpleton. The contrast between El's Swedish dialect and the hillbilly accents added a nice touch of comic incongruity. It was a high note the series never reached again. *The Blitz Kiss* (1941) is simply a collection of military gags centering around raw Army recruit Brendel. The short could hardly be labeled exceptional, yet it was inexplicably nominated for an Academy Award that year.

It became painfully evident that the unit didn't quite know what to do with Brendel. There were attempts to pair him with Elsie Ames, Monty Collins and Shemp Howard, though none of these teamings created any sparks. In his final two-reelers, El was teamed with Harry Langdon. Langdon had been the darling of the critics and moviegoing public during the 1920s, but his star had fallen by the time he signed on with Columbia. Harry and El failed to click as partners, and the results were dreary. However, Brendel's clever foot-sliding dance routine, a holdover from his vaudeville days, in *Pistol Packin'*

Lobby card for *Love at First Fright* (1941), easily the best of the Brendel series. Pictured upper left: Marion Martin, Brendel; pictured bottom right: Duke Ward, Brendel, player, Tiny Ward, Louise Carver.

Nitwits (1945) reveals a facet of his performing skills that went untapped by the unit. When Langdon died in 1944, the comedy shorts department dispensed with Brendel's services. El worked sporadically after that, appearing in an occasional feature film.

"I thought he was an appealing comedian, coy and cute," says Jules White, explaining his reason for giving Brendel a starring series. Apparently this sentiment wasn't shared by moviegoers; the Brendel shorts made little impression at the time of their release, and the series remains one of the unit's least known.

The El Brendel Series

Ay Tank Ay Go (12/4/36) D: Del Lord. Phyllis Crane, Bud Jamison. Poor El wants to woo his sweetheart, but they're on opposite sides of a hillbilly feud.

The Super Snooper (2/25/37) D: Preston Black. Monte Collins, Bud Jamison, Don Brody, Wilfred Lucas, Cy Schindell, Eddie Laughton, Al Frazier, Bob

Keats, E.L. Dale, Jerry Uhlick, Sam Lufkin, Bill Lally, William Irving, Blackie Whiteford, Frank Mason, Tommy Hicks, Brick Sullivan, Art Miles, Gale Arnold, Ethelreda Leopold. El and Monte investigate the robbery of an express company.

Yumpin' Yimminy! (3/7/41) D: Jules White. Fred Kelsey, Don Brody, Vernon Dent, Dorothy Appleby, John Tyrrell, Cy Schindell, Victor Travers. El unwittingly becomes a jewel thief's assistant.

Ready, Willing But Unable (5/30/41) D: Del Lord. Tom Kennedy, Anne O'Neal, Dudley Dickerson, Jack Norton, Bud Jamison. El accidentally hits a mannequin with his automobile; believing he's killed a man, he and Tom set out to dispose of the body. Reworked with the Three Stooges as *Three Pests in a Mess* (1945).

Love at First Fright (7/25/41) D: Del Lord. Marion Martin, Tiny Ward, Duke Ward, Louise Carver, Hank Mann, Blanche Payson, Frank Mills, Bert Young. A family of hillbillies mistake radio announcer El for a long-lost relative.

The Blitz Kiss (10/2/41) D: Del Lord. Tom Kennedy, Yolande Mollot, Bud Jamison, Cy Schindell, Symona Boniface. El gets drafted into the army. Nominated for an Academy Award.

Sweet Spirits of the Nighter (12/25/41) D: Del Lord. Tom Kennedy, Lew Kelly, Frank Lackteen, Duke York, Marjorie Deanne, Vernon Dent, Bud Jamison, Hank Mann. Patrolmen El and Tom tangle with a mad scientist who's trying to revive the dead. A reworking of Collins and Kennedy's *Midnight Blunders* (1936).

Olaf Laughs Last (6/18/42) D: Jules White. Anne Jeffreys, George Lewis, Bud Jamison, Eva McKenzie, John Tyrrell, Ethelreda Leopold, Al Thompson, Victor Travers, Lynton Brent, Charles "Heine" Conklin, Cy Schindell. El saves his girlfriend from a gang of kidnappers.

Phoney Cronies (8/27/42) D: Harry Edwards. Tom Kennedy, Dudley Dickerson, Monty Collins. El and Tom, owners of a transfer company, are hired to deliver crates to a museum in the middle of the night.

Ham and Yeggs (11/27/42) D: Jules White. Elsie Ames, Barbara Slater, Eddie Laughton. A vamp tries to marry El after he inherits $50,000.

His Wedding Scare (1/15/43) D: Del Lord. Louise Currie, Monty Collins, Vernon Dent, Dudley Dickerson, Lloyd Bridges, Stanley Blystone, Eddie

Laughton, Chester Conklin, Snub Pollard, Charles "Heine" Conklin, Stanley Brown. El and his new bride go on their honeymoon; no matter where they go, they keep running into her former husbands.

I Spied for You (4/30/43) D: Jules White. Kathryn Keys, Bud Jamison, Stanley Blystone, Vernon Dent, Barbara Slater, Johnny Kascier, Al Thompson, Bobby Barber. Seaman Brendel thwarts a ring of Nazi saboteurs.

Boobs in the Night (6/25/43) D: Del Lord. Monty Collins, Charles Middleton, Frank Lackteen. El and Monty, auxiliary Home Defense workers, encounter a mad scientist seeking a human head for his mechanical man. Remade with the Three Stooges as *Dopey Dicks* (1950).

A Rookie's Cookie (10/8/43) D: Jules White. Adele Mara, Lloyd Bridges, Bernard Gorcey, John Tyrrell, Dewey Robinson, Fred "Snowflake" Toones, Dudley Dickerson, Al Thompson. Rookie cop Brendel falls in love with a girl who's being pursued by a numbers racketeer. Working title: *Clubs Are Trumps*.

Defective Detectives (4/3/44) D: Harry Edwards. Harry Langdon, Christine McIntyre, Vernon Dent, John Tyrrell, Eddie Laughton, Snub Pollard, Dick Botiller. Private detectives El and Harry are hired to keep on the trail of a mobster who has been threatening injury to a banker and his wife.

Mopey Dope (6/16/44) D: Del Lord. Harry Langdon, Christine McIntyre, Arthur Q. Bryan, Al Thompson, Johnny Kascier. El's absentminded pal Harry has difficulty remembering a wedding anniversary. A remake of Charley Chase's *The Mind Needer* (1938).

Pick a Peck of Plumbers (7/23/44) D: Jules White. Shemp Howard, John Tyrrell, Al Thompson, Kathryn Keys, Willa Pearl Curtis, Beatrice Blinn, Frank "Billy" Mitchell, Jean Murray, Brian O'Hara, Judy Malcolm, Charles "Heine" Conklin, Joe Palma. Vagrants El and Shemp become plumber's assistants; on their first assignment, they reduce a house to shambles in search of a ring that fell down the drainpipe. Stock shot of waterlogged ceiling taken from *Andy Clyde Gets Spring Chicken* (1939). A remake of Sidney and Murray's *Plumbing for Gold* (1934); a reworking of the Three Stooges' *A-Plumbing We Will Go* (1940). Remade with the Three Stooges as *Scheming Schemers* (1956); reworked with the Three Stooges as *Vagabond Loafers* (1949).

Snooper Service (2/2/45) D: Harry Edwards. Harry Langdon, Rebel Randall, Dick Curtis, Vernon Dent, Fred Kelsey, Buddy Yarus. El and Harry, private sleuths, are hired to follow a beautiful showgirl.

Pistol Packin' Nitwits (4/4/45) D: Harry Edwards. Harry Langdon, Christine McIntyre, Brad King, Dick Curtis, Tex Cooper, Victor Cox, Charles "Heine" Conklin. El and Harry protect a pretty saloonkeeper from a gang of Western thugs. Working title: *Tenderfeet*. Reworked with the Three Stooges as *Out West* (1947). Sequence with Vernon Dent was cut from final version.

Charley Chase

In 1937 Charley Chase came to Columbia after having been dropped from the roster of his longtime home, the Hal Roach Studios. Jules White recalls, "Chase had an agent who was a very good friend of mine, so he brought Charley in." At this time, the comedy shorts department had just been divided into two units, one supervised by Jules White, the other by Hugh McCollum. Chase made nearly all of his pictures for the McCollum unit, where he was given the creative freedom to write, produce and direct two-reelers with the Three Stooges, Smith and Dale, Andy Clyde and others, in addition to appearing in his own series (although, curiously, he never directed any of his own starring shorts).

Chase's Columbia shorts are the antithesis of his work for Hal Roach. Whereas the Roach comedies stressed the situation over the individual gag, the Columbias rarely allowed the story to interfere with the gags, many of which were ruthlessly dragged in for the sake of a quick laugh. The Roach product was leisurely structured, often elegant in design; it's not uncommon to find a Chase Roach short that spends a major portion of its running time dealing with sophisticated expository plotting, building methodically to a climactic payoff. The Columbias, on the other hand, are pretty much cut-and-dried affairs, slick assembly-line vehicles in which fast-paced visuals take precedence over characterization. This rapid tempo robbed Chase's established personality of much of its humanity.

Gone too is the unique charm of the Roach comedies: the infectious background music (the Columbia comedy shorts rarely had any score), an occasional song by Chase (Charley sings in only two of his Columbias, *The Grand Hooter* and *The Big Squirt*), and the familiar stock company of supporting players (though Columbia had its own, equally talented coterie). Chase's Columbias benefit from the handsome, glowing production values that distinguish the unit's work from this period; being affiliated with a major studio, the comedy shorts department had access to expensive sets that would have been too prohibitive for an independent unit to commission. However, it's a superficial advantage; the films look good, but they're lacking in substance. Despite these shortcomings, the series was not a total loss. Indeed, a few of the entries, especially those which are closest in spirit to the Roach films, rank among the comedian's finest. But taken as a whole, this series is very much inferior to his earlier work.

Several entries are embarrassingly flat; even the staunchest Chase addicts will find little to praise in *Calling All Doctors* (1937), *The Sap Takes a Wrap*

Charley with Ann Doran, a talented comedienne who was seen in a number of Columbia two-reelers. From *Skinny the Moocher* **(1939).**

(1939) and *Teacher's Pest* (1939). *Rattling Romeo* (1939) offers some laughs but loses steam at midpoint and sputters to a disappointing finish. *Skinny the Moocher* (1939) has a typically Chaselike premise as Charley's love life is hindered by his valet's kleptomania; however, the film is marred by too many unrelated gag sequences and a completely unnecessary climactic free-for-all. *Time Out for Trouble* (1938) is the series' worst entry. Charley's fiancée (Louise Stanley) catches him in an innocent embrace with another woman and immediately calls off their engagement. Despondent and suicidal, he contracts with a gangster (Dick Curtis) to have himself "bumped off." No sooner does he finalize the arrangements when his fiancée has a change of heart and reconciles with him. Charley then tries to cancel his deal with the thug, only to be informed that all transactions are nonretractable. With the emphasis on knockabout slapstick, Charley is reduced to playing the role of a complete idiot. His incessant whining grates on the viewer's nerves, and when he grapples around on the floor with the mobster's girlfriend (Ann Doran) or dangles from an open window with a rope fastened around his ankle, it's a tragic waste of one of the screen's subtlest comic actors.

There are a handful of efforts that are quite good, however. *The Wrong Miss Wright* (1937), a remake of his silent short *Crazy Like a Fox* (1926), is one of the top entries. While on an ocean cruise, Charley falls hopelessly in love with a beautiful woman (Peggy Stratford). In order to get released from a prearranged marriage to a woman he's never seen, Charley feigns insanity, thinking this will relieve him of his marital obligation. He later discovers that the woman he's betrothed to is the same one he met on the cruise, but not until he's pulled some outrageous stunts that have alienated his prospective father-in-law (John T. Murray). *The Big Squirt* (1937) is a certified gem. Charley, a soda jerk with a mania for murder mysteries, vows he'll apprehend a public enemy. Disguising himself as a blind street musician, Chase sings "I'm a Daring Drugstore Desperado," a delightful novelty song he composed for the picture. *Pie à la Maid* (1938) is another above-average outing in which a waitress (Ann Doran) mistakes Charley for a notorious gangster (John Tyrrell). An interesting if not wholly successful touch is the addition of an organ score to the soundtrack; although it doesn't convey a genuine feeling of silent comedy (much of the humor is verbal), it's an admirable attempt to break away from the standard bill of fare.

The Heckler (1940), an atypical effort for Chase, is one of the very best. Based on the Mack Sennett short *The Loudmouth* (1933), Charley plays an unbearably obnoxious spectator at a baseball game. Chase's raucous antics in the bleacher section, heckling ballplayers and spectators alike, are hilarious; spilling soda all over one sports fan, Charley remarks, "It won't hurt you—it's a *soft* drink!" Vernon Dent lends memorable support as the poor soul sitting next to him. After an unusually strong opening, the film slows down considerably during its final third as Chase becomes involved with racketeers who want to use his heckling skills to throw a ballgame.

In *His Bridal Fright* (1940), the last Chase short released, Charley tries to obtain a rare postage stamp to win the approval of his fiancee's father (Bud Jamison). There are a few clever touches, but the film doesn't come to life until its wild car chase finale, masterfully staged by director Del Lord (who directed seventeen of the twenty Chase comedies produced by Columbia).

Chase died of a heart attack on June 20, 1940. His death was a tremendous loss to the unit; he was an all-purpose talent and was well liked and respected. Elwood Ullman, who scripted several Chase comedies, echoes the sentiments of his coworkers when he states, "Charley was a wonderful man and a magnificent talent." It's regrettable that so little of Chase's Columbia work is representative of the artistry of which this genuinely great comedian was capable.

Chase's Columbia filmography is divided into three sections: his starring series, his directorial efforts, and his screenplay credits.

The Charley Chase Series

The Grand Hooter (5/7/37) D: Del Lord. Peggy Stratford, Nena Quartaro, Harry Semels, Bud Jamison, Eddie Laughton. Charley shows more concern for

Charley (center) is about to relieve Vernon Dent of his hot dog in *The Heckler* **(1940); Monte Collins (left) watches in apparent disbelief.**

his meetings at the Lodge of Hoot Owls than he does for his marriage. Remade with Shemp Howard as *Open Season for Saps* (1944).

From Bad to Worse (6/4/37) D: Del Lord. Peggy Stratford, Bobby Watson, Bud Jamison, Lew Davis, Pat Lane, Billy McCall, Edith Craig, Olivia Moore, Ethelreda Leopold, Ruth Hilliard, Polly Chase, Elaine Waters. Aboard a train, Charley's honeymoon is interrupted by a young woman and her jealous husband.

The Wrong Miss Wright (6/18/37) D: Charles Lamont. Peggy Stratford, John T. Murray, Bud Jamison, Robert McKenzie, Eva McKenzie, Ella McKenzie. Charley feigns insanity in order to get released from a prearranged marriage. Remade with Vera Vague as *You Dear Boy* (1943). Reworked with Vera Vague as *Happy Go Wacky* (1952).

Calling All Doctors (7/22/37) D: Charles Lamont. Lucille Lund, John T. Murray, Bobby Watson, James C. Morton, Fern Emmett, Vernon Dent, Lon Poff, William Irving, Lynton Brent, Charles Dorety, Bobby Barber. Hypochondriac Charley mistakes a lunatic for a trained physician. Remade with Vera Vague as *Doctor, Feel My Pulse* (1944) and *She Took a Powder* (1951).

The Big Squirt (9/17/37) D: Del Lord. Lucille Lund, Bud Jamison, Leora Thatcher, Eddie Fetherstone, Theodore Lorch, Carol Tevis, Al Thompson, Polly Chase, Beatrice Blinn. Soda jerk Charley, a mystery story buff, fancies himself as a master criminologist. Working title: *Don't Look Now*. Remade with Bert Wheeler as *The Awful Sleuth* (1951).

Man Bites Lovebug (12/24/37) D: Del Lord. Mary Russell, John T. Murray, Frank Lackteen, Bud Jamison, Etta McDaniel. Charley, a marriage expert, tries to strengthen a friend's marriage via jealousy. Remade with Billy Gilbert as *Wedded Bliss* (1944).

Time Out for Trouble (3/18/38) D: Del Lord. Louise Stanley, Ann Doran, Dick Curtis, Eddie Fetherstone, Vernon Dent, Bud Jamison, Bess Flowers, Cy Schindell. Despondent over breaking up with his fiancee, Charley hires a gangster to kill him. Remade with Shemp Howard as *Off Again, On Again* (1945).

The Mind Needer (4/29/38) D: Del Lord. Ann Doran, Vernon Dent, John T. Murray, Bess Flowers. Absentminded Charley struggles to remember his wedding anniversary. Working titles: *The Numb Skull* and *Numb Skull Number One*. Remade with Langdon and Brendel as *Mopey Dope* (1944).

Many Sappy Returns (8/19/38) D: Del Lord. Ann Doran, John T. Murray, Fred Kelsey, John Sheehan, Vernon Dent, Lane Chandler, Kernan Cripps. Charley, a taxi driver, mistakes an escaped lunatic for his girlfriend's father. Remade with Schilling and Lane as *He's in Again* (1949).

The Nightshirt Bandit (10/28/38) D: Jules White. Phyllis Barry, Eva McKenzie, James C. Morton, Fred "Snowflake" Toones, Marjorie Deanne, June Gittelson. Professor Chase is on the lookout for a nightshirt bandit prowling the college campus. Remade with Andy Clyde as *Go Chase Yourself* (1948) and *Pardon My Nightshirt* (1956).

Pie à la Maid (12/25/38) D: Del Lord. Ann Doran, John Tyrrell, Lionel Belmore, Gaylord Pendleton, Stanley Brown, Cy Schindell. Charley becomes infatuated with a waitress who has mistaken him for a mobster.

The Sap Takes a Wrap (3/10/39) D: Del Lord. Gloria Blondell, Ethel Clayton, The Astor Trio, George Cleveland, Marjorie Deanne, Gene Morgan, Harry Wilson, James Millican, John T. Murray, Bud Jamison, John Tyrrell. Charley gives his girlfriend a mink coat he was supposed to be guarding for three showgirls; when the ladies want their coat back, Charley goes to great lengths to recover it.

Lobby card for *The Nightshirt Bandit* (1938), one of Chase's best Columbia shorts. The girl next to Charley is Marjorie Deanne.

The Chump Takes a Bump (5/5/39) D: Del Lord. At a nightclub, Charley fails to recognize his newly blonde wife. Remade with Hugh Herbert as *Wife Decoy* (1945).

Rattling Romeo (7/14/39) D: Del Lord. Ann Doran, John Tyrrell, Harry Bernard, Bud Jamison, Ben Taggart, Richard Fiske, Cy Schindell, Stanley Brown. To please his girlfriend, Charley buys an automobile.

Skinny the Moocher (9/8/39) D: Del Lord. Ann Doran, John T. Murray, Richard Fiske, Ben Taggart, John Tyrrell, Cy Schindell, Stanley Brown, James Craig, Lorna Gray. Charley, trying to make a favorable impression on his girlfriend's father, is hindered by his valet's kleptomania.

Teacher's Pest (11/3/39) D: Del Lord. Ruth Skinner, Chester Conklin, Richard Fiske, Bud Jamison, Hank Bell, Vernon Dent, Bill Wolfe. Charley is the new schoolteacher in a tough Western town.

The Awful Goof (12/22/39) D: Del Lord. Linda Winters, Lucille Lund, Dick Curtis, Bud Jamison. Charley innocently gets involved with the wife of a jealous wrestler.

The Heckler (2/16/40) D: Del Lord. Vernon Dent, Monty Collins, Bruce Bennett, Richard Fiske, Don Beddoe, Robert Sterling, Bud Jamison, Stanley Brown, Bess Flowers, John Ince, Beatrice Blinn, Linda Winters, Charles "Heine" Conklin. Charley is an obnoxious spectator at a baseball game. Remade with Shemp Howard as *Mr. Noisy* (1946).

South of the Boudoir (5/17/40) D: Del Lord. Ann Doran, Helen Lynd, Arthur Q. Bryan. Charley's wife walks out on him, so he hires a waitress to take her place when he brings his boss home for dinner. Remade with Hugh Herbert as *When the Wife's Away* (1946).

His Bridal Fright (7/12/40) D: Del Lord. Iris Meredith, Bud Jamison, Richard Fiske, Dudley Dickerson, Bruce Bennett, Jack "Tiny" Lipson, Vernon Dent, Stanley Brown. To impress his fiancee's stamp-collecting father, Charley sets out to obtain a rare postage stamp from "Pidgemania."

Directed by Charley Chase

Oh, What a Knight! (11/22/37) Herman Bing, Louise Stanley, Claud Allister. Bing, a barber, is mistaken for a society woman's new footman.

The Old Raid Mule (3/4/38) Andy Clyde, Olin Howland, Ann Doran, Vernon Dent, Bud Jamison, Bob McKenzie, Eddie Laughton. Andy feuds with his hillbilly neighbor.

Tassels in the Air (4/1/38) The Three Stooges (Moe Howard, Larry Fine, Jerry "Curly" Howard), Bess Flowers, Bud Jamison, Vernon Dent, Victor Travers. Moe is mistaken for Omay, a famous interior decorator.

Ankles Away (5/13/38) Andy Clyde, Ann Doran, Gene Morgan, Gino Corrado, Grace Goodall, Vernon Dent, Bess Flowers, John T. Murray, Symona Boniface. Andy is duped into thinking his bride-to-be has a wooden leg.

Flat Foot Stooges (5/13/38) The Three Stooges (Moe Howard, Larry Fine, Jerry "Curly" Howard), Chester Conklin, Dick Curtis, Lola Jensen. The Stooges are firemen who still rely on an old horse-drawn fire engine.

Half-Way to Hollywood (7/1/38) Tom Kennedy, Johnny Arthur, Ann Doran, Harry Holmes, Cy Schindell. Johnny writes a movie scenario and gets Tom and his wife to star with him in his amateur production.

Violent Is the Word for Curly (7/2/38) The Three Stooges (Moe Howard, Larry Fine, Jerry "Curly" Howard), Gladys Gale, Marjorie Deanne, Bud Jamison, Eddie Fetherstone, John T. Murray, Al Thompson, Pat Gleason. The Stooges, three gas station attendants, are mistaken for eminent professors by the dean of a girls' college.

Mutts to You (10/14/38) The Three Stooges (Moe Howard, Larry Fine, Jerry "Curly" Howard), Bess Flowers, Lane Chandler, Bud Jamison, Vernon Dent. Three professional dogwashers take in an abandoned baby. Working title: *Muts to You*. A remake of Sidney and Murray's *Ten Baby Fingers* (1934) and Andy Clyde's *My Little Feller* (1937). Remade with the Three Stooges as *Sock-a-Bye Baby* (1942).

A Nag in the Bag (11/11/38) Joe Smith, Charlie Dale, Dick Curtis, Stella Le-Saint, Dorothy Vernon, Bud Jamison, Gloria Blondell, Polly Chase. Drive-in restaurant operators Smith and Dale get betting fever and put all their money on a horse; because of dialect trouble, they bet on the wrong horse.

Mutiny on the Body (2/10/39) Joe Smith, Charlie Dale, Chester Conklin, Guy Usher, Vernon Dent, Cy Schindell, Marjorie Deanne. Smith and Dale, owners of the Klassy Korset Company, go to a sanitarium for rest and relaxation. Remade with the Three Stooges as *Monkey Businessmen* (1946).

Boom Goes the Groom (3/24/39) Andy Clyde, Vivien Oakland, Monty Collins, Dick Curtis. Just as he's about to get married, Andy learns that his gold mine is worth a fortune.

Saved by the Belle (6/30/39) The Three Stooges (Moe Howard, Larry Fine, Jerry "Curly" Howard), Carmen LaRoux, LeRoy Mason, Gino Corrado, Vernon Dent, Al Thompson. Three garment salesmen, peddling earthquake shock absorbers (pillows with straps) in the South American country of Valeska, are mistaken for political assassins.

Static in the Attic (9/22/39) Walter Catlett, Ann Doran, Charles Williams, Tommy Bond, Beatrice Blinn, Eddie Laughton, Bud Jamison. Walter gets a "ham" radio for his birthday.

Written by Charley Chase

Ankles Away (5/13/38) D: Charley Chase. Andy Clyde, Ann Doran, Gene Morgan, Gino Corrado, Grace Goodall, Vernon Dent, Bess Flowers, John T. Murray, Symona Boniface. Andy is duped into thinking his bride-to-be has a wooden leg.

Many Sappy Returns (8/19/38) D: Del Lord. Charley Chase, Ann Doran, John T. Murray, Fred Kelsey, John Sheehan, Lane Chandler, Vernon Dent, Kernan Cripps. Charley, a taxi driver, mistakes an escaped lunatic for his girlfriend's father. Remade with Schilling and Lane as *He's in Again* (1949).

Pie à la Maid (12/25/38) D: Del Lord. Charley Chase, Ann Doran, John Tyrrell, Lionel Belmore, Gaylord Pendleton, Stanley Brown, Cy Schindell. Charley becomes infatuated with a waitress who has mistaken him for a mobster.

The Sap Takes a Wrap (3/10/39) D: Del Lord. Charley Chase, Gloria Blondell, Ethel Clayton, The Astor Trio, George Cleveland, Marjorie Deanne, Gene Morgan, Harry Wilson, James Millican, John T. Murray, Bud Jamison, John Tyrrell. Charley gives his girlfriend a mink coat he was supposed to be guarding for three showgirls; when the ladies want their coat back, Charley goes to great lengths to recover it.

Now It Can Be Sold (6/2/39) D: Del Lord. Andy Clyde, Tommy Bond, Anita Garvin, Dick Curtis. Andy, aided by his junior G-man nephew, tangles with bank robbers.

Buster Keaton

Buster Keaton was undoubtedly the greatest comedy talent to work for Columbia. His meticulously crafted silent comedies award him that oft-maligned title, a genius of the cinema. Pictures like *Sherlock, Jr.* and *The Navigator* (both 1924) have been rediscovered by the intelligentsia as well as today's moviegoing public. After years of neglect, a growing number of Keaton buffs are learning that the prime legacy of "The Great Stone Face" is permanent and, best of all, still marvelously funny.

It's all the more disheartening, then, to discover that Keaton's Columbia shorts are the worst comedies he ever appeared in. Keaton himself concurred with this assessment. His precipitous fall from grace with MGM in the early 1930s (due to numerous personal problems, bad management, and a raging bout with alcohol) made Buster a bad risk for film employment. In 1939, Columbia was the first major studio to express revived interest in the comic as a star performer. Jules White recounts how Keaton's services were obtained:

> Buster was a very close friend of Clyde Bruckman, one of my writers. One day Bruckman came to me and said, "Buster Keaton hasn't worked for a couple of years. He's not money hungry and you can make a good deal if you're interested in him." If I was interested in him? I was thrilled at the prospect of having him work for us. Rather than call on him myself, I felt Buster would be more comfortable if Bruckman brought him in. So the two of them came to my office and before long, Keaton was signed to a contract.

Although Bruckman had been a gag writer for both Keaton and Harold Lloyd in the 1920s, his salad days were over. The Columbia two-reelers he wrote for Buster were assembly-line slapstick outings, alien to the true Keaton

Lorna Gray (left) tries to free Buster Keaton from Gino Corrado's stranglehold in *Pest from the West* (1939).

style. Unlike his contemporaries at Columbia, Charley Chase and Harry Langdon, Keaton did not submit scripts for these shorts (even though he had coauthored all of his own silent comedies). Whenever a sequence in one of these films suggests a vintage Keaton routine of yore, it can be safely presumed that Clyde Bruckman's predilection for recycling gags is at work.

Oddly enough, Buster's Columbia comedies were very popular on their initial release. Exhibitors welcomed the pictures and audience response was favorable, proving that Keaton had not lost his appeal, regardless of the unsatisfactory vehicles he was appearing in. A lot of effort went into the first one, *Pest from the West* (1939). Buster plays an idle millionaire in pursuit of a pretty young señorita (Lorna Gray) who is using him to make her employer (Gino Corrado) jealous. The film's funniest sequence has Buster mistakenly serenading Lorna beneath irascible Bud Jamison's window. As Buster strums his ukelele and croons "In a Little Spanish Town," Jamison punctuates each chorus by hurling crockery at the stoic Keaton's head. Buster plugs on with his tune, never missing a beat despite flying dishware. Though not in the same league as Keaton's silent classics, *Pest from the West* got the series off to a good start. It looked as if the Keaton shorts would maintain a high level.

Unfortunately, this wasn't the case. *Nothing but Pleasure* (1940) is a glaring example of why Keaton's Columbia work consistently misses the mark.

Considering the poor quality of *Nothing but Pleasure* (1940), Buster's forlorn expression is completely justified.

The film reprises two classic bits: the parking routine originally used in W.C. Fields' *Man on the Flying Trapeze* (1935) and Keaton's own sequence of putting a drunken woman to bed, which he had performed in *Spite Marriage* (1929) and on stage. The beauty of these routines was their deliberate pacing, as one gag neatly dovetails into the next. In *Nothing but Pleasure*, the comic "turns" are whittled down to nothing and thrown into the plotline in a haphazard fashion. What should have been hilarious becomes frustrating.

Pardon My Berth Marks (1940) is by far the best entry, a fast-paced comedy directed by Jules White. As an aspiring reporter who boards a train and becomes involved with the wife of a mobster, Buster is in top form. For once, Keaton portrays a resourceful character able to think his way out of situations. It's the closest the series ever came to recapturing the youthful Keaton spirit, "hardworking and honest," to use Buster's own terminology.

The rest of the series is annoyingly mediocre. Scared reaction comedy wasn't Buster's forte, and *The Spook Speaks* (1940) falls flat because of it. *So You Won't Squawk* (1941) features a Keatonian premise, with innocent Buster mistaken for a gang leader who's supposed to be bumped off. But the short degenerates into stock footage of car chases (taken from the 1935 Columbia feature *She Couldn't Take It*) and process shots with Buster teetering on a building ledge. Keaton was a stickler for authenticity and performed all his own dangerous stunts in silent days; now he was reduced to reacting before some very phony-looking back projection effects. *His Ex Marks the Spot* (1940) is also quite humorless, as his ex-wife (Elsie Ames) returns to make both Keaton and the viewer miserable. *The Taming of the Snood* (1940) doesn't have much of a plot, but it does contain one lengthy sequence in which Buster and Elsie Ames (an overbearing comedienne the unit spotlighted in several shorts) perform some truly breathtaking acrobatics. The film's funniest bit is also its subtlest: Buster is polite to customers of his millinery shop, but turns fiercely possessive when one tries on his porkpie hat. "*That* hat ain't for sale!" he ominously warns, grabbing his hat off a befuddled woman's head.

With *Mooching Through Georgia* (1939) the series hit rock-bottom. It has a Civil War setting: An aging Confederate soldier (Buster) relates, in flashback, how he outwitted the Yankee Army, stealing their secret war plans. Though comparisons to *The General* immediately spring to mind, *Mooching Through Georgia* comes nowhere near Keaton's 1926 masterpiece. Buster is paired with Monty Collins, and it sadly recalls the Keaton–Jimmy Durante teaming of a few years previous. Collins, a more bombastic comic, over-shadows Keaton in several scenes; at times it isn't clear who's supposed to be the star of the picture. The obvious use of a double for Buster during some stunts further weakens the humor.

She's Oil Mine was Keaton's last Columbia short. In his autobiography, Buster claimed to have vowed "not to make another crummy two-reeler" for the unit, and stood firm on his promise. In 1943 Felix Adler, a staff writer for the Columbia shorts unit, fashioned a screenplay entitled *What a Soldier!* with Buster slated for the lead. Keaton did not appear in it; the project was shelved and eventually made as *Dizzy Yardbird* (1950) with Joe Besser.

While these shorts invariably disappoint, they're important as Keaton's final starring series for any movie studio. Like his later television work and *Beach Party* epics, these films are worth a look if only because he's in them. Still, nearly all of Keaton's Columbias show a flagrant disregard for the qualities that made Buster the brilliant comedian he was.

The Buster Keaton Series

Pest from the West (6/16/39) D: Del Lord. Lorna Gray, Gino Corrado, Richard Fiske, Bud Jamison, Forbes Murray, Eddie Laughton, Ned Glass. Buster, a millionaire vacationing in Mexico, falls for a pretty señorita and sets out to win her heart.

Mooching Through Georgia (8/11/39) D: Jules White. Monty Collins, Lynton Brent, Jill Martin, Bud Jamison, Ned Glass, Jack Hill, Stanley Mack. Buster relates, in flashback, how he outwitted the Yankee Army during the Civil War. Remade with the Three Stooges as *Uncivil Warbirds* (1946).

Nothing but Pleasure (1/19/40) D: Jules White. Dorothy Appleby, Beatrice Blinn, Bud Jamison, Richard Fiske, Jack Randall, Robert Sterling, Bobby Barber. Buster and his wife travel to Detroit to buy a new car; to save money on the shipping fee, they decide to drive it back home.

Pardon My Berth Marks (3/22/40) D: Jules White. Dorothy Appleby, Richard Fiske, Vernon Dent, Cy Schindell, Eva McKenzie, Ned Glass, John Tyrrell, Bud Jamison, Jack "Tiny" Lipson, Lynton Brent, Fred "Snowflake" Toones, Stanley Brown. Buster, an aspiring reporter, boards a train and innocently becomes involved with a mobster's wife. Remade with Harry Von Zell as *Rolling Down to Reno* (1947).

The Taming of the Snood (6/28/40) D: Jules White. Dorothy Appleby, Elsie Ames, Richard Fiske, Bruce Bennett. Buster runs afoul of a jewel thief.

The Spook Speaks (9/20/40) D: Jules White. Elsie Ames, Don Beddoe, Dorothy Appleby, Lynton Brent, John Tyrrell, Bruce Bennett. Buster and Elsie are hired as housekeepers, unaware that the residence, belonging to a magician, is rigged with secret gadgets.

His Ex Marks the Spot (12/13/40) D: Jules White. Elsie Ames, Dorothy Appleby, Matt McHugh, Jack "Tiny" Lipson. Buster's ex-wife and her boyfriend come to live with him, to the dismay of his new spouse.

So You Won't Squawk (2/21/41) D: Del Lord. Eddie Fetherstone, Bud Jamison, Matt McHugh, Vernon Dent, Hank Mann, Edmund Cobb. Buster is mistaken for a gangster marked for death.

General Nuisance (9/18/41) D: Jules White. Elsie Ames, Monty Collins, Dorothy Appleby, Lynton Brent, Bud Jamison, Nick Arno, Harry Semels. Buster is smitten with a pretty army hospital nurse.

She's Oil Mine (11/20/41) D: Jules White. Elsie Ames, Monty Collins, Eddie Laughton, Bud Jamison, Harry Semels, Stanley Brown. Bumbling plumber Buster gets mixed up with an oil heiress and her jealous suitor.

Buster poses with Elsie Ames (left), Matt McHugh and Dorothy Appleby in this typical Columbia gag shot. From *His Ex Marks the Spot* (1940).

The Glove Slingers

The Glove Slingers series was a misfire, but it's noteworthy for being a noble attempt to modify the usual knockabout fare. Though visual gags were still liberally employed, the films possess stronger-than-usual storylines and are populated by characters who behave in a manner a little less bluntly cartoonish than is the norm for Columbia comedy shorts. The central figure is Terry Kelly, an earnest young man who wants to become a boxer, like his late father. The role of Terry was essayed at various times by Noah Beery, Jr., David Durand and Bill Henry. Sidney Miller, Doodles Weaver and Joe Brown, Jr. were among those who played his youthful allies; Shemp Howard, Paul Hurst, Guinn "Big Boy" Williams and Wally Vernon were a few of the supporting comics who portrayed Terry's older confidants.

The first entry, *Glove Slingers* (1939), has Terry (Noah Beery, Jr.) training for a fight in secrecy, as his mother (Dorothy Vaughn) is dead-set against her son becoming a boxer. *Glove Slingers* contains some of Jules White's most disciplined direction and proves conclusively that he could tell a story without resorting to overt slapstick. Yet the film is a bit too restrained for its own good, as performers like Shemp Howard seem listless having to give such reserved interpretations of their roles.

After this initial short, the series had no real direction to head in, so someone came up with the idea of sending Terry and his chums to college. This change in setting may have been welcomed by the scriptwriters, since the college campus offered a greater wealth of gag material than the fight arena, but it also caused the series to lose track of itself. Now that the plots centered around collegiate life, Terry was no longer an aspiring boxer, but instead a student who has a flair for pugilism. This led to highly questionable displays of moral fiber, as any conflict our hero becomes involved in is ultimately settled by fisticuffs (coincidentally, boxing gloves are always kept within arms reach).

The series did try to maintain continuity; most of the entries pick up where the previous one left off, regardless of whether different actors were essaying the principal roles. Many of these productions were able to utilize existing sets; a few, like the luxury liner in *Mitt Me Tonight* (1941), are truly impressive for comedy shorts from that period. Others have modest musical numbers, such as a tap dance in *Mitt Me Tonight* and the song "Gypsy from Poughkeepsie" sung by Rita Rio (later known as Dona Drake) in *Fresh as a Freshman* (1941). *Pleased to Mitt You* (1940) is perhaps the best in the series, although, oddly enough, it's the one that comes closest to being a typical Columbia comedy short: a disjointed parade of gag sequences.

The Glove Slingers were kayoed in 1943. The failure of this series was never forgotten; from here on in, the unit shunned any radical departure from tried-and-true formulas.

The Glove Slingers Series

Glove Slingers (11/24/39) D: Jules White. Noah Beery, Jr., Shemp Howard, Paul Hurst, Dorothy Vaughn, Betty Campbell, Cy Schindell, Elaine Waters, Julieta Naldi, Richard Fiske, Dick Curtis, Bob Ryan, Johnny Kascier. Against his mother's wishes, Terry Kelly (Beery) trains to become a boxer; his opponent turns out to be his girlfriend's brother.

Pleased to Mitt You (9/6/40) D: Jules White. David Durand, Shemp Howard, Guinn "Big Boy" Williams, Doris Donaldson, Dorothy Vaughn, Stanley Brown, Eddie Laughton, Ralph Sanford, Richard Fiske, Lynton Brent, Charles Dorety. The college savings of Terry (Durand) are stolen by his rival.

Fresh as a Freshman (1/29/41) D: Jules White. David Durand, Paul Hurst, Wally Vernon, Dorothy Vaughn, Adele Pearce, Rita Rio, Eddie Laughton, Vernon Dent, Al Thompson, June Bryde, Marjorie "Babe" Kane. Terry (Durand) arrives at Taylor College and receives a less-than-cordial welcome.

Lobby card for *Pleased to Mitt You* (1940), perhaps the best of the Glove Slingers series. Pictured (l. to r.): Doris Donaldson, Guinn "Big Boy" Williams, player, David Durand, player, and Shemp Howard.

Glove Affair (4/4/41) D: Jules White. David Durand, Dorothy Vaughn, Paul Hurst, Roscoe Ates, John Kellogg, Vernon Dent, Harry McKim, Adele Pearce, Victor Travers. Terry (Durand) protects his sweetheart's little brother from the town bully. Working title: *Then Came the Gong.*

Mitt Me Tonight (11/6/41) D: Jules White. David Durand, Sidney Miller, Doodles Weaver, George Offerman, Jr., Lorraine Miller, Eddie Laughton, Victor Travers, Dorothy Vaughn, Lynton Brent, Cy Schindell, Johnny Kascier. Terry (Durand) and his pals stowaway aboard an ocean liner.

The Kink of the Campus (12/25/41) D: Del Lord. David Durand, Sidney Miller, Joe Brown, Jr., Yvonne DeCarlo, Marjorie "Babe" Kane. Terry (Durand) is framed by a rival so that he'll be ineligible to play in the big football game.

Glove Birds (2/12/42) D: Jules White. David Durand, Sidney Miller, Joe Brown, Jr., George Offerman, Jr., Jean Porter, Dorothy Vaughn, Lynton Brent, Bud Jamison, Ned Glass, Ray Cook, William Alston. Terry (Durand) is erroneously jailed prior to an important boxing match.

A Study in Socks (5/21/42) D: Del Lord. David Durand, Marjorie Deanne, Sidney Miller, Johnny Holmes, Arthur Q. Bryan, Monty Collins, Bud Jamison. Inventor Terry (Durand) displays a disastrous gasoline formula to his girlfriend's father.

College Belles (10/16/42) D: Harry Edwards. David Durand, Sidney Miller, Joe Brown, Jr., Gwen Kenyon, Chester Conklin. Terry (Durand) and his pal stage a boxing bout to sell war bonds.

The Great Glover (12/25/42) D: Jules White. Bill Henry, Adele Mara, Sidney Miller, Joe Brown, Jr., Lloyd Bridges, Jerry Shelton, Johnny Kascier. Terry (Henry) and his friends pitch in to help the Taylor College scrap drive. Working titles: *His Girl's Worst Friend* and *Never Lead with Your Chin*.

Socks Appeal (2/19/43) D: Harry Edwards. Bill Henry, Adele Mara, Sidney Miller, Joe Brown, Jr., Dorothy Vaughn. Terry (Henry) is the proprietor of the college service shop; his rival tries to ruin his business and steal his girl.

His Girl's Worst Friend (5/14/43) D: Jules White. Bill Henry, Adele Mara, Rick Vallin, Sidney Miller, Joe Brown, Jr., June Bryde, Edward Hall. On the last day of the semester, Terry (Henry) and his pals enroll for a summer aviation course. Working title: *A Left to the Right*.

Hugh Herbert

Hugh Herbert had been a popular supporting comedian in many films, most notably in a host of Warner Brothers musicals, prior to signing on with the Columbia comedy shorts unit in 1943. His forte was dialogue humor, delivered in a nonsensical mumbling fashion, as though he allowed all of his garbled private thoughts to spill freely from his mouth. His trademark cry of "woo woo" (according to legend, it was actually "hoo hoo" but was so widely interpreted the other way that it was eventually altered) was used to convey amusement, embarrassment and astonishment.

Herbert's Columbia shorts are a mixed bag, with the good entries offset by a number of flat, predictable ones. There were reasons for the frequently disappointing results. First of all, the unit specialized in knockabout slapstick and not the type of verbal humor Herbert excelled in. His age (he was fifty-five years old when the series began), coupled with the fact that he was never much of a physical comedian to start with, prohibited him from executing the strenuous gags that were a staple of these comedies. Another, perhaps even greater reason was Herbert's attitude toward these films. Says Edward Bernds, "Most of the people I worked with in short subjects—cast, crew, everybody— were real hard workers, whereas Hugh Herbert was lazy and, worst of all, had the attitude that he was slumming, that these two-reelers were beneath his dignity, that he was a much better artist." Thus, the glaring phoniness of the stunts, a general lack of tailor-made material and Herbert's indifferent performances combined to render many of the films uninspired and lifeless.

With two units operating out of the comedy shorts department—one headed by Jules White, the other by Hugh McCollum—each series alternated between them; one short would be produced by White, the next by McCollum and so on. This modus operandi was used to balance out the schedule—that is, until 1944, when comedienne Vera Vague worked with McCollum director Harry Edwards on *Strife of the Party*. Vera considered Edwards to be such a poor director (and rightfully so) that she requested to work exclusively with Jules White. From that point on, the Vera Vague series became the sole responsibility of White's unit. To even out the schedule, the Hugh Herbert series became the property of the McCollum unit. Things ran smoothly enough until 1946, when Edward Bernds directed Herbert in *Hot Heir* (released 1947). Bernds remembers:

> Herbert made one crack that rankled me; when I asked him to please learn his lines, he said, "I can ad-lib better lines than this." Well, I suppose he could have, but since I had written the script, his remark rubbed me the wrong way. I undertook my director's prerogative to bawl him out for not knowing his lines, for not picking up his cues. He responded by telling McCollum that he didn't want to work with me anymore. I should have been more tolerant, I guess; I was making like a minor-league Frank Capra. Looking back on it, I should have let the situation pass. It just wasn't all that important and it put McCollum in an awkward position.

Since Bernds was the only director working for the McCollum unit at this time (he had replaced Harry Edwards), McCollum obtained the services of Del Lord. Lord had directed two-reelers for both units before graduating to work in 'B' features in the mid-1940s; at McCollum's request, he returned to the department and directed the next several Herbert comedies. But when Lord left the unit for good in 1949, McCollum was forced to direct a couple of the shorts himself. McCollum was fired from Columbia in 1952, so the final Herbert entry, *The Gink at the Sink*, was directed by Jules White.

The majority of the Herbert shorts are marital farces, with Hugh in hot water with his wife because of an imagined liaison with another woman (this formula was being beaten to death by Leon Errol over at RKO). *Who's Hugh?* (1943), *His Hotel Sweet* (1944), *A Knight and a Blonde* (1944) and *Woo, Woo!* (1945) are alarmingly similar in content; viewing them together, it's nearly impossible to detect where one ends and another begins. *Pitchin' in the Kitchen* (1943) is one of the better efforts. Hugh busies himself with household chores while his wife (Dorothy Appleby) goes to work in a defense plant. The film covers familiar ground—Hugh listens to a radio cooking show for instructions on the culinary art, and when the dial knob is inadvertently switched to an exercise program, he starts doing calisthenics while mixing a cake—but it benefits from Jules White's customarily swift direction and an

Hugh incurs the wrath of his rich uncle (Emil Sitka, center) and a burly neighbor (Dick Wessel, right) in *Hot Heir* (1947).

uncommonly enthusiastic performance by Herbert. *Wife Decoy* (1945), a remake of Charley Chase's *The Chump Takes a Bump* (1939), is also among the series' best. Hugh accompanies his boss (Dick Elliott) on a date with an attractive young lady (Rebel Randall); this way, if the boss's wife ever catches up with him, he can pass the woman off as Hugh's friend. Meanwhile, Hugh's wife (Christine McIntyre) has, unbeknownst to hubby, dyed her hair blonde. Winding up at the same nightclub as Hugh and his party, she begins to flirt with Herbert, who fails to recognize his spouse. Surprisingly effective direction by Harry Edwards helps to make this a very entertaining short.

A decidely superior departure from these domestic outings are a handful of "scare" comedies that teamed Herbert with Dudley Dickerson. Dickerson, a talented and vastly underrated black comedian, has never received proper recognition. Despite the fact that he was shoehorned into stereotyped roles (porters, bellhops, janitors), Dudley was such an appealing comic figure that he transcended racial barriers and gave performances that are, by any standards, genuinely hilarious. And though Dickerson appeared in many Columbia comedy shorts, the Herbert comedies mark one of the rare occasions in which he was given an equal footing with the star comedian. In *Nervous Shakedown* (1947), Hugh and Dudley encounter a couple of escaped convicts

(Kenneth MacDonald, Dick Wessel) posing as sanitarium doctors. In *Tall, Dark and Gruesome* (1948), a crate containing a live gorilla is delivered to a mountain cabin where the pair is staying, with expected results. Best of all is *One Shivery Night* (1950); two fortune-hunting thugs (Phil Van Zandt, Robert Williams) try scaring Hugh and Dudley out of the abandoned house they've been assigned to renovate. These efforts may not be terribly original, but they possess a good share of amusing, if overly mechanical, moments, and Herbert and Dickerson make a splendid team.

In spite of several flawed entries, the Herbert comedies were a hit with audiences; *Tall, Dark and Gruesome* was one of the best-received Columbia shorts for that year. It's a shame that largely interchangeable scripts and Herbert's overall lack of professional integrity hampered what should have been one of the department's funniest series.

The Hugh Herbert Series

Pitchin' in the Kitchen (9/10/43) D: Jules White. Dorothy Appleby, Vi Athens, Frank Sully, Johnny Kascier, Minerva Urecal, Symona Boniface, Al Thompson. When his wife gets a job in a defense plant, Hugh stays home and does the housework. Remade as *The Gink at the Sink* (1952).

Who's Hugh? (12/17/43) D: Harry Edwards. Christine McIntyre, Constance Worth, Eddie Gribbon, George Lewis, Vernon Dent, Charlie Hall, Barbara Pepper, Eddie Laughton, Fred Kelsey, Joe Palma, Fred "Snowflake" Toones. Hugh's wife goes to Palm Springs to file for a divorce; Hugh follows her and attempts a reconciliation.

Oh, Baby! (4/17/44) D: Jules White. Esther Howard, Bud Jamison, Lynton Brent, Jackie Warrington, Eleanor Counts, Victor Travers, Symona Boniface, Johnny Kascier, Charles Dorety, Al Thompson, Joe Palma. Hugh hates children—until he thinks he's about to become a father. Working title: *A Blissful Blunder*. A remake of Andy Clyde's *I'm a Father* (1935).

His Hotel Sweet (7/9/44) D: Harry Edwards. Isabel Withers, Christine McIntyre, Jack Norton, Johnny Kascier, Charles "Heine" Conklin. Hugh stops his friend from committing suicide—and is accused of being a home-wrecker.

A Knight and a Blonde (11/17/44) D: Harry Edwards. Isabel Withers, Christine McIntyre, Lorin Raker, John Tyrrell. Hugh has difficulty eluding a sleepwalking blonde.

Woo, Woo! (1/5/45) D: Jules White. Christine McIntyre, Dick Curtis, Harry Barris. Hugh, the "Chief Worrier" of Why Worry Inc., is hired by a pretty young wife to make her husband jealous. Working title: *I Should Worry*.

Wife Decoy (5/18/45) D: Harry Edwards. Christine McIntyre, Rebel Randall, Dick Elliott, Marilyn Johnson, Jack Rice, Snub Pollard, Robert Williams, Joe Palma, Charles Dorety. At a nightclub, Hugh fails to recognize his newly blonde wife. A remake of Charley Chase's *The Chump Takes a Bump* (1939).

The Mayor's Husband (9/20/45) D: Harry Edwards. Christine McIntyre, Vernon Dent, Robert Williams, Dick Curtis, Isabel Withers. Gangsters pry incriminating evidence from Hugh through the use of a gun moll.

When the Wife's Away (2/1/46) D: Edward Bernds. Vernon Dent, Christine McIntyre, Frank "Billy" Mitchell, Helen Lynd, Brian O'Hara. Hugh, branch manager of Korny Krunchies Breakfast Food, brings the boss home to dinner on his anniversary. A remake of Charley Chase's *South of the Boudoir* (1940).

Get Along Little Zombie (5/9/46) D: Edward Bernds. Christine McIntyre, Dick Curtis, Dudley Dickerson, Jack Roper, Jessie Arnold. There's a monster running around loose in the house Hugh is showing to two prospective clients.

Honeymoon Blues (10/17/46) D: Edward Bernds. Christine McIntyre, Jacqueline Dalya, Emil Sitka, Judy Malcolm, Dave Pepper, Eva Novak, Victor Travers, Eddie Dunn, Gino Corrado. On his wedding night, detective Herbert is hired to recover some love letters a woman has been using to blackmail a wealthy oil man.

Hot Heir (2/13/47) D: Edward Bernds. Christine McIntyre, Emil Sitka, Dick Wessel, Dorothy Granger, Charles "Heine" Conklin, Johnny Kascier. Hugh innocently becomes involved with his neighbor's wife, just as his rich uncle comes to visit. Remade with the Three Stooges as *Gents in a Jam* (1952).

Nervous Shakedown (3/13/47) D: Del Lord. Dudley Dickerson, Kenneth MacDonald, Dick Wessel, Frank Lackteen, Vernon Dent. Hugh and Dudley stay at Dr. Flint's Sanitarium, unaware that two escaped convicts are using the place for a hideout. Working title: *A-Haunting We Will Go*.

Should Husbands Marry? (11/13/47) D: Del Lord. Christine McIntyre, Matt McHugh, Vernon Dent, Marion Martin, Dudley Dickerson, Dorothy Granger. Hugh's loudmouth pal crashes a dinner party Hugh is throwing for his boss.

Tall, Dark and Gruesome (4/15/48) D: Del Lord. Dudley Dickerson, Christine McIntyre, Charles "Heine" Conklin. A crate containing a live gorilla is delivered to a mountain cabin Hugh has rented.

Christine McIntyre registers annoyance as Hugh winds up wearing his breakfast in *The Gink at the Sink* (1952), Herbert's last film.

A Pinch in Time (11/11/48) D: Del Lord. Christine McIntyre, Matt McHugh, Kenneth MacDonald, Symona Boniface, Vernon Dent, Lynne Lyons, Emil Sitka, Charles "Heine" Conklin, Robert Williams, Chester Conklin. A blonde plants a stolen necklace on an unsuspecting Hugh. A remake of Walter Catlett's *Blondes and Blunders* (1940).

Trapped by a Blonde (4/7/49) D: Del Lord. Christine McIntyre, Matt McHugh. Hugh goes on a camping trip with his brother-in-law and innocently gets involved with the sheriff's wife.

Super-Wolf (10/13/49) D: Del Lord. Christine McIntyre, Henry Kulky, Jack Rice, Vernon Dent. Hugh is a dead ringer for a criminal terrorizing the city.

One Shivery Night (7/13/50) D: Del Lord. Dudley Dickerson, Phil Van Zandt, Robert Williams, Vernon Dent. A pair of fortune-hunting thugs try to scare Hugh and Dudley out of an abandoned mansion they've been hired to renovate.

A Slip and a Miss (9/9/50) D: Hugh McCollum. Jean Willes, Gay Gail, John R. Hamilton, Victoria Horne, Minerva Urecal, Dick Curtis. When his wife begins divorce proceedings, Hugh tells his side of the story to the judge.

Woo-Woo Blues (7/14/51) D: Richard Quine. Victoria Horne, Ben Welden. Hugh's former girlfriend tries to blackmail him with old love letters.

Trouble In-Laws (10/11/51) D: Hugh McCollum. Charles Williams, Kitty McHugh, Jean Bates, Vernon Dent, Dick Wessel, Mike Mahoney. Hugh, an advertising man, tries to get a local strong man to endorse a breakfast food.

The Gink at the Sink (6/12/52) D: Jules White. Christine McIntyre, Frank Sully. Hugh can't find a job, so his wife goes to work, leaving him to do the household chores. A remake, with stock footage, of *Pitchin' in the Kitchen* (1943).

Vera Vague

When actress Barbara Jo Allen conceived the character of Vera Vague, little did she realize that she would be identified with the role for the remainder of her career. Vera was a shrill-voiced, giddy spinster, and this character gave Miss Allen enormous popularity on radio. When she began appearing in films, incongruities were immediately apparent: Barbara Jo was an attractive woman and far too youthful to play an old maid. Vera's persona was then modified to that of an amiable man-chaser. She was usually cast as the leading lady's best friend, and in such feature films as *Priorities on Parade* (1942) and *Girl Rush* (1944) she found herself playing opposite the likes of Jerry Colonna, Alan Carney and Paul Hurst. By this time, the creation had overshadowed the creator, and Miss Allen billed herself solely as Vera Vague.

Jules White hired her for a series of comedy shorts in 1943. The resulting two-reelers are among the unit's weakest efforts, with a handful of entertaining shorts shining through the general mediocrity. For the most part, the fault lay in the scripts: The material rarely took her gender into consideration, as it was interchangeable with any other contract comedian. Vera proved to be adept at handling physical comedy, but when she gets entangled in a towel rack or smacked on the chin with a garage door (both occur in *Strife of the Party*) it's unsettling to see a woman on the receiving end of such abuse.

Her first effort, *You Dear Boy* (1943), is an undistinguished remake of Charley Chase's *The Wrong Miss Wright* (1937). Vera feigns insanity to free herself from a prearranged marriage to a man she's never seen, only to discover that her betrothed (Douglas Drake) is the same man she fell in love with while on a vacation. It's worth noting that *You Dear Boy* marks one of the few times Vera used her real voice, which was beautifully rich and clear, in films. *Doctor, Feel My Pulse* (1944), the second Vague short, is the series' best; in this remake

Jack Norton (left) and Eddie Kane examine Vera in *Doctor, Feel My Pulse* (1944), the best of the Vague two-reelers.

of Charley Chase's *Calling All Doctors* (1937), director Jules White improved upon the original by eschewing the slapstick elements in favor of situation and characterization. Vera plays a hypochondriac who mistakes a lunatic (Jack Norton) for a trained medico; no matter how screwy his "treatment" appears to be, she consents to whatever the "doctor" advises. In one very funny sequence, Vera develops a nervous tic that results in an involuntary "winking" reaction; every male she passes thinks she's coming on to them, and before long she's being followed by a parade of admirers.

During the filming of *Strife of the Party* (1944), the third entry, Vera found Harry Edwards to be such an incompetent director that she requested to work solely with Jules White. There were two units operating out of the comedy shorts department at the time—one run by White, the other by Hugh McCollum—and each series would alternate between them. Edwards worked only for the McCollum unit, so when the Vera Vague series became the responsibility of the White unit, the Hugh Herbert series went to McCollum in order to balance out the production schedule. White, with whom Vera enjoyed working, directed all of the remaining Vague two-reelers.

In *The Jury Goes Round 'N' Round* (1945), Vera is the only juror on a murder trial who believes the defendant is innocent. One by one she manages to cajole her fellow jurors over to her side. The results are diverting, but not enough to justify the Academy Award nomination the short received that year. The series garnered its second Academy Award nomination for *Hiss and Yell* (1946), a heavy-handed and frequently distasteful outing. Vera catches a glimpse of magician Bluebeard the Great (Barton Yarborough) decapitating a stage mannequin and erroneously believes she's witnessed a murder. It's hard to fathom why the Academy chose this entry over the other two-reel comedies produced by the department; although 1946 was not a banner year for comedy shorts, there were certainly a number of efforts superior to it. Nevertheless, this is the only Columbia comedy shorts series to have been honored with *two* nominations.

Headin' for a Weddin' (1946), one of the better Vague shorts, has Vera and a rival (Claire Carleton) vying for the affections of a handsome millionaire cowboy (William Hall). Vera and Claire made a spirited team, and their energy compensates for the film's deficiencies. As time went on, the Vague comedies were allocated virtually nonexistent production values. Vera plays twins in *Cupid Goes Nuts* (1947), one an introverted spinster, the other a man-crazy WAC. It's a solid premise, bolstered by an exuberant performance by Fritz Feld as an amorous beau, but the action takes place almost entirely on one set.

The series finished in 1952. Most of the entries had been on par with *She Snoops to Conquer* (1944), *Calling All Fibbers* (1945) and *Reno-Vated* (1946) which show Vera striving mightily to cope with thankless material. Regardless, she remained a thorough professional; says Jules White, "Vera was a real lady and a joy to work with."

The Vera Vague Series

The following are all of Vera's Columbia two-reelers. This listing does not include the *Vera Vague Laff Tours*, a series of one-reel comic travelogues produced by another short subjects unit at the studio.

You Dear Boy (11/4/43) D: Jules White. Minerva Urecal, Douglas Drake, Grace Lenard, Eva McKenzie, Charles "Heine" Conklin, Eddie Laughton, Al Thompson, Symona Boniface, John Tyrrell. Vera feigns insanity to get released from a prearranged marriage. A remake of Charley Chase's *The Wrong Miss Wright* (1937). Reworked as *Happy Go Wacky* (1952).

Doctor, Feel My Pulse (1/21/44) D: Jules White. Jack Norton, George Lewis,

Christine McIntyre, Ann Doran, Bud Jamison, John Tyrrell, Eddie Kane, Judy Malcolm, Slim Gaut, Charles "Heine" Conklin, Johnny Kascier, Victor Travers, Robert "Bobby" Burns. Hypochondriac Vera mistakes a lunatic for a trained physician. A remake of Charley Chase's *Calling All Doctors* (1937). Remade as *She Took a Powder* (1951).

Strife of the Party (10/13/44) D: Harry Edwards. Lorin Raker, Joe Forte, Gwen Donovan, Vernon Dent, Symona Boniface, Joe Palma, Charles "Heine" Conklin. Vera's neighbors turn out to be a gang of crooks.

She Snoops to Conquer (12/29/44) D: Jules White. Weldon Heyburn, Vernon Dent, Bud Jamison, Rebel Randall, John Tyrrell, Charles "Heine" Conklin. Vera, an inquiring reporter, tangles with Nazi spy Otto Shultz.

The Jury Goes Round 'N' Round (6/1/45) D: Jules White. Barton Yarborough, Vernon Dent, Mike Mazurki, June Bryde, Frank Alten, Elberta Casey, Judy Malcolm, Joe Palma, Victor Travers, Blackie Whiteford. Vera, a juror on a murder case, is the only one who believes the defendant is innocent. Nominated for an Academy Award.

Calling All Fibbers (11/29/45) D: Jules White. Etta McDaniel, Frank Sully, Vernon Dent, John Tyrrell. Vera pretends to have been injured in an auto accident in order to get out of two conflicting engagements. Working title: *Lying Liars*. A remake of Walter Catlett's *Fibbing Fibbers* (1936).

Hiss and Yell (2/14/46) D: Jules White. Barton Yarborough, Fred Kelsey, Symona Boniface, Emil Sitka, John Tyrrell, Charles "Heine" Conklin, Johnny Kascier, Victor Travers. When Vera sees a magician decapitate a dummy, she thinks she's witnessed a murder. Working title: *She Lost Her Head*. Nominated for an Academy Award.

Headin' for a Weddin' (8/15/46) D: Jules White. Claire Clarleton, William Hall, Jack Rice, Vernon Dent, Joe Palma, Al Thompson, Charles "Heine" Conklin, Blackie Whiteford. Vera and Claire vie for the affections of a handsome millionaire cowboy. Working title: *Don't Fence Me Out*.

Reno-Vated (11/21/46) D: Jules White. Monty Collins, Ray Walker, Victor Travers, Emil Sitka. After Vera divorces her husband, she marries her lawyer. Stock shot of waterlogged ceiling taken from *Andy Clyde Gets Spring Chicken* (1939).

Cupid Goes Nuts (5/1/47) D: Jules White. Fritz Feld, Chester Clute. Vera plays twin sisters of opposite personalities. Working title: *Two of a Kind*.

A Miss in a Mess (1/13/49) D: Jules White. Stephen Roberts, Judy Malcolm,

Vera loosens Frank Alten's necktie and rips his shirt to shreds in the process in this scene from *The Jury Goes Round 'N' Round* (1945), which was nominated for an Academy Award for Best Short Subject of that year. Also pictured (l. to r.): Vernon Dent, Elberta Casey, June Bryde (seated), Joe Palma, Barton Yarborough, Blackie Whiteford, Victor Travers, Judy Malcolm, player.

Lois Austin, Pat O'Malley, Johnny Kascier. Vera's fiance is the spitting image of an escaped axe-murderer. Working title: *The Battered Bride*. A remake of Harry Langdon's *His Marriage Mixup* (1935).

Clunked in the Clink (7/13/49) D: Jules White. Christine McIntyre, Douglas Fowley, Vernon Dent. Vera's husband thinks she's been killed in a plane crash, unaware that she was arrested for speeding on the way to the airport. Working title: *Loose in the Calaboose*.

Wha' Happen? (11/10/49) D: Jules White. Dorothy Granger, Tim Ryan, Stanley Blystone, Stephen Roberts, Al Thompson. Suffering from amnesia, Vera thinks she's responsible for a burglary.

Nursie Behave (5/11/50) D: Jules White. John Merton, Sherry Moreland, Jack Pickard. Vera, a hospital nurse, is assigned to care for a district attorney who was injured in an auto accident. Working title: *Nurses Versus Hearses*.

She Took a Powder (8/11/51) D: Jules White. George Lewis, Christine McIntyre. Vera's fiance tries to cure her of her hypochondria. Working title:

The Pill Eater. A remake, with stock footage, of *Doctor, Feel My Pulse* (1944).

Happy Go Wacky (2/7/52) D: Jules White. Minerva Urecal, Grace Lenard, Chester Conklin, Blackie Whiteford, Joe Palma. Nurse Vera is hired by a patient to help him get rid of some unwelcome relatives living at his house. Working title: *Empty Head.* A reworking, with stock footage, of *You Dear Boy* (1943).

Shemp Howard

Shemp Howard had been one of the original Three Stooges (during their apprenticeship with Ted Healy) before embarking upon a solo career in 1932. After several supporting roles in feature films and comedy shorts (including a few of the Andy Clyde and Glove Slingers entries) he was given a starring series at Columbia in 1944. Shemp was a born comedian, capable of producing genuinely hilarious moments, yet his Columbia shorts tend to stifle his considerable comic abilities rather than showcase them. Shemp was frequently saddled with material unsuited for him, as in *A Hit with a Miss* (1945), a lifeless remake of the Three Stooges' *Punch Drunks* (1934).

Shemp's first effort, *Pick a Peck of Plumbers* (1944), paired him with El Brendel; in this remake of Sidney and Murray's *Plumbing for Gold* (1934), El and Shemp are plumber's assistants who reduce a house to rubble while trying to recover a ring that has slipped down a drainpipe. The results are only middling; Shemp and El fail to connect as a team, and the material is so mechanical it could have been done by any other contract players. The film occasionally brightens when Shemp tosses in a few extemporaneous bits of business, but he's never permitted to really cut loose.

Where the Pest Begins (1945) does allow him to ad-lib freely, and the film is better because of it. The slim plot—Shemp tries to ingratiate himself to his new neighbors (Tom Kennedy, Christine McIntyre)—provides him with enough elbow-room to inject several of his inimitable asides. *Society Mugs* (1946), a remake of the Three Stooges' *Termites of 1938* (1938), teams Shemp with Tom Kennedy (who receives above-the-title billing with Shemp); though not up to the standards of the original, it's pleasant foolishness, and the two comics work well together. *Mr. Noisy* (1946), a remake of Charley Chase's *The Heckler* (1940), is the best of the series. The material worked well with Chase, and it worked even better with Shemp. The role of an obnoxious sports spectator seemed tailor-made for Shemp's salty demeanor, and he played it to the hilt. Vernon Dent repeated his memorable role as the luckless fellow sitting next to him during a baseball game.

After *Bride and Gloom* (1947), one of the better entries, Shemp rejoined the Stooges, replacing his younger brother Curly, who had suffered a stroke. Shemp's solo efforts offer an interesting, though largely disappointing look at this gifted and unjustly underrated comedian.

Ladies' man Shemp Howard with Rebel Randall (left) and Christine McIntyre. From *Society Mugs* (1946).

The Shemp Howard Series

Pick a Peck of Plumbers (7/23/44) D: Jules White. El Brendel, John Tyrrell, Al Thompson, Kathryn Keys, Willa Pearl Curtis, Beatrice Blinn, Frank "Billy" Mitchell, Jean Murray, Brian O'Hara, Judy Malcolm, Charles "Heine" Conklin, Joe Palma. Vagrants El and Shemp become plumber's assistants; on their first assignment, they reduce a house to a shambles while searching for a lost ring. Stock shot of waterlogged ceiling taken from *Andy Clyde Gets Spring Chicken* (1939). A remake of Sidney and Murray's *Plumbing for Gold* (1934); a reworking of the Three Stooges' *A-Plumbing We Will Go* (1940). Remade with the Three Stooges as *Scheming Schemers* (1956); reworked with the Three Stooges as *Vagabond Loafers* (1949).

Open Season for Saps (10/27/44) D: Jules White. Christine McIntyre, George Lewis, Early Cantreen, Jack "Tiny" Lipson, Harry Barris, Al Morino. Shemp is more concerned about his lodge meetings than he is about his marriage. A remake of Charley Chase's *The Grand Hooter* (1937).

Off Again, On Again (2/16/45) D: Jules White. Christine McIntyre, Dick Curtis, Grace Lenard, Russell Trent, Joe Palma, John Tyrrell, Judy Malcolm, Charles Willey, Frances Haynes, Charles "Heine" Conklin, Al Thompson. Despondent over breaking up with his fiancee, Shemp hires a gangster to kill him. A remake, with stock footage, of Charley Chase's *Time Out for Trouble* (1938).

Where the Pest Begins (10/4/45) D: Harry Edwards. Tom Kennedy, Christine McIntyre, Rebel Randall, Harry Tenbrook. Shemp antagonizes his new next-door neighbor.

A Hit with a Miss (12/13/45) D: Jules White. Charles Rogers, Robert Williams, Marilyn Johnson, Joe Palma, Charles "Heine" Conklin, John Tyrrell, Wally Rose, Arthur Housman, Blackie Whiteford, George Gray. Shemp, a mild-mannered waiter, goes berserk every time he hears the tune "Pop Goes the Weasel." A remake, with stock footage, of the Three Stooges' *Punch Drunks* (1934).

Mr. Noisy (3/22/46) D: Edward Bernds. Matt Willis, Vernon Dent, Brian O'Hara, Walter Soderling, Daniel Kerry, Wally Rose, John Ince, Claire James, Marilyn Johnson, Don Gordon, Bess Flowers, Tom Coleman, Victor Travers, Fran O'Connor. Shemp is an obnoxious spectator at a baseball game. A remake, with stock footage, of Charley Chase's *The Heckler* (1940).

Jiggers, My Wife (4/11/46) D: Jules White. Christine McIntyre, Symona Boniface, Tom Kennedy, Early Cantreen, Cy Schindell. Shemp's suspicious wife thinks he's seeing another woman.

Society Mugs (9/19/46) D: Edward Bernds. Tom Kennedy, Christine McIntyre, Rebel Randall, Vernon Dent, Charles Williams, Etta McDaniel, Bess Flowers, Gene Roth, Snub Pollard, Helen Benda. Exterminators Shemp and Tom are mistaken for professional escorts. A remake of the Three Stooges' *Termites of 1938* (1938).

Bride and Gloom (3/27/47) D: Edward Bernds. Christine McIntyre, Jean Donahue, Dick Curtis, Vernon Dent, Emil Sitka. Shemp's fiancee leaves him when she sees him with a pretty blonde.

Schilling and Lane

Of all the partnerships concocted by the unit, the Gus Schilling–Richard Lane teaming stands out as the best of these calculated combinations. Schilling, the jittery, unsteady worrier, and Lane, the brash, blustery loudmouth, complimented each other nicely. Veterans of stage and screen, Gus and Dick brought an explosive energy level to the films, which compensates for the series' shortcomings. The main problem was that they were never given consistent personalities — and to allow them enough time to "find" themselves was a luxury the tight schedules simply couldn't permit. A number of their comedies are remakes of earlier shorts, with few, if any, revisions. Because of this practice, their character traits would often vary from picture to picture.

Richard Lane recalled that working in these comedy shorts was a logical extension of his feature film work for the studio: "I was doing some other things for Columbia, like playing Inspector Farraday in the *Boston Blackie* series, so when I was asked to appear in those little comedies, it seemed like the natural thing to do." For two performers who had never operated as a team previously, Schilling and Lane quickly developed a good rapport. "Gus was wonderful, a great comic," Lane commented. "He didn't quibble; if the script called for us to be physical, we were physical. Whatever we had to do was fine with him. I don't think I ever heard him complain about anything."

Their first effort, *High Blood Pleasure* (1945), is a perfect example of the team's fever-pitch delivery working wonders on run-of-the-mill material. En route to a baseball game, the boys are stopped for speeding; thinking quickly, Dick passes himself off as his twin brother, a prominent surgeon, and tells the motorcycle cop (Harry Semels) that he's rushing Gus to the hospital for an emergency operation. When the officer insists on escorting them to the hospital, Dick is forced to continue the charade all the way to the operating room. *High Blood Pleasure* is a lesser entry, but Gus and Dick perform with such gusto that the film is not without merit. Lane's double-talk rendition of "Little Red Riding Hood" is a highlight.

Though the quality of their shorts range from enjoyable *(Hot Water, Training for Trouble)* to disappointing *(Ain't Love Cuckoo?, Flung by a Fling)*, the team's vitality never flagged. *Pardon My Lamb Chop* (1948) is distinguished by a lively version of the burlesque chestnut "Mike's Place," a routine made famous by Abbott and Costello in *Lost in a Harem* (1944). Dick, a crazed salesman, persuades Gus to accompany him into an imaginary tavern run by his friend "Mike." Once there (actually, they never leave Schilling's living room), Dick argues with him and eventually murders the nonexistent barkeeper as a quizzical Gus, caught up in the insanity of the moment, tries to defend his partner's actions. In *Wedding Belle* (1947) Dick, an errant husband, tries to shake the romantic overtures of his old flame, a whip-cracking circus performer named Zorita (Lynne Lyons, in a wonderful comic role), by pretending to have come down with a severe case of "jungle fever." Elwood Ullman's screenplay and Edward Bernds' direction combine to make *Wedding Belle* one of the series' finest.

Two Nuts in a Rut (1948) is their best short. Dick plays a harried movie producer, Gus his assistant. After editing his new production, Dick hands Gus a two-foot strip of celluloid and announces, "This is all I like in the whole picture!" "Yes," observes Gus, "but is it enough to preview?" To escape the stress of the business, Dick decides to vacation at a Palm Springs hotel. Upon their

Dr. Schilling and Mr. Lane: Gus (standing) masquerades as a medical specialist when Dick feigns a case of "jungle fever" in *Wedding Belle* (1947).

arrival, however, Gus spreads the word that a big, influential movie producer is in town; before long, several would-be starlets are clamoring for screen tests. To relieve his partner's headaches, Gus has Dick transferred to another section of the hotel. Dick, unaware of this change, returns to his old room, which has since been rented to a wrestling champion (Dick Wessel), and gets caught in a compromising situation with the wrestler's wife (Christine McIntyre). With familiar plot gimmicks given snappy new twists, *Two Nuts in a Rut* is first-rate all the way.

The most fascinating entry in the series is *Pardon My Terror* (1946), which was originally written for the Three Stooges. But when Curly Howard suffered a stroke during the production of *Half-Wits Holiday* (filmed in 1946, released 1947), the next planned Stooges short, *Pardon My Terror*, was made with Gus and Dick instead. The script was altered slightly, with Lane taking Moe's part and the Curly and Larry roles combined for Schilling. Edward Bernds, who wrote and directed the picture, explains:

> If I had more time, I could have tailored the script to suit them. But as I remember the circumstances, we were committed to go with the Stooges; the sets were up, we were on the schedule — which was sacred to the production office — and we even had some of the cast obligated to the film. In the business it's called "play or pay" — if you don't use them, you pay anyway. So after Curly had a stroke and it was evident he wouldn't be able to make the picture, Hugh McCollum checked all the schedules to see which contract players were readily available. It turned out to be Gus and Dick. I believe I only had two or three days to change the script, and much of the Stooge-type humor stayed in. It turned out okay, though it probably would have been better with the Stooges because it wasn't ideal Schilling and Lane material.

In *Pardon My Terror*, Gus and Dick, operators of the Wide Awake Detective Agency (appropriately, they're asleep when we first see them), are hired to solve the mystery behind the disappearance of millionaire Jonas Morton (Vernon Dent). Their search leads them to the Morton mansion, where they encounter a motley gang of crooks (Kenneth MacDonald, Lynne Lyons, Dick Wessel) who are after the old man's fortune. The result is an atypical short for the team, with Lane pushing and slapping Schilling around more than usual. Although it really isn't ideal Schilling and Lane material, it's doubtful that the Stooges could have produced better results (in the last few films prior to his stroke, Curly's languid performances weakened several potentially funny scenarios). The story was redone to much better effect with the Three Stooges as *Who Done It?* (1949), made after Shemp Howard had taken Curly's place as "third Stooge."

The series ended with *Hold That Monkey* (1950), a remake of Collins and Kennedy's *Gum Shoes* (1935). Schilling went on to other projects, returning to the unit in 1953 for a brief role as an attorney in the Andy Clyde short *Oh Say Can You Sue*. Lane had a prolific career in movies and on television, where he achieved fame as the ringside announcer for the weekly wrestling bouts and roller derby games.

"Those comedy shorts were a delight to do," said Lane, "and that whole crew was a lot of fun to work with." For Ed Bernds, the feeling is mutual:

> I have nothing but fond memories of Gus Schilling and Dick Lane. They were inventive, they were constructive, they worked hard, they did the little improvisations that make a director look good. When I saw some of the Schilling and Lanes recently, I was amazed and delighted with the tempo of the pictures. They really moved! When actors can belt out the dialogue at high speed and pick up the cues sharply and incisively, that shows that they're well prepared and don't have to wait for the lines to filter out through an imperfect memory. They were always full of energy, always thinking laughs and comedy; it was a real pleasure to work with them.

The Schilling and Lane Series

High Blood Pleasure (12/6/45) D: Jules White. Vernon Dent, Lynton Brent, Harry Semels, Symona Boniface, Johnny Kascier, Victor Travers, Cy Schindell, Blackie Whiteford. To avoid getting a speeding ticket from a motorcycle cop, Dick poses as a surgeon rushing Gus to the hospital for emergency surgery. A remake of Collins and Kennedy's *Just Speeding* (1936).

Ain't Love Cuckoo? (6/6/46) D: Jules White. Barbara Slater, Terry Howard, Jean Donahue, Judy Malcolm, Emil Sitka, John Tyrrell, Johnny Kascier, Al Rosen. The Schillings and the Lanes think their mates have been killed in the war, and inadvertently marry each other's spouses.

Hot Water (7/25/46) D: Edward Bernds. Christine McIntyre, Dick Curtis, Rebel Randall, Helga Storme, Judy Malcolm, Vernon Dent. Trying to keep a bachelor apartment while their wives are away, Gus and Dick fall into possession of stolen jewelry.

Pardon My Terror (9/12/46) D: Edward Bernds. Christine McIntyre, Lynne Lyons, Kenneth MacDonald, Dick Wessel, Phil Van Zandt, Vernon Dent, Emil Sitka, Dudley Dickerson. When a millionaire mysteriously disappears, private eyes Gus and Dick are called in on the case. A reworking of Walter Catlett's *You're Next* (1940). Remade with the Three Stooges as *Who Done It?* (1949) and *For Crimin' Out Loud* (1956).

Training for Trouble (7/3/47) D: Jules White. Monty Collins, Sidney Field (Sid Fields), Sherry O'Neil, Nina Bara, Joe Palma. Gus, Dick and their pet monkey make life miserable for a troupe of entertainers traveling by train. A remake, with stock footage, of the Three Stooges' *A Pain in the Pullman* (1936).

Judy Malcolm collars Richard Lane (left) and Gus Schilling in *Ain't Love Cuckoo?* (1946). Miss Malcolm, who was seen in several Columbia shorts, had been Schilling's partner in burlesque. She had a running gag in most of the Schilling and Lane comedies: Appearing out of nowhere, she'd walk up to Gus, slap him across the face and scream, "How dare you remind me of somebody I hate!"

Wedding Belle (8/9/47) D: Edward Bernds. Christine McIntyre, Lynne Lyons, Sammy Stein, Billy Curtis, Symona Boniface, Judy Malcolm, Vernon Dent, Victor Travers, Johnny Kascier. The return of Dick's old flame creates new stress in his already strained marriage.

Two Nuts in a Rut (2/19/48) D: Edward Bernds. Christine McIntyre, Dick Wessel, Claire Carleton, Lynne Lyons, Symona Boniface, Vernon Dent, Emil Sitka, Ted Stanhope, Johnny Kascier. Dick, a movie producer, tries to have a peaceful vacation but is constantly hounded by aspiring actresses.

Pardon My Lamb Chop (6/10/48) D: Jules White. Dorothy Granger, Judy Malcolm, Cy Schindell. Gus, in an attempt to show kindness towards his fellow man, invites salesman Dick Lane into his home.

He's in Again (1/13/49) D: Edward Bernds. Christine McIntyre, Vernon Dent, Robert Williams, Jack Overman. Gus, a cab driver, mistakes Dick, an escaped lunatic, for his girlfriend's father. A remake of Charley Chase's *Many Sappy Returns* (1938).

Flung by a Fling (5/12/49) D: Jules White. Christine McIntyre, Grace Lenard, Nanette Bordeaux, Judy Malcolm, Johnny Kascier. The boys, attending a war veterans' convention, try to prevent their wives from meeting an old flame. A remake of Alan Mowbray's *French Fried Patootie* (1941).

Hold That Monkey (2/16/50) D: Jules White. Jean Willes, Margie Liszt, Joe Palma. Hotel detectives Gus and Dick encounter a trained gorilla. A remake, with stock footage, of Collins and Kennedy's *Gum Shoes* (1935).

Sterling Holloway

Sterling Holloway's distinctive voice (its mellow, whispery timbre sounded like a case of arrested adolescence) and comic appearance (he looked like the archetypal country bumpkin) made him a welcome addition to many movies and TV shows. His series for Columbia gave him a rare opportunity to play lead roles instead of the fleeting, subordinate parts he usually essayed.

The Holloway comedies tend to soft-pedal overt slapstick in favor of situational humor. A perfect example is *Scooper Dooper* (1947), the best of the series. Sterling is a small-town lad who secures a job in the filing department of a big-city newspaper. Yearning to be an investigative reporter, he finally gets a chance to prove his mettle when he's sent (as a practical joke) to get the goods on a suspected diamond smuggler. Under director Edward Bernds' expert guidance, the short plays like a mini-feature, offering character development and a logical chain of events.

In *Flat Feat* (1948) the accent is also on plot, as Sterling is a bumbling police rookie determined to follow in the footsteps of his prestigious father. *Man or Mouse* (1948) is a tad more raucous than the others, as Holloway goes to great lengths to impress his girlfriend's muscle-bound father; albeit basically a one-joke idea , it's very pleasant fare. As with other Columbia comedy shorts series from this period, old scripts were dusted off for reuse. *Moron Than Off* (1946), a remake of Harry Langdon's *I Don't Remember* (1935), and *Hectic Honeymoon* (1947), a remake of Johnny Downs' *Groom and Bored* (1942), have their moments, although they are decidedly inferior to the original versions.

The Holloway shorts aren't hilariously funny, but the best of the group are agreeable, leisurely paced, coherent efforts—a refreshing departure from the chaotic overkill prevalent in much of the unit's work.

The Sterling Holloway Series

Mr. Wright Goes Wrong (8/1/46) D: Jules White. Christine McIntyre, Dee Green, Arthur Q. Bryan, Helen Dickson, Al Thompson, Tommy Kingston, Emil Sitka, Judy Malcolm. Sterling uses his friend's name to obtain a hotel suite and, in doing so, gets involved in his friend's troubles.

Noel Neill, best known for her portrayal of Lois Lane in the *Superman* serials and television series, costarred with Sterling Holloway in *Man or Mouse* (1948).

Moron Than Off (11/28/46) D: Jules White. Monty Collins, Eleanor Counts, Edythe Elliott, Symona Boniface, Blackie Whiteford, Emil Sitka, Joe Palma, Al Thompson, Victor Travers, Cy Schindell, Johnny Kascier. Sterling's poor memory causes nothing but problems; his luck seems to change when he wins the Irish Sweepstakes. A remake, with stock footage, of Harry Langdon's *I Don't Remember* (1935).

Scooper Dooper (2/27/47) D: Edward Bernds. Jean Donahue, Joan Blair, Dick Elliott, Charles Williams, Symona Boniface, Joe Palma, Harold Brauer, Cy Schindell. Sterling, an aspiring newspaper reporter, tries to get the goods on a suspected diamond smuggler.

Hectic Honeymoon (9/18/47) D: Edward Bernds. Jean Willes, Christine McIntyre, Dick Wessel, Harry O. Tyler, Symona Boniface, Harold Brauer, Dudley Dickerson, Phil Arnold, Fred "Snowflake" Toones. Newlywed Sterling has to keep his marriage a secret from his matrimony-hating boss. A remake of Johnny Downs' *Groom and Bored* (1942).

Man or Mouse (1/15/48) D: Jules White. Noel Neill, Edgar Dearing. Sterling's girlfriend attempts to build him into a strongman to impress her muscle-bound father. Working title: *Mass of Muscle.*

Flat Feat (6/24/48) D: Edward Bernds. Patricia White, Dick Wessel, Cliff Clark, Cy Schindell, Wally Rose, Symona Boniface, Harold Brauer, Blackie Whiteford. Police officer Holloway has a difficult time living up to his father's reputation.

Harry Von Zell

Harry Von Zell's comedies are a pleasant surprise. For someone who was essentially a verbal performer, he was able to handle physical humor with flair and possessed an affable screen presence that made even the weakest efforts tolerable. Von Zell recounted how this series came about:

> In the forties I was working as a free-lance announcer for NBC. I delivered commercials assigned to me and was called upon to report the news prepared by the writers' staff in the news department. Eventually I was contacted by Jules White, who was "head man" of the short subjects department at Columbia Pictures. He had heard me on the air and had a proposal to make. His idea was to produce a series based on the experiences encountered by a well-known radio personality, and [he] wished to place me under contract to play the role. I was not enthused by the idea, but when he explained that he was prepared to assign me a staff of expert comedy writers and $500 per subject, I changed my mind.

Unfortunately, the first effort, *So's Your Antenna* (1946), is the series' weakest entry. Mild-mannered Von Zell plays a gangster character named "Hoodlum Harry" for a radio broadcast; when a pair of bank robbers (Dick Wessel, Joe Palma) overhear him rehearsing, they mistake him for the genuine article. The film merely limps along from one aimless gag sequence to another, with much of the footage devoted to a protracted encounter between Harry and a stir-crazy ex-convict (Tom Kennedy).

His second effort, *Meet Mr. Mischief* (1947), is a marked improvement. Harry is an incurable practical joker who finds himself pursued by a religious fanatic (Ralf Harolde) who wants to decapitate Harry and bring the dismembered head back to his tribe in Asia. The contrived plot is rendered amusing thanks to breezy direction and assured performances.

Radio Romeo (1947) is the best of the series. Harry conducts an "Advice to the Lovelorn" radio program; when a pretty listener (Lynne Lyons) comes to him for solace, he has a lot of explaining to do to his jealous wife (Christine

Christine McIntyre tries to prevent a scuffle between husband Harry Von Zell (left) and an irate hotel detective (Dick Wessel) in *Radio Romeo* (1947).

McIntyre). The script and direction by Edward Bernds make familiar material fresh and funny. *Rolling Down to Reno* (1947), directed by Jules White, is also first-rate. In this remake of Buster Keaton's *Pardon My Berth Marks* (1940), Harry inadvertently insults a notorious public enemy (Kenneth Mac-Donald) during a radio broadcast and, fearing retaliation, decides to leave town. Traveling by train, Harry has a run-in with MacDonald's wife (Christine McIntyre) and gets caught up in a compromising situation with her when the public enemy shows up.

The Sheepish Wolf (1948), another top-notch outing, has Von Zell entertaining an attractive client (Christine McIntyre) in hopes of landing a radio contract. Harry's intentions are misconstrued by his wife (Lynne Lyons) and brother-in-law (Lennie Bremen), as well as the young woman's sword-wielding husband (George Lewis); the result is a frenzied chase that employs plenty of "high and dizzy" comedy as Harry and his pursuer teeter along the ledge of an apartment building. "We never went wrong with a 'high and dizzy,' " comments director Ed Bernds.

The Harry Von Zell shorts proved to be one of the best series the department produced in the 1940s. For Von Zell, they were certainly beneficial:

Eventually, the exposure I received from these films led to my affiliation with George Burns and Grace Allen—and you know the results of that "marriage."

The Harry Von Zell Series

So's Your Antenna (10/10/46) D: Jules White. Tom Kennedy, Dick Wessel, Joe Palma, Emil Sitka, Lew Davis. Harry, a radio actor, is mistaken for a gangster.

Meet Mr. Mischief (1/23/47) D: Edward Bernds. Ralf Harolde, Christine McIntyre, Charles Wilson, Dudley Dickerson, Emil Sitka, Phil Arnold, Fred Kelsey, Vernon Dent, Symona Boniface. Practical joker Harry is pursued by a headhunter.

Rolling Down to Reno (9/4/47) D: Jules White. Christine McIntyre, Kenneth MacDonald, Symona Boniface, Dudley Dickerson, Emil Sitka, Phil Arnold, Charles "Heine" Conklin, Lew Davis. Radio commentator Von Zell unwittingly antagonizes a public enemy over the airwaves. Working title: *Rolling Down to Rio*. A remake, with stock footage, of Buster Keaton's *Pardon My Berth Marks* (1940).

Radio Romeo (12/25/47) D: Edward Bernds. Christine McIntyre, Lynne Lyons, Dick Wessel, Matt Willis, Emil Sitka, Ted Stanhope, Symona Boniface, Allan Ray, Charles Wilson, Phil Arnold. Harry conducts an "Advice for the Lovelorn" radio program and becomes involved in a young woman's marital problems.

The Sheepish Wolf (5/27/48) D: Edward Bernds. Christine McIntyre, George Lewis, Lynne Lyons, Lennie Bremen, Harry O. Tyler, Vernon Dent, Emil Sitka, Symona Boniface, Fred Sears, Red Breen, Victor Travers. In hopes of landing a radio contract, Harry's boss has him entertain a pretty client.

Radio Riot (2/10/49) D: Edward Bernds. Dee Green, Emil Sitka, Earl Hodgins, Lee Kendall, Kenneth MacDonald, Johnny Kascier. Harry's boss orders him to be courteous to a hillbilly oil millionaire client and his family.

Microspook (6/9/49) D: Edward Bernds. Emil Sitka, Christine McIntyre. Harry announces a radio show from a haunted house.

His Baiting Beauty (1/12/50) D: Edward Bernds. Christine McIntyre, Dick Wessel, Emil Sitka, Jean Willes, Minerva Urecal. Harry leaves town to participate in the opening ceremonies of a new radio station, but his wife thinks he's going there to meet another woman.

Vernon and Quillan

In 1948, comedians Wally Vernon and Eddie Quillan were paired for a series that ran until 1956. Quillan recalls the beginning of this series:

> I got a call from Columbia Pictures asking me if I could meet with Jules White, who wanted to talk to me about making some two-reel comedies. I had known Jules for over twenty years, from the time I made two shorts for his brother Jack, so it was like meeting an old friend. He told me what he had in mind, then asked me what I thought of Wally Vernon. I had made one picture with Wally at Universal titled *Margie* (1940). I told Jules that I thought we'd make a fine team. He was pleased with my reaction and shortly afterwards a deal was made.

Vernon's career spanned minstrel shows, vaudeville and burlesque prior to his entering films in the 1930s; he was no stranger to the Columbia comedy shorts department, having appeared in one of the "Glove Slingers" entries (*Fresh as a Freshman*, 1941). Quillan was also a veteran of the stage and screen; he started in show business as a child performer and later starred in films for Mack Sennett, RKO, MGM and Universal. Experienced practitioners of the art of the comic pratfall, Vernon and Quillan were the most physically graceful team the unit ever concocted. A few of their two-reelers even afforded them the opportunity to display their considerable dancing skills.

The current inavailability of nearly all the Vernon and Quillan shorts has been maddening, making it impossible at this time to fully assess the series. Judging from the handful of shorts offered by 16mm rental companies, these efforts run hot and cold, bolstered by the appealing expertise of these two seasoned performers. But because so little of this work is accessible, it would be unfair to evaluate the entire series on the strength of what may ultimately turn out to be the team's lesser efforts.

A Fool and His Honey (1952) is the best of the Vernon and Quillan shorts now available. Wally, a philandering husband, comes to the erroneous conclusion that his wife (Jean Willes) has been fooling around with his pal Eddie. After a crazy turn of events, Eddie innocently winds up in the Vernons' bedroom; a frantic chase ensues, culminating in a hotel gymnasium (the doubles used for this sequence match the action beautifully). Jules White directed with speed and assurance; *A Fool and His Honey* remains a tightly-knit, enjoyable outing.

Other entries currently available for screening are from the unit's final years, during the period in which threadbare budgetary allotments forced Jules White to cannibalize earlier shorts in order to make ends meet. *He Took a Powder* (1955) uses a great deal of footage from an earlier Vernon and Quillan effort, *He Flew the Shrew* (1951); the low budget is painfully evident in the "new" sequences (one farm setting consists of a canvas backdrop with a few wooden crates, barrels and clusters of hay scattered about). *Nobody's Home* (1955), largely comprised of stock footage from *House About It* (1950),

Wally Vernon (left) gets ready to clobber Eddie Quillan with an Indian club in *A Fool and His Honey* **(1952).**

contains some admirable stunt work by Quillan, as well as some incredibly heavy-handed visual gags (a bump on Vernon's forehead is pressed flat with a trowel). *Come on Seven* (1956) is a grab-bag of new scenes mixed with footage from *Fun on the Run* (1951) and Collins and Kennedy's *Free Rent* (1936). All of these entries are mediocre, but so were the majority of the comedy shorts made in this patchwork fashion. Until the late 1940s through early 1950s Vernon and Quillan shorts can be viewed, judgment must be reserved on what may possibly be a very entertaining series.

The Vernon and Quillan Series

Crabbin' in the Cabin (5/13/48) D: Jules White. Dorothy Granger, Lynne Lyons, Kathleen O'Malley, Virginia Belmont. Wally and Eddie's hunting trip is spoiled by the unexpected arrival of their spouses. Remade as *A-Hunting They Did Go* (1953).

Parlor, Bedroom and Wrath (12/16/48) D: Jules White. Christine McIntyre, Billy Gray, Laura Lee Michel, Lonnie Thomas, Vernon Dent. Wally tries to rest at home—until brother-in-law Eddie and his kids come to visit. Remade as *Doggie in the Bedroom* (1954).

Let Down Your Aerial (11/17/49) D: Edward Bernds. Jean Willes, Matt McHugh, Vernon Dent, Stanley Blystone, Harriett Bennett. Wally helps Eddie put up the aerial for his new television set. Remade as *His Pest Friend* (1955), and with the Three Stooges as *Goof on the Roof* (1953).

House About It (7/20/50) D: Jules White. Jean Willes, Margie Liszt, Stanley Blystone. The Vernons and the Quillans all move into the same house. Working title: *Home on the Rage*. A remake, with stock footage, of Collins and Kennedy's *Bury the Hatchet* (1937). Remade as *Nobody's Home* (1955).

He Flew the Shrew (1/11/51) D: Jules White. Jean Willes, Emmett Lynn. Wally can no longer tolerate his wife's nagging, so he hits the road with hobo pal Eddie. Working title: *Fragrant Vagrant*. Remade as *He Took a Powder* (1955).

Fun on the Run (5/10/51) D: Jules White. Mary Castle, Joy Windsor, Rebel Randall, Pete Thompson, Bob Casson, Nanette Bordeaux, Charles "Heine" Conklin, Alyn Lockwood, Barbara Bartay. Vaudevillians Wally and Eddie head for Reno in search of work. Working title: *A Hitch in Time*. Uses stock footage from Collins and Kennedy's *Free Rent* (1936). Remade as *Come on Seven* (1956).

A Fool and His Honey (1/10/52) D: Jules White. Jean Willes, Frank Sully, Emil Sitka, Diane Mumby, Violet Murray, Ginger Sherry, Barbara Carroll. Wally mistakenly thinks Eddie is fooling around with his wife.

Heebie Gee-Gees (4/10/52) D: Edward Bernds. Iris Adrian, Margie Liszt, Rudy Lee, Dick Curtis, Mike Mahoney, Emil Sitka. Wally and Eddie use the house cleaning money to bet on a horse race.

Strop, Look and Listen (12/11/52) D: Jules White. Fred Kelsey, Lyn Thomas, Ginger Sherry, Emil Sitka. Wally and Eddie are barbers who invent a new flexible steel razor.

He Popped His Pistol (5/14/53) D: Jules White. Nanette Bordeaux, Kenneth MacDonald. The boys own a shoe store and accidentally wrap all their money inside a customer's shoe box.

A-Hunting They Did Go (10/24/53) D: Jules White. Dorothy Granger, Lynne Lyons, Kathleen O'Malley, Virginia Belmont, Joe Palma. The boys go off on a hunting weekend, followed closely by their wives. A remake, with stock footage, of *Crabbin' in the Cabin* (1948).

Doggie in the Bedroom (1/7/54) D: Jules White. Christine McIntyre, Billy Gray, Laura Lee Michel, Lonnie Thomas, Joe Palma, Vernon Dent. Wally tries to rid himself of visiting brother-in-law Eddie and his noisy children. A remake, with stock footage, of *Parlor, Bedroom and Wrath* (1948).

His Pest Friend (1/20/55) D: Jules White. Jean Willes, Vernon Dent, Matt McHugh. Wally and Eddie install a new television set and use the money saved for a party. A remake, with stock footage, of *Let Down Your Aerial* (1949).

Nobody's Home (6/9/55) D: Jules White. Jean Willes, Margie Liszt, Stanley Blystone. The Vernons and the Quillans discover they've purchased the same house from a crooked real estate agent, so they all try to live harmoniously under one roof. A remake of *House About It* (1950) and Collins and Kennedy's *Bury the Hatchet* (1937), using stock footage from both.

He Took a Powder (10/27/55) D: Jules White. Jean Willes, Emmett Lynn, Maxine Gates, Barbara Bartay. Wally leaves his wife and travels with his pal Eddie, a gentleman hobo. Working title: *Life Without Wife*. A remake, with stock footage, of *He Flew the Shrew* (1951).

Come on Seven (2/23/56) D: Jules White. Rebel Randall, Alyn Lockwood, Mary Castle, Joy Windsor, Nanette Bordeaux, Barbara Bartay, Frank Sully. Wally and Eddie travel to Reno to try to raise money for a poor child's operation. A remake, with stock footage, of *Fun on the Run* (1951). Also uses footage from Collins and Kennedy's *Free Rent* (1936).

Joe Besser

It's no secret that the later Columbia comedy shorts were largely comprised of footage from earlier two-reelers, but nowhere is this practice more evident than in the Joe Besser series. From 1949 to 1956, only ten Besser shorts were produced, yet the last four are merely "remakes" of the first four, with very little new footage added. Most of these films are military comedies, with Joe continually at odds with his top sergeant (Dick Wessel or Henry Kulky). Besser was paired a few times with Jim Hawthorne (billed simply as "Hawthorne"), a radio humorist whom Jules White had hired to serve as Besser's comic straight man.

After *Army Daze* (1956) Besser became a member of the Three Stooges, taking the place of Shemp Howard, who had died of a heart attack in 1955. Like Besser's Stooge films, his solo shorts benefit tremendously from his spirited performances, although his panache fails to salvage these uninspired, graceless comedies.

Military intelligence: Sergeant Henry Kulky (center) is at wit's end with rookies Joe Besser (right) and Jim Hawthorne (left) in *Aim, Fire, Scoot* (1952).

The Joe Besser Series

The following are all of Besser's Columbia shorts produced by either the Jules White or Hugh McCollum units. This listing does not include Besser's *Cuckoorancho* (1938), a Columbia two-reeler produced in New York by Ben K. Blake.

Waiting in the Lurch (9/8/49) D: Edward Bernds. Christine McIntyre, Vernon Dent, Rodney Bell, Andre Pola, James Logan, Charles Hamilton, Joe Palma. Joe's bride-to-be frowns on his mania for chasing fire engines. Working title: *Left in the Lurch*. Remade as *The Fire Chaser* (1954).

Dizzy Yardbird (3/9/50) D: Jules White. Dick Wessel, Brian O'Hara, Jessie Arnold, Bill Wallace, Jim Brown, Emil Sitka, Nick Arno. Joe's sergeant struggles to mold him into a model soldier. Original script title: *What a Soldier!* Remade as *G.I. Dood It* (1955).

Fraidy Cat (12/13/51) D: Jules White. Jim Hawthorne, Steve Calvert, Tom

Kennedy, Joe Palma, Eddie Baker. Joe and Hawthorne encounter a trained gorilla while guarding an antique shop. Working title: *Silly Sleuths*. A remake of the Three Stooges' *'Dizzy Detectives* (1943). Remade as *Hook a Crook* (1955).

Aim, Fire, Scoot (3/13/52) D: Jules White. Jim Hawthorne, Henry Kulky, Angela Stevens, Charles "Heine" Conklin. Joe and his sergeant fall for the same girl. Working title: *Daffy Draftees*. Remade as *Army Daze* (1956).

Caught on the Bounce (10/9/52) D: Jules White. Maxine Gates, Esther Howard, Edward Coch, Jr. Joe and his family make plans to visit his wealthy aunt. Working title: *Gullible's Travels*.

Spies and Guys (4/4/53) D: Jules White. Angela Stevens, Emil Sitka. Private Besser is sent on a secret mission with a WAC lieutenant.

The Fire Chaser (9/30/54) D: Jules White. Christine McIntyre, Vernon Dent, Rodney Bell, James Logan, Andre Pola, Charles Hamilton, Joe Palma. Joe's passion for following fire engines is driving his fiancee crazy. A remake, with stock footage, of *Waiting in the Lurch* (1949).

G.I. Dood It (2/17/55) D: Jules White. Dick Wessel, Phil Van Zandt, Emil Sitka, Brian O'Hara, Bill Wallace, Jim Brown, Nick Arno. Joe's pet dog relates, in flashback, his master's adventures in the Army. A remake, with stock footage, of *Dizzy Yardbird* (1950).

Hook a Crook (11/24/55) D: Jules White. Jim Hawthorne, Steve Calvert, Tom Kennedy, Joe Palma, Eddie Baker, Dan Blocker, Barbara Bartay, Lela Bliss. Private detectives Joe and Hawthorne are hired to recover some stolen jewels. Working title: *Daffy Detectives*. A remake, with stock footage, of *Fraidy Cat* (1951), and the Three Stooges' *Dizzy Detectives* (1943).

Army Daze (3/22/56) D: Jules White. Jim Hawthorne, Angela Stevens, Henry Kulky, Phil Van Zandt, Charles "Heine" Conklin. Joe and Hawthorne are drafted into the army. Working titles: *Army Days* and *Whacky in Khaki*. A remake, with stock footage, of *Aim, Fire, Scoot* (1952).

Mini-Series

Throughout the department's existence, several performers supplemented their incomes by appearing in two-reelers in between other assignments. "We usually signed them to a two-picture deal, with an option for more," says Jules White. "That way, if they received what they felt was a better offer elsewhere, they'd be free to accept it since they weren't bound to a long-term contract with us." The Radio Rogues, Alan Mowbray, and Eddie

Foy, Jr., were among those who starred in a few comedy shorts for the unit, then moved on to other projects.

Leon Errol's brief stay at Columbia resulted in four shorts, the best of which is *Hold Your Temper* (1933), an amusing essay in frustration humor: Leon, the normally cheerful president of a novelty company, struggles to maintain his composure in the face of all the galling mishaps that occur as the day progresses. The other Errol shorts — *Perfectly Mismated* (1934), *One Too Many* (1934) and the bizarre *Honeymoon Bridge* (1935) — are misfires, filled with intriguing ideas that never lead anywhere. After an argument with studio management, Errol left Columbia and found a home at RKO, where he starred in a long-running series of two-reel comedies.

Polly Moran was featured in *Oh, Duchess!* (1936) and *Sailor Maid* (1937). These below-average outings did nothing to restore the popularity she enjoyed in the early 1930s in her films with Marie Dressler.

Columbia's New York office arranged to have the legendary vaudeville team Joe Smith and Charlie Dale appear in two-reelers. *A Nag in the Bag* (1938) and *Mutiny on the Body* (1939) were made in Hollywood, produced by Hugh McCollum and directed by Charley Chase (Jules White was not a fan of the team's Jewish dialect humor and had no interest in becoming involved with their pictures). Smith and Dale were adept at visual comedy, but since dialogue routines were their hallmark, these shorts do not show them off to particularly good advantage.

Roscoe Karns starred in a couple of two-reelers that showcased his hard-boiled, wisecracking personality. In *Black Eyes and Blues* (1941) he's so obnoxious that the viewer never takes an interest in him or his plight. When his wife, played by Dorothy Appleby, files for a divorce, she seems fully justified in her actions. *Half Shot at Sunrise* (1941) makes better use of Karns' boorish demeanor, as Roscoe and his son (Bobby Larson) create havoc in a movie theatre. In one effectively insane sequence, Roscoe cracks peanuts so loudly that the actor on the screen (Stanley Brown) stops dead in his tracks and screams, "If you don't cut out that noise, we'll stop the show!"

Johnny Downs, always an agreeable performer, starred in two shorts. His *Groom and Bored* (1942) is fast and funny, one of the better Columbia shorts to emerge from that period.

Billy Gilbert made three comedies. With the proper material Gilbert could be hilarious, but outings like *Shot in the Escape* (1943), a mundane remake of Laurel and Hardy's *We Faw Down* (1928), are unworthy of this fine comedian.

The vivacious Una Merkel joined forces with lovely Gwen Kenyon in *Quack Service* (1943). Though the women made an attractive duo, the results were unimpressive. Una was also teamed with Harry Langdon, and both were ill-served in *To Heir Is Human* (1944).

Slim Summerville starred in two efforts. *Garden of Eatin'* (1943) is tedious, marred by Harry Edwards' sloppy, leaden direction. *Bachelor Daze* (1944), on the other hand, is a low comedy delight that pairs Slim with

Columbia stalwart Emmett Lynn; under director Jules White's guidance, they make a sublime team. Regrettably, it was only a one-time partnership.

Joe DeRita, later known as "Curly Joe" of the Three Stooges, made four shorts as a solo comic. At this point in his career, DeRita was the poor man's Lou Costello, with none of Lou's engaging appeal. When Joe performs a brief cross-talk routine with a tall, mustachioed straight man in *Slappily Married* (1946), comparisons to Abbott and Costello are unavoidable. DeRita's blubbering mannerisms render these films intolerable.

The unit even managed to sign Billie Burke for a couple of shorts. *Billie Gets Her Man* (1948) offers breezy entertainment; instead of involving Miss Burke in the roughhouse antics, director Edward Bernds wisely placed the bulk of the slapstick in the hands of such capable supporting players as Emil Sitka, Dick Wessel and Patsy Moran, allowing Billie's scatterbrained character to retain her femininity.

Bert Wheeler achieved great success in the 1930s as half of the popular Wheeler and Woolsey comedy team. After Robert Woolsey's death in 1938, Wheeler's stock in the industry plummeted, and he found it difficult to secure movie roles. His last theatrical film appearances were as the star of two Columbia shorts, *Innocently Guilty* (1950) and *The Awful Sleuth* (1951). Jules White, an admirer of Wheeler's work, proudly says, "I gave him a job at a time nobody else wanted him." Wheeler was grateful for the employment, but these pictures did not result in any offers from other studios.

The pairing of Max Baer and Maxie Rosenbloom, ex-pugilists turned thespians, was the unit's final attempt to create a comedy team. The Baer-Rosenbloom series ended after four shorts; as both men had shallow comic personalities and limited acting skills, the scripts adhered to tried-and-true formulas. Their films are currently unavailable for reappraisal; *Rootin' Tootin' Tenderfeet* (1952), a remake of Laurel and Hardy's classic *Way Out West* (1937), sounds the most intriguing.

The "mini-series" entries are notable mainly for the array of performers who appeared in them. As for overall quality, these shorts are often minor footnotes in prolific careers.

Leon Errol

Hold Your Temper (12/15/33) D: Sam White. Dorothy Granger, Arthur Hoyt, James C. Morton, Gertrude Sutton, Phil Dunham, Charlie Hall, Bud Jamison, Robert "Bobby" Burns, Spec O'Donnell, Eddie Borden. Leon begins the day with a sunny disposition but grows increasingly irritable as time wears on.

Opposite: The one-sheet for *To Heir Is Human* (1944), which pairs a pert Una Merkel with an aging Harry Langdon.

Leon Errol (left) resorts to drastic measures to settle a neighborly dispute with James C. Morton in *Hold Your Temper* (1933).

Perfectly Mismated (11/20/34) D: James W. Horne. Dorothy Granger, Vivien Oakland, Fred Malatesta, Phil Dunham, Lucille Ball, Arthur Rankin, James Blakely, Allyn Drake, Ruth Brooks, Frank Yaconelli, Billy West, Charles King. Leon's ex-wife moves into the apartment next to his. Working title: *Scrambled Wives.*

One Too Many (12/28/34) D: Robert McGowan. Vivien Oakland, William Irving, Bud Jamison, Jack Norton, Johnny Kascier, Harry Semels. Leon's wife tries to do something about hubby's fondness for alcohol.

Honeymoon Bridge (10/3/35) D: Del Lord. Geneva Mitchell, Harry Myers, Bud Jamison, Fred "Snowflake" Toones, William Irving, Bess Flowers, Al Thompson, Robert "Bobby" Burns. Leon is driven crazy by his wife's addiction to bridge playing.

The Radio Rogues:
Jimmy Hollywood, Eddie Bartell, Henry Taylor

Do Your Stuff (6/15/35) D: James G. Parrott. Lois January, Edward LeSaint, Carlton E. Griffin, Herb Ashley, James C. Morton, Billy West, Robert McKenzie, George Gray, Charles Phillips, Lew Davis, Billy Engle, George Cleveland, Rita Ross, Catherine Courtney, Edna Lyall, Bud Jamison, Sam Lufkin, Roger Gray, Betty McMahan, Celeste Edwards, Louise Dean, Joan Dix, Robert "Bobby" Burns. The Radio Rogues, salesmen for a cure-all tonic called "Nervoto," decide to go to Hollywood and cure invalids with mirth, melody and music instead of medicine. Remade with Joe DeRita as *Jitter Bughouse* (1948).

Star Gazing (9/26/35) D: Benny Rubin. Robert "Bobby" Burns, William Irving, Eddie Laughton. As proprietors of the All Cities Hotel, the Radio Rogues do impressions of movie stars in order to increase business.

Yoo Yoo Hollywood (11/14/35) D: Benny Rubin. Jean Manners, James C. Morton. The Radio Rogues crash Hollywood and manage to ruin director Cecil Ernst Capra's masterpiece.

Polly Moran

Oh, Duchess! (10/9/36) D: Charles Lamont. Vernon Dent, Mary Blake, Al Thompson, Jack "Tiny" Lipson, Symona Boniface, Bob McKenzie, Eva McKenzie. Polly is a fish peddler known to her customers as "The Duchess"; Vernon, the father of her daughter's fiance, mistakes her for genuine royalty.

Sailor Maid (2/12/37) D: Charles Lamont. Frank Mills, Cy Schindell, Al Thompson, Eddie Laughton, Ted Lorch, Blackie Whiteford. Immigrant Polly looks for an American husband so she won't be deported.

Joe Smith and Charlie Dale

A Nag in the Bag (11/11/38) D: Charley Chase. Dick Curtis, Stella LeSaint, Dorothy Vernon, Bud Jamison, Chester Conklin, Gloria Blondell, Polly Chase. Drive-in restaurant operators Joe and Charlie get betting fever and put all their money on a horse; due to dialect trouble, they bet on the wrong one.

Mutiny on the Body (2/10/39) D: Charley Chase. Chester Conklin, Guy Usher, Vernon Dent, Cy Schindell, Marjorie Deanne. Joe and Charlie, owners of the Klassy Korset Company, go to a sanitarium for rest and relaxation. Remade with the Three Stooges as *Monkey Businessmen* (1946).

Chester Conklin (center) shares his race track acumen with Charles Dale (left) and Joe Smith in *A Nag in the Bag* (1938).

Roscoe Karns

Black Eyes and Blues (4/18/41) D: Jules White. Elsie Ames, Richrad Fiske, Don Beddoe, Dorothy Appleby, Eddie Laughton, John Tyrrell, Stanley Brown, Lynton Brent. Roscoe's wife heads for Reno to get a divorce.

Half Shot at Sunrise (9/4/41) D: Del Lord. Ann Doran, Marion Martin, Bobby Larson, Vernon Dent, Bess Flowers, Bud Jamison, Monty Collins, Jack "Tiny" Lipson, Symona Boniface, John Tyrrell, Stanley Brown, Claire James, Victor Travers, Eddie Laughton, Ted Lorch, Marjorie "Babe" Kane, Frank Mills, Hank Mann, Bert Young. After his wife walks out on him, obnoxious Roscoe takes his son to the movies and creates havoc in the theatre.

Alan Mowbray

French Fried Patootie (6/27/41) D: Jules White. Greta Granstedt, Mae Busch, Kitty McHugh, Lorin Raker, Johnny Kascier. Alan tries to keep his wife from meeting an old flame of his. Working title: *Wee Wee Fifi*. Remade with Schilling and Lane as *Flung by a Fling* (1949).

Judging by the look on Alan Mowbray's face, his troubles have just begun in *Three Blonde Mice* (1942). Dorothy Appleby strains to eavesdrop.

Three Blonde Mice (1/22/42) D: Jules White. Monty Collins, Ann Doran, Dorothy Appleby, Mary Ainslee, Sally Cairns, Bud Jamison. To avoid getting a traffic ticket, Alan poses as an expectant father rushing to see his wife; when the cop follows him, he's forced to produce a wife and child. A remake of Walter Catlett's *Elmer Steps Out* (1934).

Johnny Downs

Groom and Bored (4/9/42) D: Del Lord. Marjorie Deanne, Arthur Q. Bryan, Walter Soderling, Helen Lynd, Bud Jamison, Symona Boniface, Dudley Dickerson, Eddie Laughton, Fred "Snowflake" Toones, Stanley Brown. Johnny tries to keep his marriage a secret from his boss, who feels that matrimony interferes with business. Remade with Sterling Holloway as *Hectic Honeymoon* (1947).

Kiss and Wake Up (10/2/42) D: Jules White. Adele Mara, Frank Sully. To make his fiancee jealous, Johnny has a friend masquerade as a girl.

Billy Gilbert, Barbara Slater, Cliff Nazarro and Grace Lenard form a jovial conga line in this publicity pose for *Shot in the Escape* (1943).

Billy Gilbert

Shot in the Escape (8/6/43) D: Jules White. Cliff Nazarro, Grace Lenard, Barbara Slater, Kathryn Keys, Charlie Hall. Billy and Cliff get their clothes wet when they try to help a woman across a muddy street; while drying off in her apartment, her jealous husband shows up.

Crazy Like a Fox (5/1/44) D: Jules White. Jack Norton, Esther Howard, Dan Seymour, Blackie Whiteford, Lynton Brent, Eddie Laughton, Duke Ward, Judy Malcolm, Charles "Heine" Conklin, Victor Travers. Publicity man Norton persuades taxi driver Billy to substitute for an uncooperative potentate. A remake of Andy Clyde's *Am I Having Fun!* (1936).

Wedded Bliss (8/18/44) D: Harry Edwards. Christine McIntyre, Vernon Dent. Billy tries to fix a friend's matrimonial dilemma. A remake of Charley Chase's *Man Bites Lovebug* (1937).

Una Merkel

Quack Service (9/3/43) D: Harry Edwards. Gwen Kenyon, Monty Collins, Dudley Dickerson, Vernon Dent, Blanche Payson, Bud Jamison, Snub Pollard, Stanley Brown, Al Thompson. Process servers Una and Gwen are assigned to serve papers to a prominent physician.

To Heir Is Human (1/14/44) D: Harold Godsoe. Harry Langdon, Christine McIntyre, Lew Kelly, Eddie Gribbon, Vernon Dent, John Tyrrell. Una, an aspiring private detective, locates Harry, a missing heir, and accompanies him to a forbidding mansion where he is to collect the inheritance.

Slim Summerville

Garden of Eatin' (10/22/43) D: Harry Edwards. Bobby Larson, Chester Conklin, Marjorie "Babe" Kane, Christine McIntyre, Snub Pollard, Vernon Dent, Al Thompson, Jack "Tiny" Lipson. Slim is nearly lynched in a tough Western town after being falsely accused of kidnapping.

Bachelor Daze (2/17/44) D: Jules White. Emmett Lynn, Minerva Urecal, Vernon Dent, Victor Travers, Al Thompson, Frank Sully, Charles Dorety. Slim, prompted by his pal Emmett, makes romantic overtures to the local widow.

Eddie Foy, Jr.

Dance, Dunce, Dance (10/18/45) D: Jules White. Judy Malcolm, John Tyrrell, Jack Norton, Robert Williams, Symona Boniface, Maude Prickett, Peggy Miller. A Hollywood producer mistakes Foy, a starving actor, for a masseur.

Foy Meets Girl (10/5/50) D: Richard Quine. Jean Willes, Iris Adrian, Dick Wessel. Foy rents his apartment to a pretty young woman and her wrestler husband.

Wedding Yells (2/8/51) D: Jules White. Lyn Thomas, Dorothy Ford, Emil Sitka, Peter Thompson, Stanley Blystone. Foy's boss has him stand in for a client as a bridegroom by proxy. Working title: *Proxy Honeymoon*.

Joe DeRita

Slappily Married (11/7/46) D: Edward Bernds. Christine McIntyre, Dorothy Granger, Dick Wessel, Jean Donahue, Florence Auer, Symona Boniface. Joe's wife thinks that he's been flirting with another woman and moves out on him. A remake of Andy Clyde's *A Maid Made Mad* (1943).

Slim Summerville (left) and Emmett Lynn are hilarious in *Bachelor Daze* (1944).

The Good Bad Egg (3/20/47) D: Jules White. Dorothy Granger, Norman Ollestead, Al Thompson, Frank Mills, Robert "Bobby" Burns, Vernon Dent, Charles Phillips, Lew Davis, Symona Boniface, Victor Travers. Joe's stepson ruins his plans to demonstrate his new invention. A remake, with stock footage, of Andy Clyde's *Knee Action* (1937).

Wedlock Deadlock (12/18/47) D: Edward Bernds. Christine McIntyre, Patsy Moran, Esther Howard, Charles Williams, Dorothy Granger, William Newell. Just as Joe and his bride are getting settled into their new home, her family comes to visit. A remake of Monte Collins' *Unrelated Relations* (1936).

Jitter Bughouse (4/29/48) D: Jules White. The Nov-Elites (Joe Mayer, Art Terry, Frankie Carr), Christine McIntyre, Emil Sitka, Patsy Moran. Joe and The Nov-Elites cure mental disorders with music. Working title: *Notes to You*. A remake of The Radio Rogues' *Do Your Stuff* (1935).

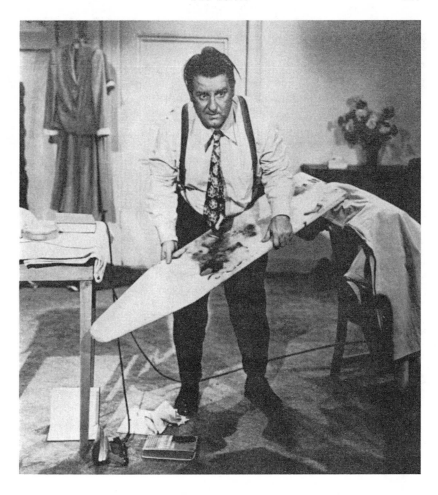

Joe DeRita struggles to reconstruct an ironing board and to create laughter in *Slappily Married* (1946); he fails miserably on both counts.

Billie Burke

Silly Billy (1/29/48) D: Jules White. Virginia Hunter, Myron Healy, Tim Ryan, Ruby Dandridge, Emil Sitka, Blackie Whiteford, Cy Schindell. Billie invites the father of her daughter's fiance to her home, mistaking him for the fiance. Working title: *Strife with Mother.*

Billie Gets Her Man (9/9/48) D: Edward Bernds. Patsy Moran, Dick Wessel, Emil Sitka, Gay Nelson, Jimmy Lloyd, Andre Pola, Symona Boniface, Stanley Ince, Cy Schindell, Harold Brauer, Johnny Kascier, Wanda Perry, Teddy Mangean, Virginia Ellsworth, Dee Green, Maudie Prickett, Charles "Heine"

Billie Burke welcomes her former sweetheart (Emil Sitka) in *Billie Gets Her Man* (1948).

Conklin. Billie is trying to decide whether to marry an old school friend, now a millionaire, when she gets the mistaken idea that her daughter is pregnant.

Max Baer and Maxie Rosenbloom

Two Roaming Champs (8/12/50) D: Edward Bernds. John Merton, Rita Conde, James Logan, Emil Sitka, Symona Boniface. Detectives Baer and Rosenbloom are hired to check on a millionaire's greedy relatives.

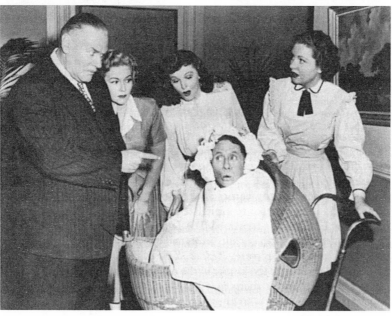

Top: A rose between two thorns: Max Baer, Jean Willes and Maxie Rosenbloom in *Rootin' Tootin' Tenderfeet* (1952). Bottom: Vernon Dent sees through Bert Wheeler's disguise in *Innocently Guilty* (1951) as Christine McIntyre (left), Nanette Bordeaux and Kathleen O'Malley react.

Wine, Women and Bong (2/22/51) D: Jules White. Christine McIntyre, Jean Willes, Nanette Bordeaux, Johnny Kascier, Charles "Heine" Conklin. Telling their wives that they have to work late, the two Maxes sneak off to a nightclub.

The Champ Steps Out (11/15/51) D: Edward Bernds. Emil Sitka, Jean Willes, Ralph Volkie, Dave Stan. Having just returned from an expedition in Asia Minor, a millionaire hires the two Maxes, operators of the Kayo Detective Agency, to guard his rare discoveries.

Rootin' Tootin' Tenderfeet (2/14/52) D: Jules White. Jean Willes. The boys are out West, looking for an heiress to whom they have to deliver a deed. Working title: *Westward Hokum*.

Bert Wheeler

Innocently Guilty (8/21/50) D: Jules White. Vernon Dent, Christine McIntyre, Nanette Bordeaux, Margie Liszt, Kathleen O'Malley, Joe Palma. Bert innocently becomes involved with his boss' wife. A remake of Andy Clyde's *It Always Happens* (1935) and *His Tale Is Told* (1944).

The Awful Sleuth (4/19/51) D: Richard Quine. Jean Willes, Minerva Urecal, Ben Welden, Tom Kennedy, Vernon Dent, Ralph Volkie. Soda jerk Bert, with the aid of his wife and mother-in-law, captures three criminals. A remake of Charley Chase's *The Big Squirt* (1937).

Single Entries

For various reasons, a handful of performers made only one starring comedy short for the unit. Franklin Pangborn, George Givot, Johnny Arthur and Wally Brown were able to fit only a single Columbia two-reeler into their schedules.

Some of these solitary entries were failed attempts at initiating a new series. In 1954 the unit tried to capitalize on the renewed popularity of Hal Roach's *Our Gang* shorts (renamed *The Little Rascals*) on television. Jules White rounded up a group of child actors and christened them "The Mischief Makers." The resulting picture, *Kids Will Be Kids*, is unquestionably the worst two-reel comedy in the history of the department, bar none. No matter how bad other Columbia shorts may be, at least they featured professional performers who could strive to inject some life into the flaccid material. But the Mischief Makers aren't capable of doing that much; they're possibly the most inept young thespians ever to set foot in front of a motion picture camera. None of them appears to have had any prior acting experience, and their hopelessly futile attempts to utter coherent sentences provide a few unintentional laughs (they're never quite sure where the dialogue begins or

Emil Sitka (second from right) lends a much-needed touch of professionalism to the Mischief Makers' *Kids Will Be Kids* (1954), unquestionably the worst two-reel comedy the unit ever produced.

ends). This intended series of kiddie comedies never went any farther than this initial entry. Mercifully, the majority of these moppets did not pursue acting careers, although mischief maker Sally Jane Bruce popped up the following year in *The Night of the Hunter* (1955) as one of the two children terrorized by Robert Mitchum.

Italian comic Harry Mimmo came to the attention of Columbia's New York office via an appearance on the Ed Sullivan television show. He was signed for one comedy short, *Down the Hatch* (1953), which was filmed in 3-D, though never officially released to theatres in this format (Columbia has recently struck up a 3-D print). Mimmo's humor was more in dialect than in visual comedy, and he was not an ideal candidate for slapstick. "I should have toned down his mannerisms," says Jules White, who feels he gave too much of a free rein to Mimmo's quirky dialect shtick.

Muriel Landers starred in *Tricky Chicks* (1957), billed as a *"Girlie Whirls"* comedy featurette. A stab at something different, it was ultimately done in by a low budget and poor scripting. Miss Landers sings two songs, "The Heat

Is On" and "I'm Taking a Slow Burn," both of which suffer from nonexistent production values.

These single entry efforts are strictly curios, brimming with under-developed ideas and overused gimmicks.

Franklin Pangborn

The Captain Hits the Ceiling (7/6/35) D: Charles Lamont. Geneva Mitchell, Bud Jamison, Stanley Blystone, Arthur Housman. Pangborn has a run-in with a burly sea captain who turns out to be his fiancee's father.

Monte Collins

Unrelated Relations (1/9/36) D: Del Lord. Ruth Skinner, Mary Foy, Ken Hollis, Louise Carver, Jack Kenney, Frank Taylor, Jack "Tiny" Lipson, Tommy Bond. Just as Monte and his bride move into their new home, the bride's family drops in. Working title: *Honeymoon Hardships*. Remade with Joe DeRita as *Wedlock Deadlock* (1947).

Guinn "Big Boy" Williams

The Champ's a Chump (6/20/36) D: Sam White. Louis Prima, Fred Kohler, Jr., Shirley Chambers, Harley Wood, Bobby Barrie, Richard "Tex" Brodus, James C. Morton, Fay Holderness, Sonny LaMont, Noral Whittinghill, George Tait, John Huddleston, Bill Brand, Bud Hervey, Jim Gonzales, Don Wyler, Don Ackerman, Bob Milton, Ted O'Shea, James Notaro, Jack Ellison, Sol Haines, Frank Edmunds, Jack Douglas, Russell Ash, Jerry Brashin, Bud Carpenter, Ward Arnold, Ken Gatewood, Rita Dunn, Belle Richards, Ethelreda Leopold, Valerie Hall, Joyce Mathews, Gertie Messenger, Angela Blue, Marion Shelton, Edith Haskins, Gay Waters. Williams enrolls in college, in an effort to sign a collegiate boxer to a contract.

Herman Bing

Oh, What a Knight! (11/22/37) D: Charley Chase. Louise Stanley, Claud Allister. Bing, a barber, is mistaken for a society woman's new footman.

Opposite top: The unit's third and final 3-D comedy short: *Down the Hatch* (1953) starring Harry Mimmo (center). Secondary players Maxine Gates, Joe Palma, Phil Van Zandt and Rita Conde are supposed to be reacting to the Limburger cheese in Mimmo's possession, but they may very well be passing judgment on the comedian's performing skills. Bottom: Muriel Landers (center) stars in *Tricky Chicks* (1957), a "Girlie Whirls" comedy featurette. Bek Nelson is on the far right.

Tom Kennedy and Johnny Arthur

Half-Way to Hollywood (7/1/38) D: Charley Chase. Ann Doran, Harry Holmes, Cy Schindell. Johnny writes a movie scenario, then gets Tom and his wife to star with him in his amateur production.

Danny Webb

A Star Is Shorn (4/21/39) D: Del Lord. Mary Treen, Ethelreda Leopold, Eugene Anderson, Jr., Victor Travers, Dudley Dickerson, Cy Schindell, Gene Stone, Raymond Brown, Al Thompson. A beauty contest winner (Leopold), her roommate (Treen) and their agent (Webb) attempt to crash Hollywood in grand style.

George Givot and Cliff Nazarro

Two Saplings (3/5/43) D: Harry Edwards. George and Cliff, owners of a bankrupt Greek restaurant, visit a bank for a loan and foil a robbery.

Wally Brown and Tim Ryan

French Fried Frolic (12/8/49) D: Jules White. Christine McIntyre, Nanette Bordeaux, Emil Sitka, Kathleen O'Malley, Grace Lenard. Wally and Tim are a couple of not-too-successful insurance salesmen. Working title: *A French Folly*.

Harry Mimmo

Down the Hatch (11/26/53) D: Jules White. Phil Van Zandt, Rita Conde, Maxine Gates, Emil Sitka, Joe Palma, Johnny Kascier. A gang of smugglers try to get immigrant Harry to conceal a stolen ruby. Working title: *Wid a Beeg Respect*. Filmed in 3-D.

The Mischief Makers

Kids Will Be Kids (12/9/54) D: Jules White. Daisy, Sally Jane Bruce, Emil Sitka. The Mischief Makers enter their pet dog Daisy in a contest. Working title: *Best Dog Wins*.

Muriel Landers

Tricky Chicks (10/24/57) D: Jules White. Richard Wessel, Bek Nelson, Benny Rubin, William Leslie, Chris Fortune. Government investigators suspect Muriel and Bek of being enemy agents. Working titles: *Girlie Whirls* and *Hotter Than Hot*.

Television and
Theatrical Revivals

In its formative years, television provided movie studios with an outlet for a backlog of product long considered unmarketable — specifically, short subjects. The Laurel & Hardy and Our Gang shorts in particular met with great response. But the only Columbia shorts to enjoy a renewed popularity through TV exposure were the Three Stooges comedies.

ABC was the first to express an interest. According to Gary H. Grossman in *Saturday Morning TV* (Dell Publishing, 1981), the network purchased exclusive rights to thirty of the early Three Stooges two-reelers in October 1949. But things really didn't begin to happen until January 1958, when Screen Gems, Columbia's television subsidiary, offered a package of seventy-eight Stooge shorts to TV markets. The comedies were a resounding success, earning surprisingly respectable ratings, and soon after forty more titles were added to the package. Before long, all 190 Stooge shorts were made available, although many stations voluntarily withdrew a number of titles due to their high levels of comic violence and/or racial slurs.

This quantity of Stooge films enabled stations to air them on a Monday-through-Friday basis. These afternoon programs were geared towards children, who comprised the largest share of the Stooges' TV audience. Those of you who grew up during this era will fondly recall the local kiddie show host who introduced the Stooge comedies. In New York (WPIX, Channel 11), it was Officer Joe Bolton. Bolton, whose program was set in a fictional police station, was himself a fan of the Stooges and was more knowledgeable about the team than most of the other hosts. Moe Howard made several guest appearances on Bolton's show; on one occasion he and Bolton sang "Swingin' the Alphabet," a novelty song performed by the Stooges in *Violent Is the Word for Curly* (1938). In the early 1960s, Chicago's WGN (Channel 9) had Andy Starr (played by Bob Bell), the elderly custodian of the mythical Odeon Theater. As Starr, Bell's makeup gave him more than a passing resemblance to Andy Clyde, whose comedy shorts were frequently aired during this time slot. In the eyes of many young viewers, the two men were one and the same.

195

Due to the heated outcry from parental groups, the hosts of these programs repeatedly issued warnings about the comic violence in the films: "Remember boys and girls, the Stooges are professional actors and know how to do these things. Don't go trying them out on your playmates." The debate about TV's influence on impressionable young minds has been raging for years. Let us go on record by saying that we, the authors, watched the Stooge comedies on television when we were children and it had no detrimental effect on our tender psyches (although our friends may not concur with this assessment). We believe that most children don't take this cartoon violence seriously at all and are intelligent enough to make the distinction between comic exaggeration and genuine violence.

Encouraged by the success of the Stooge pictures, Screen Gems put together a package of some 200 two-reel comedies featuring the work of Andy Clyde, Buster Keaton, Harry Langdon, Vera Vague, Hugh Herbert, El Brendel, Harry Von Zell and others. This package, however, met with lukewarm response. Stations that had clamored for the Stooge shorts were unenthused about this new batch of comedies, and usually relegated them to oddball time-slots, such as filler for delayed sports broadcasts. Part of the problem was that outside of the Andy Clyde series (79 titles) none of these other series offered more than two dozen entries. Therefore, stations couldn't present a daily program showcasing a single series. Or perhaps it was felt that these two-reelers didn't have the appeal of the Stooge shorts. Whatever the reasons, these films have never been telecast in many parts of the country. One exception was the aforementioned Andy Starr program, which alternated between Stooge shorts and Andy Clyde and Buster Keaton comedies.

The popularity of the Stooge comedies on television prompted Columbia to release *Three Stooges Fun-O-Rama* (1959), which was nothing more than a collection of the Joe Besser–Stooge shorts being passed off as a theatrical feature film. In 1974 Columbia released to theatres *The Three Stooges Follies*, which consisted of unedited short subjects, three with the Stooges: *Yes, We Have No Bonanza* (1939), *Violent Is the Word for Curly* (1938) and *You Nazty Spy!* (1940). Two-reelers with Buster Keaton *(Nothing but Pleasure*, 1940) and Vera Vague *(Strife of the Party*, 1944) were included, as well as Chapter One of the 1943 *Batman* serial and footage of Kate Smith singing "We're All Americans." The decision to throw in these additional titles proved disastrous as rowdy Stooge fans, who have little to no tolerance for anything that doesn't feature the celebrated trio, jeered loudly during the non–Stooge films. More recently, Columbia has struck up brand-new 35mm prints of Stooge shorts with Curly, which has resulted in countless Stooge festivals at revival theatres.

But except for a handful of scattered titles available through 16mm rental companies, the non–Stooge Columbia shorts remain inaccessible.

Selected Biographies

The key word here is *selected*. For various reasons, a number of people have been omitted. In some instances it was for the sake of brevity: we automatically excluded those starring comedians whose series totaled ten entries or less (Walter Catlett, Buster Keaton, Harry Von Zell, Sterling Holloway, et al.). The primary reason for omission, however, was the lack of information available. Studio records were generally inaccessible; the few studio biographies we came across were inconclusive. Because of Hollywood's caste system, short subjects personnel were largely ignored by the publicity mill; there was virtually no mention of them in fan magazines, and trade journals gave them a passing nod at best.

Our sleuthing uncovered only sketchy pieces of information on a few supporting players we wish we could have included. All that we were able to learn about Dorothy Appleby, a pert brunette who enlivened many Columbia shorts, was that her screen career began in the early 1930s; she was seen in such pictures as *King of the Wild Horses* (1933), *School for Girls* (1934), *Charlie Chan in Paris* (1935), *Riff Raff* (1936), *Stagecoach* (1939) and *High Sierra* (1941). She retired from acting in the early 1940s; rumor has it that she married and settled in Chicago. Richard Fiske, who was usually cast as a comic heavy, was killed in World War II. Reportedly, Marjorie Deanne, who appeared in the two-reelers during the late 1930s and early 1940s, died of heart failure in 1970. Beautiful blonde Ethelreda Leopold came to movies via a modeling career (she was spotted in a lipstick ad); in addition to the Columbia shorts, she appeared in several feature films, among them *Nothing Sacred* (1937), *Hollywood Hotel* (1937), *Gold Diggers in Paris* (1938), *Ball of Fire* (1941) and *Pardon My Sarong* (1942). Barbara Slater, who played Miss Lulu in *Half-Wits Holiday* (The Three Stooges, 1947), had been a model and chorus girl. She was also seen in *Louisiana Purchase* (1941) and as the florist shop girl in Charlie Chaplin's *Monsieur Verdoux* (1947).

As for the individuals who *are* profiled, we tried to be as accurate as possible, not an easy task in view of the often contradictory data we were faced with. Fortunately, the personal recollections of Ed Bernds, Emil Sitka, Jules White and other veterans of the unit helped to clear up some of the confusion. If we haven't been completely successful in separating fact from fiction, we will stand as corrected and hope the reader will forgive.

Felix Adler

Not to be confused with the circus clown bearing the same name, screenwriter Felix Adler was born in Chicago, Illinois, in 1891. After an extensive vaudeville career as dancer, singer and comedian, he was signed by Mack Sennett as a title writer in the early 1920s. By 1926 he supplanted Arthur Ripley as chief scenario writer of Sennett's comedies, possessing a storehouse of stage turns and burlesque blackouts in his memory that would serve him for the next thirty years.

During the talkie era he was in great demand, not only as a staff writer for the Columbia comedy shorts department (1935–57), but as a coauthor of a number of Laurel & Hardy features, including such classics as *Way Out West* (1937) and *Block-Heads* (1938). He also contributed special comedy sequences to other films, like Abbott & Costello's *The Naughty Nineties* (1945).

Adler retired from the industry in the late 1950s after some scant television work. He died of abdominal cancer at the Motion Picture Country Home on March 25, 1963.

Barbara Jo Allen (see Vera Vague)

Edward Bernds

Edward Bernds was born July 12, 1905, in Chicago, Illinois. During his high school years, he purchased a crystal set and developed an avid interest in radio. In his junior year, Bernds went to work for a local radio station, WENR, one of several that began springing up in the area at that time. He remained there until March 1927 when an affair of the heart took precedence over his position with the station: "A girl I met at Crane Junior College had gone to Los Angeles with her family, so I left WENR and drove to California in my beat-up Ford. I got a job at KELW in Burbank, and got married on August 20, 1927." Radio operators in Chicago were earning twice as much as operators in the Los Angeles area, so Ed and his wife, Betty, drove back to Chicago where he secured a job at WLS. Then, after a couple of months, he went to another station, WCFL.

But it was his brief WLS stint that proved to be beneficial. Howard Campbell, the man who hired Bernds at WLS, secured the job of chief engineer at the new sound department of United Artists Studio in Hollywood. Bernds picks up the story:

> Sound in movies — talking pictures — burst upon the scene late in 1928. Sound recording for movies was a new technique. There were no experienced sound technicians; the people with the skills closest to those required were broadcast operators, so most of us came from radio stations. Campbell recruited me to come to Hollywood.
> At United Artists I worked with Douglas Fairbanks on *The Iron Mask*,

with Mary Pickford on *Coquette*, with both Doug and Mary on *The Taming of the Shrew* and with the legendary D.W. Griffith on *Lady of the Pavements*. In August 1929, I quit UA and went to work for Columbia. MGM may have the biggest and richest studio, but UA, with Fairbanks, Pickford, Chaplin and Griffith, was royalty, and presumably no one in his right mind would quit aristocratic United Artists for Poverty Row Columbia. I did, and I'm pretty sure I was in my right mind.

First of all, Howard Campbell, who had recruited me, was fired as chief engineer of the United Artists sound department. Many factors entered into his downfall, but he was actually dismissed, I believe, because he affronted Mary Pickford and that, at UA, was the kiss of death. The man put in charge in his place didn't like me much, and I wasn't exactly fond of him. Those things happen. So I left United Artists for Poverty Row, which at the time was roughly equivalent to being exiled to Siberia in the dead of winter.

After a handful of "B" pictures at Columbia, Bernds was assigned as Frank Capra's sound man, a position he held from 1930 to 1939, working on such Capra films as *Rain or Shine* (1930), *Dirigible* (1931), *The Bitter Tea of General Yen* (1933), *Lady for a Day* (1933), *It Happened One Night* (1934), *Mr. Deeds Goes to Town* (1936), *Lost Horizon* (1937), *You Can't Take It with You* (1938) and *Mr. Smith Goes to Washington* (1939). "The only Capra picture from his period I didn't work on was *Miracle Woman* (1931). I'm not sure how I missed that one."

Bernds' expertise as a sound engineer and his affiliation with the Capra films quickly earned him the title of the studio's top sound mixer. He also worked on many other Columbia productions, including Howard Hawks' *Twentieth Century* (1934), Leo McCarey's *The Awful Truth* (1937), "B" entries such as the *Blondie* series, and two-reelers with the Three Stooges, Andy Clyde, Charley Chase and Buster Keaton.

However, Bernds' real desire, from the first day he set foot in a movie studio, was to become a director. In 1944 he got his chance:

I saw Frank Capra one night at a restaurant; he knew I wanted to get into directing and asked me what I was doing about it. When I told him I was still a sound man, Frank made me promise that I'd talk to Harry Cohn, the head of Columbia, that evening. When I finally spoke with Cohn, he said to me, "Look, you're the number one sound man at this studio. If I let you direct, you'll be starting at the bottom." I stood firm with my decision to be a director. Cohn relented, but was quick to add, "If this doesn't work out, don't come crying to me."

My first stab at directing was an O.W.I. short produced by Hugh McCollum. This was a one-reel propaganda short on the necessity of security during wartime — you know, a slip of a lip will sink a ship, that sort of thing. This was in August 1944. It was part of a series of films all the major studios made for the armed services and government agencies; these pictures were free of charge to those organizations. So you see, they were taking absolutely no risk by having me direct one. But the film managed to win some great comments from top people in the O.W.I. McCollum received letters from Stanton Griffis, who was Ambassador to Spain during the post-war years, and Elmer Davis, head of the O.W.I. McCollum was thrilled; he had never gotten this kind of recognition. It really made me look good in his eyes.

Bernds was then allowed to write several two-reel comedies for McCollum's unit and was eventually permitted to direct them as well. In addition to the comedy shorts, he soon began to branch out into feature film work, writing and directing the later *Blondie* entries.

When McCollum was fired from Columbia in 1952, Bernds, out of loyalty to the man fondly referred to as "Mac," also left. Upon leaving his home base of over twenty years, Ed found it difficult at first to secure work with another studio. The primary reason was the release of *Gold Raiders*, a low-budget western comedy starring George O'Brien and the Three Stooges, which he had directed:

> I should have never made that picture. When the shooting schedule was cut down successively from a respectable twelve days to ten, eight, and finally five days, I should have walked out on the project. I didn't because the producer, Bernard Glasser, pleaded that he would lose everything he owned if I didn't do the picture. *Gold Raiders* was made in December 1950, between Christmas and New Year's Day, but not released in the Los Angeles area until June 1952, and that's when the Hollywood Daily Variety and the Hollywood Reporter printed murderous reviews on it. Among other things, they singled out my direction as being particularly awful. Those reviews did me a lot of harm, because I left Columbia about that time; I was trying to get established at other studios, so it killed a couple of promising deals I had pending.

Fortunately, producer Ben Schwalb, whom Bernds had known in passing during his Columbia days, offered him a position writing and directing Bowery Boys features over at Allied Artists. Bernds got Elwood Ullman, a talented comedy writer with whom Ed had collaborated on a number of two-reelers, in on the deal. Among their efforts: *Loose in London* (1953), *Private Eyes* (1953), *The Bowery Boys Meet the Monsters* (1954), *Jungle Gents* (1954), and *Bowery to Bagdad* (1955), Bernds' personal favorite.

Later in the decade, Bernds directed pictures for 20th Century–Fox and the newly formed American International Pictures, in addition to his assignments at Allied Artists. During this period, he forsook comedies in favor of westerns *(The Storm Rider, Escape from Red Rock, Quantrill's Raiders)*, science-fiction films *(World Without End, Space Master X-7, The Queen of Outer Space, Return of the Fly)* and dramas dealing with juvenile delinquency *(Reform School Girl, Joy Ride, High School Hellcats)*.

In the 1960s, he was reunited with the Three Stooges, directing *The Three Stooges Meet Hercules* (1962), *The Three Stooges in Orbit* (1962) and all of the live-action introductory segments for "The New Three Stooges" (1965), a made-for-TV cartoon series. Bernds also wrote, with Elwood Ullman, the script for *Tickle Me* (1965) with Elvis Presley.

Now retired, Ed Bernds resides in Van Nuys, California. Flattered by the interest in his work, he comments, "When we were making these films, no thought was given as to how these things would look years later. It was just our job and we tried to do it to the best of our abilities. We didn't expect to be remembered for these pictures — but it's nice to know that people still enjoy them."

Joe Besser (see The Three Stooges)

Preston Black (see Jack White)

Stanley Blystone

Born in 1895, William Stanley Blystone began his screen career in 1915. His brothers also found work in the movie business: John G. Blystone became a director, Jasper Blystone an assistant director.

Blystone began appearing in the Columbia shorts in the mid-1930s and continued to do so, in between feature film roles, until the early 1950s (although, since stock footage from earlier shorts was used in many of the later efforts, he was seen in them for quite some time after that). Because of his large stature and low, gravelly voice, he was usually cast as a gruff, authoritarian figure, such as the firehouse captain in *False Alarms* (The Three Stooges, 1936).

During the 1950s, Blystone continued to play supporting roles in features and made numerous appearances on television. He died of a heart attack, at age 61, on July 16, 1956; he had collapsed on the sidewalk near Desilu Studios, where he was set to play a part in a Wyatt Earp TV film.

Symona Boniface

Born in 1894, Miss Boniface was a stage performer, producer and playwright in addition to being a movie actress. With her *grande dame* appearance, she typified the pompous society matron; she invariably played this kind of role in the Columbia shorts of the 1930s and 40s, as her dignity was continually deflated by the Three Stooges and other comedians. Her best remembered role was as Mrs. Smythe Smythe, the dowager who gets pelted by a pie conveniently hanging from the ceiling in the Three Stooges short *Half-Wits Holiday* (1947).

She died on September 2, 1950 in Woodland Hills, California; however, because of the liberal use of stock footage from earlier shorts, she was seen in several Three Stooges comedies throughout the 1950s.

El Brendel

Born Elmer G. Brendel on March 25, 1890, in Philadelphia, Pa., El had been a stage performer (he appeared in vaudeville with his wife, Sophie Flo Bert) prior to entering films in 1926. He was featured in a few silent pictures, including *Wings* (1927); with the advent of sound, he successfully parlayed his characterization of a simple-minded Swede into a popular comic figure in early talkies. Under contract to Fox, he was seen in such productions as *The Cockeyed World* (1929), *Sunny Side Up* (1929), *Happy Days* (1930), *The Big Trail* (1930), *Just Imagine* (1930), *Delicious* (1931) and *Women of All Nations* (1931).

By the mid-1930s, the novelty of Brendel's humor was beginning to wear thin, and Fox cast him in "B" pictures and two-reelers. In 1936 he starred in a couple of comedy shorts for Columbia, then went on to play supporting roles in a few feature films, including *Little Miss Broadway* (1938), *Valley of Giants* (1938), *If I Had My Way* (1940), *Captain Caution* (1940) and *Gallant Sons* (1940).

In 1941 he returned to Columbia for a starring series of comedy shorts, which occasionally teamed him with Tom Kennedy and, later, Harry Langdon. When his series came to an end in 1945, Brendel had difficulty securing film work, and wound up playing supporting roles in *The Beautiful Blonde from Bashful Bend* (1949), *Paris Model* (1953), *The She-Creature* (1956) and *The Madcaps* (1964). He also appeared on television, in Joan Davis' series and an episode of "Destry."

Brendel died of a heart attack on April 9, 1964, at the Hollywood Presbyterian Hospital.

Lynton Brent

Lynton Wright Brent was born August 2, 1903, in Chicago, Illinois. He was a stage actor during the 1920s, appearing in productions of *Sally, Irene, The Student Prince, Hamlet, Paid in Full* and *Hoyt's Revue*. Entering films in the 1930s, Brent worked for Monogram, Mascot, Republic, Educational, Paramount, RKO and Columbia; he was seen as a supporting player in the Columbia comedy shorts from the mid-1930s on through the early 1940s.

Clyde Bruckman

Clyde Bruckman was born in 1895. His career as a comedy writer spanned four decades; during that period, he worked with nearly every major film comedian in the business. He became a member of Buster Keaton's writing staff in 1921, working on such classic comedies as *The Three Ages* (1923), *Our Hospitality* (1923), *Sherlock, Jr.* (1924) and *The Navigator* (1924). With Keaton, Bruckman co-directed *The General* (1926).

Bruckman went on to direct two-reelers for Hal Roach (including several

Supporting player Lynton Brent was also an architect and artist. In this 1934 photo, he poses beside one of his paintings, "Orient."

with Laurel & Hardy), Harold Lloyd's first three sound pictures, and W.C. Fields in *The Fatal Glass of Beer* (1933) and *The Man on the Flying Trapeze* (1935).

The Man on the Flying Trapeze marked Bruckman's swan song as a director. According to *The Hollywood Reporter*, W.C. Fields, assisted by actor/screenwriter Sam Hardy, took over direction of the picture (then known under its working title *Everything Happens at Once*) for two days due to Bruckman's "absenteeism" (read: *alcoholism*). By doing so, Fields managed to keep the film in production, but it also served to point out to the industry that Bruckman could no longer be entrusted with directing a picture; for the remainder of his career, Bruckman served only as a writer.

Bruckman started with the Columbia comedy shorts unit in 1934, directing the Three Stooges in *Horses' Collars* (released 1935); by the late 1930s, he was writing scripts for many of the two-reelers. In the 1940s he also wrote screenplays for Universal, for such pictures as *Swingtime Johnny* (1943), *Twilight on the Prairie* (1944) and *South of Dixie* (1944).

But by this time, Bruckman became more and more dependent upon the practice of lifting gag sequences from earlier films (even those that were written by others) and arbitrarily inserting them into screenplays he was working on. This penchant for borrowing material proved disastrous, as he took the magician's coat routine from Harold Lloyd's *Movie Crazy* (1932), which Bruckman had directed, and reused it — word for word — in *Loco Boy Makes Good* (The Three Stooges, 1942). He also worked Lloyd routines into his screenplays for two Universal pictures, *Her Lucky Night* (1945) and *She Gets Her Man* (1945).

On March 7, 1946, Lloyd sued Columbia, seeking $500,000 in damages. When the court compared the *Movie Crazy* and *Loco Boy Makes Good* scripts, they were identical, and Lloyd won the case. Lloyd also sued Universal for several million dollars, again because of Bruckman scripts. Bruckman was fired from Universal; his alcoholism worsened, and it soon became apparent to the Columbia shorts unit that he could no longer function as one of their coterie of gag writers (he did, however, continue to receive story credit for those comedies that were remakes of his earlier screenplays).

Aside from scripting episodes of the TV series "The Buster Keaton Show" (1951) and "The Abbott and Costello Show" (1953), Bruckman had difficulty securing writing assignments; the Lloyd incidents and his heavy drinking rendered him unemployable. One day in 1955, Bruckman, despondent over his inability to find work, borrowed a pistol from his old friend Buster Keaton (he told Keaton that he wanted to use it for target practice) and killed himself in a restaurant restroom (some reports claim it was a telephone booth). His suicide note read: "I have no money to pay for a funeral." A tragic end for one who spent a lifetime creating laughter.

Charley Chase

In recent years, a growing number of film enthusiasts have embraced Charley Chase as an unsung comic genius who has been unjustly overlooked for generations. In his later films, the caliber of his work began to decline sharply; but at his best, Chase was a terrific comic innovator, both in front of and behind the camera, and his finest work remains wonderfully fresh and funny.

Born on October 20, 1893, in Baltimore, Maryland, Chase honed his performing skills in vaudeville and became quite a versatile entertainer. Allegedly discovered by producer Al Christie, Chase entered films in 1912. In 1914 Mack Sennett hired him as a supporting comedian; by the following year, Chase started phasing himself out of acting and, under the pseudonym Charles Parrott, began directing comedy shorts. In 1916 he left Sennett's and became a writer-director for Fox Pictures' comedy unit.

Charley joined the King Bee Film Company in April 1918, replacing Arvid E. Gillstrom as director of the Billy West comedies. West had achieved some measure of success as a Charlie Chaplin imitator; despite the inevitable comparisons to the Chaplin pictures, the West shorts were amusing comedies in their own right. In December of that year, Chase was hired to direct additional Billy West comedies, this time for the newly-established Bulls Eye Film Corporation. Chase went over to Paramount in 1919, directing a series of domestic comedies starring Mr. and Mrs. Carter DeHaven (a popular husband and wife team, the parents of actress Gloria DeHaven). By 1920 Chase was freelancing; his directorial credits during this period include two Lloyd Hamilton shorts for Jack White's Mermaid Comedies, which were released through Educational Pictures.

Early in 1921, Charley was hired by Hal Roach, the only comedy producer of his day who was considered a serious rival to Mack Sennett. Chase quickly sprang into action, writing and directing a number of inventive Snub Pollard comedies. In late 1923, Chase resumed his acting career, starring in his own series for Roach.

The Chase comedies were a great success. Charley was unique in that he didn't resort to the outlandish makeup and costumes worn by so many of his contemporaries. Dapper in appearance, he excelled in the comedy of human folly; much of his humor stemmed from his valiant efforts to maintain his composure in the midst of an embarrassing situation. Though often wildly complex and contrived, these situations were basically credible and provided a perfect match for the comedian's engaging "everyman" persona.

Andrea Leeds, best known for her performance in *Stage Door* (1937), costarred in a couple of Chase shorts in the mid-1930s. Miss Leeds remarks, "It is claimed that comedy is one of the most difficult aspects of acting. Mr. Chase was a master . . . he was helpful, considerate and delightfully funny on and off camera."

Chase worked steadily at the Hal Roach Studios for fifteen years. In 1936 Roach, sensing that the era of the two-reel comedy was drawing to a close, decided to concentrate on feature film production. Apparently Chase didn't fit into these new plans, and later that year he left the studio.

Charley joined the Columbia comedy shorts department in 1937. He wrote, coproduced and directed several two-reelers, in addition to starring in his own series. "Charley was a warm, wonderful, naturally funny man," says Elwood Ullman, who wrote many of the Chase Columbias. "He had us in stitches all the time."

Chase's association with the unit was a happy one, and lasted until his death from a heart attack on June 20, 1940, in Hollywood.

Andy Clyde

Andy Clyde was born March 25, 1892, in Blairgowrie, Scotland. His father was a theatrical producer and manager, so Andy developed an interest in the theatre at a very young age. He became friends with a young Scottish performer named James Finlayson; it was Finlayson who was instrumental in getting Andy into films. By 1919, Finlayson had emigrated to the United States and was appearing in Mack Sennett's Keystone Comedies; he persuaded Andy to join him in California, and got him small roles in the Sennett pictures. Within a few years, Clyde went from bit parts to supporting player and, occasionally, starring roles, most notably in a series of imaginative two-reelers with Billy Bevan *(Circus Today, Muscle Bound Music, Ice Cold Cocos)*.

In the late 1920s, Andy hit upon an "old man" characterization that was to be his trademark for the remainder of his career. With the advent of talkies, he was Sennett's top attraction; but late in 1932, a contractual dispute prompted Clyde to part company with Sennett and sign on with Educational Pictures.

Andy joined Columbia's comedy shorts unit in 1934; his starring series, second only to the Three Stooges in output and longevity, lasted until 1956. During this time, Andy also played supporting roles in many feature films, including *The Little Minister* (1934), *Annie Oakley* (1935), *It's a Wonderful World* (1939), *Abe Lincoln in Illinois* (1940) and several *Hopalong Cassidy* westerns with William Boyd.

When his series for Columbia ended, Andy continued to work steadily, appearing on such TV shows as "The Real McCoys," "No Time for Sergeants" and "Lassie." He died in his sleep on May 18, 1967, in Hollywood; he was survived by his wife of thirty-four years, Elsie Maud Tarron, a former Mack Sennett bathing beauty.

Monte Collins

Monte Francis Collins, Jr., was born December 3, 1898, in New York City. A stage and vaudeville performer, he made his film debut as an extra in *Forty Minutes from Broadway* (1920). During the 1920s, Collins appeared in many feature films, among them *Our Hospitality* (1923) with Buster Keaton, *Tumbleweeds* (1925) with William S. Hart, and Cecil B. De Mille's *The King of Kings* (1927); in 1925 he starred in a series of comedy shorts for Fox. By the late 1920s, he was paired with Vernon Dent for a series of one-reel comedies for Educational Pictures; these shorts were directed by Jules White, who would soon head the Columbia comedy shorts department.

In the early 1930s, Collins was active in both features and shorts, primarily at Educational and Radio Pictures (soon to be renamed RKO). He joined the Columbia shorts unit in 1934, appearing as a supporting player as well as a starring comedian (his series with Tom Kennedy ran from 1935 to 1938). Later, he wrote the comedies in addition to performing in them.

In the early and mid-1940s, Collins continued his association with the unit and also played supporting roles in feature films, including *Buck Benny Rides Again* (1940), *You'll Never Get Rich* (1941), *Three Girls About Town* (1941) and *House of Errors* (1942). He even wrote the screenplay for a Maria Montez picture, *Tangier* (1946).

Collins left Columbia in 1947. He and Robert Paige produced a feature, *The Green Promise* (1949), which was released thru RKO. In 1950 he supplied additional material for Laurel and Hardy's last film, the ill-fated *Atoll K* (released 1951); his credit simply read "Gags by Monty Collins."

Early in 1951, industry trade journals announced that Collins had signed a deal to start in TV production. But he didn't live to begin this new phase of his career; he died of a heart attack on June 1, 1951, in Hollywood.

Gino Corrado

Gino Corrado was born in Florence, Italy; he attended the College of Strada, then moved to the United States, attending St. Bede College in Peru, Illinois. He entered motion pictures in the 1920s, appearing in such films as *The Ten Commandments* (1923), *La Boheme* (1926), *The Volga Boatmen* (1926), *Sunrise* (1927) and *The Iron Mask* (1929). For a while, he changed his name to Eugene Corey, in hopes of moving on to more substantial roles.

But during the 1930s, Gino's movie roles were reduced to bit parts. Because of his accent and physical appearance, he was usually cast as barbers, hotel clerks or headwaiters. He played small supporting roles in many feature films, including *Scarface* (1932), *Chained* (1934), *Wonder Bar* (1934), *Top Hat* (1935), *A Night at the Opera* (1935), *Anna Karenina* (1935), *The Big Broadcast of 1937* (1936), *Gone with the Wind* (1939), *Foreign Correspondent* (1940), *Kitty Foyle* (1940), *The Mark of Zorro* (1940), *Citizen Kane* (1941), *The Talk of the Town* (1942), *The Pride of the Yankees* (1942), *Casablanca* (1942), *Hello, Frisco, Hello* (1943), *Saratoga Trunk* (1945), *My Wild Irish Rose* (1947), *Road to Rio* (1947), *Blondie in the Dough* (1947) and *Living It Up* (1954).

From the late 1930s through the mid-1940s, Corrado was a supporting player in several Columbia shorts, costarring with Collins and Kennedy, Buster Keaton and the Three Stooges. Unlike his feature film roles, these two-reelers gave Gino ample opportunity to display his considerable comedic skills.

In 1949 Gino became the maitre d'hotel at the Italia Restaurant in Beverly Hills. He told a reporter at the time, "I took the job with the understanding that if anything came along in the way of a movie role, I'd have the privilege of taking it." Commenting on the lack of movie roles for him, Gino added, "They have stopped building big restaurant and nightclub sets in pictures in order to economize. And if there are no restaurants and nightclubs, how can there be headwaiters?"

Gino Corrado died at age eighty-seven on December 23, 1982.

Dick Curtis

Born on May 11, 1902, Dick Curtis made his film debut in 1918 as an extra in *The Unpardonable Sin*. He became a stage actor and returned to movies in the 1930s, appearing in such pictures as *Shooting Straight* (1930), *Girl Crazy* (1932), *King Kong* (1933), *The Man They Could Not Hang* (1939) and many "B" Westerns.

He was featured in Columbia shorts from the late 1930s on through the early 1950s, playing supporting roles as comic heavies (usually western villains or jealous husbands).

He died on January 3, 1952, in Hollywood.

Vernon Dent

Vernon Dent was born February 16, 1895, in San Jose, California. During his youth he was educated at schools in the San Jose and Oakland area. As a young boy Vernon loved the stage, and when the opportunity came, he joined a local acting troupe and also spent time in the community theatres. He possessed a beautiful tenor voice and often got jobs as a singer. In fact, Vernon was singing in a trio (with Fred Bell and Harry Highsmith) at the Jewel City Cafe in Seal Beach, California, when former Mack Sennett comedian Hank Mann discovered him and decided Dent was good comic material. Vernon was hired by Hank in December 1919, and supported Mann in a series of comedies marketed by Arrow for release.

Vernon learned much of his comic craft from Mann, and the experience obtained was thorough enough for Vernon to receive his own starring series in 1921, "Folly Comedies," released by the Pacific Film Company. Also starring with Dent in this series was Duane Thompson, described by film historian Raymond Lee as "a cute teenager." Upon completion of this series late in 1921, Vernon free-lanced, appearing in a few Fox Sunshine Comedies, the 1922 feature *Hail the Woman*, and two Larry Semon shorts.

In the spring of 1923, Vernon arrived at the Mack Sennett Studios. Sennett had been aware of the considerable talents of this stocky but youthful twenty-eight year old for some time now, and gladly put Vernon under contract as a supporting player in the Sennett stock company. His first assignment was playing Mabel Normand's small-time lover in the seven-reel feature *The Extra Girl* (1923). His work at Sennett's for the rest of the 1920s was quite diversified, and practically anything can be said on his variety of performances. For a man his size (5' 9" tall and 250 pounds) Vernon was capable of performing some marvelous physical comedy. Vernon was also astute enough to realize that to be in demand he would have to be able to represent assorted "types" and characters—so he became a master of makeups.

Dent's career took a memorable turn when he became the main support in Sennett's series of Harry Langdon comedies. In this group of films, Vernon firmly established himself; their immense popularity in the 1920s brought

A 1947 portrait of Vernon Dent as he appears in the Andy Clyde short, *Two Jills and a Jack*.

major stardom to Langdon and also a modicum of fame for Dent. From 1924 to 1926 the mold was solidly set: Langdon played the bumbling little man to Dent's towering symbol of authority, power, villainy or whatever the role called for. In comedies like *Picking Peaches* (1924), *All Night Long* (1924), *His Marriage Wow* (1925) and *Saturday Afternoon* (1926), Vernon supplied many amusing moments.

When Langdon left Sennett's in 1926, Dent's remaining work was spent in some of Sennett's romantic comedies with Ralph Graves and Thelma Parr, and he was also featured in several of the "Smith Family" entries. But the Billy Bevan series seemed to be Vernon's mainstay at Sennett's, as he supported Bevan in such comedies as *Hoboken to Hollywood* (1926) and *The Best Man* (1928).

Vernon's contract coincided with Sennett's own distribution lease with Pathé; when the Pathé contract expired and talkies were on the horizon, Sennett, whose fortunes were already faltering, failed to renew any contracts. Vernon appeared in only eight Sennett releases from 1929 to 1932; in addition, he wrote material and even songs for Bing Crosby when Der Bingle had his series at Sennett's. Perhaps Dent's best-remembered work from this early talkie period is his role as one of the black-cloaked villains in the feature *Million Dollar Legs* (1932), Paramount's zany tribute to slapstick comedy.

It was a happy coincidence when, in 1932, Vernon was reunited with his old friend Harry Langdon for a series of two-reelers for Educational Pictures. Dent's value was noted, for he was prominently featured in almost the entire series, and always received billing after Langdon. Langdon and Dent complemented each other better than ever, and the easygoing, informal atmosphere helped to fashion first-rate gems like *The Big Flash* (1932), *Knight Duty* (1933) and *Hooks and Jabs* (1933). Nell O'Day, who was cast as Harry's leading lady in a few of these two-reelers, recalls: "Vernon was a lovely man; he couldn't have been nicer. He and Harry were very fond of each other. They were wonderful to work with." In 1933 producer-director Arvid E. Gillstrom, the man responsible for these Langdon comedies, brought the series to Paramount; when Gillstrom died soon after, the series came to an abrupt end.

Dent joined the Columbia short subjects department in 1935. This association proved to be as rewarding as his Sennett period, with Vernon remaining at Columbia until 1953 (though he appeared in several two-reelers, via stock footage, for years after that). In that space of time Vernon was seen in a vast number of shorts, proving time and time again that he was one of the screen's greatest comic foils.

Also at this time Vernon appeared in many feature films, such as *The Shadow* (1937), in which he played gangster Dutch Schultz. Other credits include *The Awful Truth* (1937), *Start Cheering* (1938), *Beasts of Berlin* (1939), *Mr. Smith Goes to Washington* (1939), *San Antonio Rose* (1941), *My Favorite Blonde* (1942), *Her Primitive Man* (1944) and *The Harvey Girls* (1946).

Known for his genuine kindness, Vernon had many friends in Hollywood. "Vernon was a great guy," recalls Edward Bernds. "When I was a fledgling director, he reached out to me, helped me, and treated me as if I were an old pro." Eunice Dent, who married Vernon in August 1938, reflects upon her late husband's love of people:

> In the two-reelers, Vern was always cast as a nasty man because he was adept at projecting that kind of image onscreen; in actuality, he was quite the reverse. There wasn't a mean bone in his body. He got along with everyone. Very rarely did he meet someone whom he couldn't get along with.
>
> Vernon was very gregarious; he had a great many friends, both in and out of the movie business. Of course, he and Harry Langdon were quite close. Of all the Three Stooges, Vern kept in closest contact with Moe. Shemp was also a good friend. Jules White used to be our neighbor;

Vernon and Jules liked each other very much. Vern was also fond of Jules' brother Jack.

When I married Vern he had the concession to MacArthur Park, which was Westlake Park then. It was a political thing, having to do with the mayor and the parks commissioner. Vernon knew everybody. The mayor gave Vernon this little plot, so we knew that when there'd be a new administration Vernon would be out of the picture. But it wasn't our livelihood so we didn't depend upon it. He did this as a lark. We had juke boxes and ice cream. It was very lucrative and a lot of fun. Vernon loved that. He loved giving out ice cream to the kids. He'd get kids from the high school to help on weekends, that's how busy things would get. Even I had to come down and pitch in. We had that for about six years.

Sadly, Vernon went blind in the mid-1950s, forcing him to retire from films. Eunice Dent recalls:

Vernon was a diabetic, which was the cause of his blindness. He drank far too much Coca-Cola. When we had the concession he'd drink the syrup and add his own seltzer. That was one of the reasons for his blindness. I couldn't curb his cravings for sweets, although I tried.

After Vernon lost his sight, I remember someone from the Braille Institute calling me, saying, "We'd like to talk to your husband. Sometimes we can help in the adjustment." The woman called me back after she saw Vernon and said, "I've never seen anything like it. I didn't even know he was blind when he came in. If there's anyone who doesn't need psychotherapy, it's your husband." He was that well adjusted.

Not all of Vernon's co-workers knew about his handicap. Emil Sitka wasn't aware of it until he saw Dent at Shemp Howard's funeral in November 1955:

Vernon came into the parlor, wearing a yarmulke like everyone else since this was a Jewish ceremony. He was led in by his arm, and brought up to Shemp's casket. The man accompanying Vernon told him, "This is Shemp." Vernon was staring straight ahead at the wall—it was then that I realized he was blind. Vernon felt Shemp's hand, then his face very gently. Everyone else had been filing past the casket quickly, but Vernon took his time, giving a last goodbye to his friend. It was one of the most moving things I ever saw.

Vernon died on November 5, 1963; contrary to previously published reports, he was not a Christian Scientist and did not die because he refused to take insulin. Says Eunice Dent:

Those stories aren't true at all. Vernon was not a Christian Scientist; while he certainly believed in God, he didn't belong to any particular faith. And he was always in robust health up until he died; he just had a sudden heart attack.

Despite his disability in his later years, Vernon Dent never lost his cheery outlook on life, and was quite free with his reminiscences on the "good old days" of moviemaking, some of which have been captured in print in Mack Sennett's *King of Comedy* (1954) and Raymond Lee's *Not So Dumb* (1970). To read Vernon's words are to listen to an optimist, a man who spent his life giving people laughter, and who, in his final years, could look back without the slightest regret.

Dudley Dickerson

This talented and underrated black comedian was born Dudley Henry Dickerson on November 27, 1906, in Oklahoma. Dickerson appeared in many feature films, including *The Virginia Judge* (1935), *Green Pastures* (1936), *All American Co-Ed* (1941), *The Man Who Came to Dinner* (1941), *The Adventures of Mark Twain* (1944), *Peggy* (1950) and *The Alligator People* (1959).

From the late 1930s on through the mid-1950s, Dudley was seen as a supporting player in several Columbia shorts. Although he continually fell victim to the stereotyping prevalent in films from this period—playing porters, bellhops and the like—Dudley managed to imbue these limited roles with an engaging appeal and came across as a genuinely funny performer, regardless of race. He brought a wonderful energy to the restrictive (and frequently condescending) nature of "scared reaction" comedy. Dudley is best known for his hilarious role as the bewildered cook ("This house has sure gone crazy!") in *A-Plumbing We Will Go* (The Three Stooges, 1940).

He died of a cerebral thrombosis on September 23, 1968.

Jean Donahue (see Jean Willes)

Ann Doran

Born July 28, 1913 (some sources claim 1911 and 1914) in Amarillo, Texas, Miss Doran made her film debut in *Robin Hood* (1922) with Douglas Fairbanks. She went to high school in San Bernadino, California; after attending the University of Southern California (USC) and the University of California at Los Angeles (UCLA), she returned to films in 1934.

Ann joined the Columbia comedy shorts unit in 1936, and was cast opposite Harry Langdon, Andy Clyde, the Three Stooges and, most notably, Charley Chase. Her last appearance in a Columbia short was in *Doctor, Feel My Pulse* (Vera Vague, 1944).

Miss Doran played supporting roles in many feature films, including *Charlie Chan in London* (1934), *Way Down East* (1935), *Mr. Deeds Goes to Town* (1936), *Nothing Sacred* (1937), *You Can't Take It with You* (1938), *Blondie* (1938), *Mr. Smith Goes to Washington* (1939), *Penny Serenade* (1941), *Meet John Doe* (1941), *Sun Valley Serenade* (1941), *Yankee Doodle*

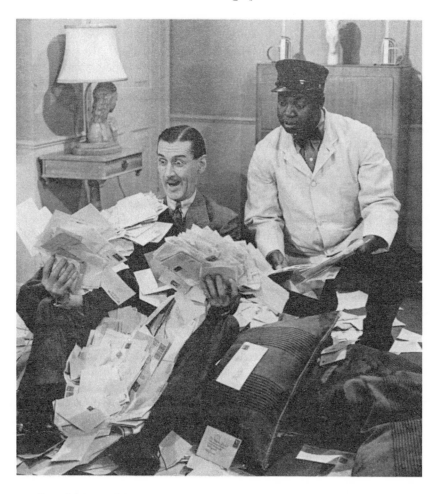

Dudley Dickerson (right) looks on as Charley Chase pores over his love letters in *His Bridal Fright* (1940).

Dandy (1942), *Old Acquaintance* (1943), *My Favorite Brunette* (1947), *The Snake Pit* (1948), *Riding High* (1950), *The Eddie Cantor Story* (1953), *The High and the Mighty* (1954), *Them!* (1954), *Voice in the Mirror* (1958), *The Carpetbaggers* (1964) and *Rosie!* (1968). Her best remembered role was as James Dean's mother in *Rebel Without a Cause* (1955).

She also made numerous appearances on television throughout the 1950s and 1960s; in the 1970s she was a regular on "Longstreet" and "Shirley" with Shirley Jones, and was featured in a few episodes of "M*A*S*H."

Still active in the business, Miss Doran has to her credit the recent movies *Little Mo* (Made for TV, 1978), *All Night Long* (1981) and *First Monday in October* (1981).

Harry Edwards

Harry Edwards was born in Calgary, Canada, in 1889. After a two-year stint in the U.S. Army, Edwards drifted to Los Angeles and became a prop-man at Universal Studios in 1913. On an occasion when the scheduled director failed to show up, Edwards was handed the megaphone and acquired a new career. Efficiency and expedience often supplanted genuine talent in the formative years of filmmaking, and Edwards was no exception.

After a gradual ascension from Henry Lehrman's L-KO Comedy unit in 1914 to Fox's Sunshine Comedies in 1917, Edwards eventually found himself at Mack Sennett's in 1924. Almost immediately he became resident director of the Harry Langdon series. Langdon was experiencing the first wave of an enormous popularity; when he left Sennett in November of 1925 to form the Harry Langdon Corporation, Edwards signed on as director. The first release, *Tramp, Tramp, Tramp* (1926), a six-reel feature, was hailed as the comedy hit of the year. Edwards, who according to Frank Capra found the feature length schedule too demanding, returned to Sennett's.

Edwards continued as a Sennett director until sound came in, whereupon his contract was cancelled. Unable to secure steady employment, he freelanced through most of the 1930s for Universal and Paramount, ending up at Columbia in 1939. While his contract with the Columbia comedy shorts unit offered steady work as staff writer and director, a basic insecurity combined with alcoholic problems resulted in some poorly made comedies.

It must be noted that Harry Langdon, who was also making shorts for Columbia, was Edwards' staunchest defender at this time. Indeed, after Langdon's death in late 1944, Edwards' dismissal was not very far off.

Edwards died May 26, 1952, of carbon tetrachloride poisoning, after having directed his first television production.

Bess Flowers

Having appeared in hundreds of feature films and short subjects, Bess Flowers is accurately referred to as the "Queen of the Hollywood Extras." Her roles varied from leads to supporting parts to bits and walk-ons. Although she was usually seen only briefly during a crowd scene (almost always as a member of the hoi polloi), the statuesque Miss Flowers always managed to stand out.

Born in Sherman, Texas, in 1900, Bess studied drama at the Carnegie Institute of Technology before journeying to Hollywood in 1922. Securing work almost immediately, she was seen in films for the next four decades. Her feature credits include *Hollywood* (1923), *A Woman of Paris* (1923), *It Happened One Night* (1934), *Private Worlds* (1935), *My Man Godfrey* (1936), *One in a Million* (1936), *The Awful Truth* (1937), *Holiday* (1938), *Ninotchka* (1939), *Meet John Doe* (1941), *Life Begins for Andy Hardy* (1941), *Springtime in the Rockies* (1942), *Girl Crazy* (1943), *Crazy House* (1943), *Mr. Skeffington*

Bess Flowers (seond from right) in a scene from *Society Mugs* (1946). Also pictured are Helen Benda, Tom Kennedy and Shemp Howard.

(1944), *Ghost Catchers* (1944), *Double Indemnity* (1944), *Billy Rose's Diamond Horseshoe* (1945), *Undercurrent* (1946), *The Secret Life of Walter Mitty* (1947), *The Barkleys of Broadway* (1949), *All About Eve* (1950), *Ghost Chasers* (1951), *The Bad and the Beautiful* (1952), *The Greatest Show on Earth* (1952), *The Caddy* (1953), *A Star Is Born* (1954), *Rear Window* (1954), *Hot Shots* (1956), *The Eddy Duchin Story* (1956), *Pal Joey* (1957) and *Good Neighbor Sam* (1964).

She also appeared in several Columbia shorts. One of her most memorable roles was as the newly rich Mrs. Smirch, who mistakes Moe Howard for Omay, a famous interior decorator, in *Tassels in the Air* (The Three Stooges, 1938).

Miss Flowers died on July 28, 1984, at the Motion Picture Country Home in Woodland Hills, California.

Hugh Herbert

Born on August 10, 1887, in Binghamton, New York, Hugh Herbert had been a stage actor, vaudeville performer and playwright prior to entering films in the late 1920s. He also had a brief career as a dialogue supervisor and screenwriter (though not to be confused with longtime screenwriter F. Hugh Herbert).

Herbert was a popular supporting comedian in many films of the 1930s and 40s, appearing in such pictures as *Hook, Line and Sinker* (1930), *Friends and Lovers* (1931), *Million Dollar Legs* (1932), *Diplomaniacs* (1933), *Dames* (1934), *Wonder Bar* (1934), *Gold Diggers of 1935* (1935), *A Midsummer Night's Dream* (1935), *Colleen* (1936), *Gold Diggers in Paris* (1938), *The Villain Still Pursued Her* (1941), *Hellzapoppin'* (1941), *The Black Cat* (1941), *Kismet* (1944), *So This Is New York* (1948), *A Song Is Born* (1948) and *The Beautiful Blonde from Bashful Bend* (1949).

His starring series of Columbia shorts ran from 1943 to 1952.

Herbert died of a heart attack on March 13, 1952, in North Hollywood.

Esther Howard

Born in 1893, Miss Howard had appeared on Broadway before going to Hollywood. Her feature film credits include *Merrily We Go to Hell* (1932), *Klondike Annie* (1936), *The Great McGinty* (1940), *Sullivan's Travels* (1941), *The Palm Beach Story* (1942), *Hail the Conquering Hero* (1944), *The Big Noise* (1944), *The Great Flamarion* (1945), *Detour* (1945), *The Champion* (1949) and *The Beautiful Blonde from Bashful Bend* (1949). Her best known role was as the drunken old floozy in RKO's *Murder, My Sweet* (1944).

She appeared in the Columbia shorts steadily from 1935 on through the early 1940s (usually cast as Andy Clyde's wife or sweetheart), returning to the unit briefly in the 1950s.

She died of a heart attack on March 8, 1965, at age 72, in Hollywood.

Shemp Howard (see The Three Stooges)

Bud Jamison

The roly-poly character actor best remembered for his roles in the Three Stooges shorts, in which he was often cast as a policeman, was born William Jamison on February 15, 1894, in Vallejo, California. He spent four years in stock companies and vaudeville before entering films in 1914. From 1915 to 1916 he was a supporting player in the majority of Charlie Chaplin's comedies for Essanay; he also appeared in several Harold Lloyd comedies.

Jamison worked steadily throughout the 1920s, appearing in such pictures as *Dante's Inferno* (1924), *The Cyclone Rider* (1924), *Ladies Beware* (1927), *Play Safe* (1927), and the Harry Langdon features *The Chaser* (1928) and *Heart Trouble* (1928).

In the 1930s Jamison was seen in two-reel comedies with Zasu Pitts,

Andy Clyde (right) helps Bud Jamison out of a tight spot in *Mister Smarty* (1936).

Thelma Todd, Clark & McCullough, Charley Chase, Buster Keaton, Bing Crosby, Edgar Kennedy and W.C. Fields.

Bud joined the Columbia shorts unit in 1933 and was featured in many of the two-reelers until 1944. He was one of the unit's most indispensable supporting players, capable of essaying a wide range of comic personalities (pompous barristers, jovial Irish cops and a French fur trapper, to name a few), all of which were played to perfection. During this period he also had supporting roles in several feature films, including *Ticket to Paradise* (1936), *Melody of the Plains* (1937), *Blondie* (1938), *Topper Takes a Trip* (1939), *Li'l Abner* (1940), *Her Cardboard Lover* (1942), *Holiday Inn* (1942), *True to Life* (1943) and *Billy Rose's Diamond Horseshoe* (1945).

After completing a bit part in *Nob Hill*, a 20th Century–Fox feature released in 1945, Jamison, a Christian Scientist, fell ill; he died on September 30, 1944, in Hollywood.

Fred Kelsey

Fred Kelsey was born on August 20, 1884, in Sandusky, Ohio. Entering films in 1909, he appeared in a countless number of feature films and short subjects. His feature credits include *The Four Horsemen of the Apocalypse* (1921), *Paths to Paradise* (1925), *The Gorilla* (1927), *Harold Teen* (1928), *Guilty as Hell* (1932), *Gold Diggers of 1933* (1933), *Twentieth Century* (1934), *One Frightened Night* (1935), *Diamond Jim* (1935), *A Damsel in Distress* (1937), *Happy Landing* (1938), *King's Row* (1941), *The Man Who Came to Dinner* (1941), *Gentleman Jim* (1942), *The Adventures of Mark Twain* (1944), *Christmas in Connecticut* (1945), *How Do You Do?* (1945), *My Reputation* (1946), *Nora Prentiss* (1947), *The Noose Hangs High* (1948), *Hans Christian Andersen* (1952) and *O. Henry's Full House* (1952).

He began appearing in the Columbia shorts in 1934 and remained a member of their stock company of supporting players until the early 1950s; he was usually cast as a befuddled cop or police inspector. Kelsey died on September 2, 1961, in Hollywood.

Tom Kennedy

Tom Kennedy was born in New York City in 1884. A former professional wrestler, he entered films in 1915, appearing in Mack Sennett's Keystone Comedies. He went on to play supporting roles in many features and shorts; his feature film credits include *Scaramouche* (1923), *Mantrap* (1926), *Tillie's Punctured Romance* (1928), *See America Thirst* (1930), *Monkey Business* (1931), *Pack Up Your Troubles* (1932), *She Done Him Wrong* (1933), *42nd Street* (1933), *Hollywood Party* (1934), *Bright Lights* (1935), *Poppy* (1936), *Go Chase Yourself* (1938), *The Day the Bookies Wept* (1939), *Remember the Night* (1940), *The Princess and the Pirate* (1944) and *The Paleface* (1948).

Kennedy joined Columbia's comedy shorts unit in 1935 for a starring series with Monte Collins; when the series ended in 1938, he continued to appear in the two-reelers, on and off, until 1953.

Throughout the 1950s and early 60s, Kennedy played roles on television and in such feature films as *Let's Go Navy* (1951), *Invasion U.S.A.* (1952), *Once Upon a Horse* (1958), *Some Like It Hot* (1959) and *It's a Mad, Mad, Mad, Mad World* (1963). He died of bone cancer on October 6, 1965, in Woodland Hills, California.

Fred Kelsey in a typical role: playing a comic policeman in the Vera Vague short *Hiss and Yell* (1946).

Frank Lackteen

Frank Lackteen was born August 29, 1894, in Kubber-Ilias, Asia Minor. The thin, slightly-built actor, who was frequently cast in sinister roles (both straight and comic), was seen in films as early as 1916. Among his feature credits are *Less Than Dust* (1916), *The Pony Express* (1925), *Cracked Nuts* (1931), *Escape from Devil's Island* (1935), *Anthony Adverse* (1936), *The Charge of the Light Brigade* (1936), *Mummy's Boys* (1936), *Juarez* (1939), *The Rains Came* (1939), *The Sea Wolf* (1941), *Moonlight and Cactus* (1944),

Singin' in the Corn (1947), *The Mysterious Desperado* (1949), *Kim* (1950), *King of the Khyber Rifles* (1953), *The Bounty Killer* (1954), *Flesh and the Spur* (1956), *The Atomic Submarine* (1959), *Three Came to Kill* (1960), *The Underwater City* (1962) and *Requiem for a Gunfighter* (1965).

Lackteen played supporting roles in Columbia shorts during the 1940s and 1950s, in addition to his many appearances in serials. He died of cerebral and respiratory illnesses on July 8, 1968, in Woodland Hills, California.

Richard Lane

Richard Lane was born May 28, 1899, in Rice Lake, Wisconsin. The son of a farm family, Lane began to foster an interest in performing at the age of eight. "My third-grade teacher saw me as a precocious kid, able to recite at the drop of a hat," he recalled. "I had a poem for everything . . . I was a real ham." He began doing repertory theater in the summers, and secured jobs by billing himself as "Richard Lane: Singing and Dancing Juvenile—Will Travel." By the time he was a teenager, he was a seasoned performer.

Lane held a number of jobs, staggering in their variety. He toured Europe with a circus, doing an "iron jaw" routine in which he hung by his teeth from a moving bar at the top of the circus tent; he faked his way into a band touring Australia, pretending to be able to play the drums ("By the time they found out, it was too late"); played the Palace in New York, doing a song-and-dance act; and appeared with the immortal Al Jolson in *Big Boy* at the Winter Garden Theatre.

Journeying to Hollywood in the 1930s, Lane embarked upon an equally varied film career, appearing in such pictures as *The Outcasts of Poker Flat* (1937), *Bringing Up Baby* (1938), *Carefree* (1938), *The Day the Bookies Wept* (1939), *Union Pacific* (1939), *Hellzapoppin'* (1941), *Time Out for Rhythm* (1941), *It Ain't Hay* (1943), *Here Comes the Coeds* (1945), *The Bullfighters* (1945) and *Take Me Out to the Ballgame* (1949). His most famous movie role was that of Inspector Farraday in Columbia's *Boston Blackie* series. Also at Columbia, he was teamed with Gus Schilling for a comedy shorts series that ran from 1945 to 1950.

Starting in the late 1940s, Lane figured prominently in the television industry, working as a newsman for KTLA, pitching used cars on "The Spade Cooley Show," and—as people best remember him—as the ringside announcer for the weekly wrestling matches and roller derby games. With his familiar cry of "Whoa, Nellie!" Lane's distinctive broadcasting style helped to popularize these events with television audiences. He remained on television until his semiretirement in 1976.

His last movie appearance was in *The One and Only* (1978). After a brief illness, Lane died on September 5, 1982, in Newport Beach, California.

Harry Langdon

Harry Langdon was born June 15, 1884, in Council Bluffs, Iowa. Both of his parents were officers in the Salvation Army, but their son opted instead to be a traveling entertainer. Leaving home at the age of twelve to join the circus, Harry subsequently worked in minstrel shows, acrobatic troupes, and knockabout burlesque. In 1903 he began a twenty-year stint in vaudeville, touring with his first wife, Rose, in a comedy sketch entitled "Johnny's New Car." He eventually fashioned a second routine, "After the Ball," written in 1913 by Langdon and Joe Smith (of the team of Smith & Dale). An essay in frustration on the golfing links, it proved exceeding popular, inspiring numerous imitations on the stage. Langdon's automobile sketch was revived in 1920 for a Broadway musical revue, *Jim Jam Jems*, costarring Joe E. Brown, Frank Fay, and Ned Sparks. While appearing at the Orpheum Theatre in 1923, Harry was signed for movies by independent producer Sol Lesser. A projected first release, *The Sky Scraper*, was announced in the trade papers; unfortunately, Lesser did not always copyright his releases, but in 1925 a Langdon short with that title was offered for state's rights release. Extant photographs do indeed show a rather callow Langdon sporting aviation garb before a biplane, but as of this writing no release has been authenticated.

Late in 1923 Lesser sold Langdon's contract to Mack Sennett, who immediately promoted the comic as "Sennett's Greatest Find Since Charlie Chaplin." Surprisingly, this boastful hyperbole eventually proved true: by 1926 Langdon was *the* exciting new comedy attraction in films. Leaving Sennett's, Langdon formed the Harry Langdon Corporation, producing six feature films — *Tramp, Tramp, Tramp* (1926), *The Strong Man* (1926), *Long Pants* (1927), *Three's a Crowd* (1927), *The Chaser* (1928) and *Heart Trouble* (1928) — and bankrupting himself in the process when he assumed the additional burden of directing the final three releases. With talkies on the horizon and three successive box office failures, Langdon spent the next fifteen years playing supporting roles in features — as in Lewis Milestone's *Hallelujah, I'm a Bum* (1933) starring Al Jolson — and leads in comedy shorts for most of the major short subjects departments in Hollywood at the time: Hal Roach, Educational, Paramount, RKO, and Columbia. Nell O'Day, Harry's lovely leading lady in three shorts for Educational and one for Paramount, has fond memories of working with the comedian: "Mr. Langdon was absolutely charming. He had very much the same kind of personality offscreen that he had as his character in films — a sort of sweet helplessness."

Langdon's final years were exceptionally busy: a tour of Australia as "Moonface" in the road company of Cole Porter's *Anything Goes* in 1936; a stopover in England, where he directed a feature comedy titled *Wise Guys* (1937); then back to the States, where he coauthored four Laurel & Hardy features: *Block-Heads* (1938), *The Flying Deuces* (1939), *A Chump at Oxford* (1940) and *Saps at Sea* (1940). As late as 1943 Harry was touring in the East with former screen moppet Edith Fellows in an act that revived material from his vaudeville routines of forty years previous. Langdon continued to be active in pictures and completed his final Columbia short, *Pistol Packin' Nitwits*, only weeks before his death of a cerebral hemorrhage on December 22, 1944. As a courtesy to the Langdon family and as a symbol of their lifelong friendship, Harry's onscreen cohort, Vernon Dent, handled all the funeral arrangements.

Eddie Laughton

Born in Sheffield, England, in 1903, Eddie Laughton was a vaudeville performer prior to being placed under contract to Columbia. His feature film credits include *Smashing the Spy Ring* (1938), *The Lone Wolf Spy Hunt* (1939), *Beware, Spooks!* (1939), *The Talk of the Town* (1942), *The Boogie Man Will Get You* (1942), *The Girl in the Case* (1944), *The Lost Weekend* (1945), *The Shocking Miss Pilgrim* (1947) and *Chicken Every Sunday* (1949).

Laughton was a supporting player in Columbia shorts from the late 1930s until the mid-1940s; during this period, he also served as the straight man for the Three Stooges when the team made personal appearances in between film assignments.

Laughton died of pneumonia on March 21, 1952, in Hollywood.

Ted Lorch

Theodore A. Lorch was born in Springfield, Illinois, in 1873. After performing on the stage and in vaudeville, Lorch entered films in the 1920s; his feature credits include *Gasoline Gus* (1921), *Shell Shocked Sammy* (1923), *The Sea Hawk* (1924), *Black Jack* (1927), *King of Kings* (1927), *Show Boat* (1929), *Spite Marriage* (1929), *The Runaway Bride* (1930), *Black Beauty* (1933), *Hold 'Em Yale* (1935), *Romance Rides the Range* (1936) and *Stagecoach* (1939).

Lorch also appeared in numerous short subjects. His best-known roles are as the High Priest in the first *Flash Gordon* serial (1936) and as Professor Sedletz, who believes that heredity is a greater influence on a person's behavior than environment, in the Three Stooges comedy *Half-Wits Holiday* (1947). He died on November 12, 1947, in Hollywood.

Del Lord

Del Lord was born in Grimsley, Canada, in 1895. He journeyed West with stage actor William Collier, Sr., and doubled for him in the first picture Collier made on the Coast. Later, Lord worked as an extra in Mack Sennett's Keystone Comedies and, while still in his teens, became the driver of the Keystone Kops paddy wagon. It was during this period that young Del impressed Sennett with his ability to stage truly spectacular auto stunts and

Eddie Laughton (right) shows Charley Chase that he's also a member of the Lodge of Hoot Owls in *The Grand Hooter* (1937).

chases. From Keystone, Lord went to work for Fox Studios; before long, he was commissioned to direct, unassisted, comedians Bobby Dunn and Glen Cavender.

By the early 1920s he was back at Sennett's, directing two-reel comedies with Billy Bevan, Ben Turpin and others on the lot. During the years 1927 and 1928 Lord worked for First National, United Artists and Educational Pictures. By 1929 he was back with Sennett, directing a series of comedies starring Jack Cooper.

In the early 1930s Lord free-lanced, intermittently directing shorts for Sennett as well as the *Vitaphone Varieties* for First National and several of Hal Roach's *Taxi Boys* comedies. By 1932 he was again with Sennett, who was now distributing his films through Paramount. However, Sennett's studio was then on its last legs; in 1933 Sennett declared bankruptcy and Lord, unable to secure other directorial assignments, found a job selling used cars.

In 1935 Lord went to work for Columbia's comedy shorts unit. Jules White recalls, "Arthur Ripley came to me one day and said, 'Do you know who's selling used cars on Ventura Boulevard? Del Lord!' So I got in contact with Del and told him, 'We've got a comedy starting tomorrow — and I want you to come in and direct it.' " Lord turned out some of the finest work in the history of the unit, directing Andy Clyde, the Three Stooges, Charley Chase, Harry Langdon and other comedians on the roster. During this time he also worked on feature films, directing *Trapped by Television* (1936), *What Price Vengeance* (1937) and second unit work for Tay Garnett's *She Couldn't Take It* (1935) and Frank Capra's *Mr. Deeds Goes to Town* (1936).

Throughout the 1940s, Lord produced (with Hugh McCollum) and directed two-reelers for the department; he also directed a few low-budget Columbia programmers, such as *Kansas City Kitty* (1944) with Joan Davis, *She's a Sweetheart* (1944) with Larry Parks and Jane Frazee, *Rough, Tough and Ready* (1945) with Chester Morris and Victor McLaglen, and *I Love a Bandleader* (1945) with Phil Harris. In 1949 he left the comedy shorts unit to concentrate on feature film work.

Little is known about Lord's activities during the 1950s and 1960s. In 1952 he directed Buster Keaton in *Paradise for Buster*, a thirty-nine minute industrial film produced by Wilding Picture Productions for John Deere and Company.

Del Lord died on March 23, 1970, in Vista, California.

Emmett Lynn

Emmett Lynn was born February 14, 1897, in Muscatine, Iowa. His career spanned movies, stage, vaudeville, burlesque and radio. He started in films when he was a teenager, working for Biograph in 1913.

Emmett is best known for his many appearances in "B" Westerns, playing the unshaven, toothless saddletramp sidekick of such cowboy stars as Don "Red" Barry and Allan "Rocky" Lane. A familiar face in films of the 1940s and 1950s, his feature credits include *Scatterbrain* (1940), *Along the Rio Grande* (1941), *Baby Face Morgan* (1942), *The Spoilers* (1942), *Bluebeard* (1944), *Rustlers of Devil's Canyon* (1947), *The Scarf* (1951), *Monkey Business* (1952), *Pickup on South Street* (1953), *Living It Up* (1954) and *A Man Called Peter* (1955).

Lynn appeared as a supporting player in Columbia comedy shorts from the 1940s and 1950s, most notably in several Andy Clyde comedies.

He died of a heart attack on October 20, 1958, in Hollywood.

Hugh McCollum

Hugh McCollum was born March 9, 1900, in Ridley Park, Pennsylvania. He attended the Episcopal Academy in Philadelphia and spent one year at the University of Pennsylvania.

He journeyed West and, in 1921, worked as a clerk at the Hotel Ambassador in Los Angeles. In 1922 he became an assistant to John McCormick of First National Pictures; from 1924 to 1925 he served as assistant to R.A. Rowland at First National's New York office. By 1926 McCollum was back on the West Coast, once again as an assistant to McCormick. From 1927 to 1928 he served as a business manager for various film companies, including First National.

In February 1929, McCollum became secretary to Harry Cohn, the head of Columbia Pictures. In 1933 he was assistant to Sam Briskin, Columbia's production chief; in 1934 he became the business manager for Columbia's short subjects department.

McCollum was elevated to the position of short subjects producer in 1937, sharing production chores equally with Jules White. Affectionately referred to as "Mac," McCollum was primarily concerned with business matters and left most of the creative decisions to others (although he did suggest and veto ideas and even wound up directing a handful of the comedies himself). Very often, he shared his producer's credit with writer-director-comedian Charley Chase and director Del Lord.

In 1952 he was ousted in a power play instigated by Jules White, who then assumed responsibility of the entire unit. McCollum later became production manager for Gene Autry's Flying A Productions, which made Autry's films. He died in 1963.

Kenneth MacDonald

Born Kenneth Dollins in Portland, Indiana, in 1901, MacDonald began his career in the 1920s, acting in stage productions all over the United States. He came to Hollywood in the early 1930s and appeared in bit parts in several films. In 1933 he wrote "The Case of Kenneth MacDonald," a self-promotional booklet he distributed to motion picture producers; it was an attempt to secure larger roles, and the effort paid off. He went on to play supporting roles in many films throughout the 1930s, most notably in Columbia Charles Starrett westerns.

He began appearing in the Columbia comedy shorts in 1946. His suave demeanor, vibrant vocal timbre and flawless delivery made him a perfect foil for comedians like the Three Stooges and Hugh Herbert. Like many of the supporting players who were seen in both features and shorts, MacDonald was given a greater opportunity to display his comic timing in these little two-reelers than in the more "prestigious" feature productions. He remained a fixture of the comedy shorts stock company until 1955.

MacDonald's later feature credits include *The Caine Mutiny* (1954), *Francis in the Navy* (1955), *The Ten Commandments* (1956), *The She-Creature* (1956), *The Ladies' Man* (1961), *The Errand Boy* (1961), *The One and Only Genuine Original Family Band* (1968) and *Which Way to the Front?* (1970). He also made numerous television appearances, including the role as the judge in sixty episodes of the *Perry Mason* series. His final appearance was in "The Test," an episode of *The F.B.I.* series.

MacDonald died on May 5, 1972, at age 70, at the Motion Picture Country Home in Woodland Hills, California; he had been a patient there for several months.

Character actor Kenneth MacDonald (second from right) was a superb comic villain in many Columbia shorts. Here he's seen with Moe Howard (left) and Larry Fine in this shot from the Three Stooges comedy *Loose Loot* (1953).

Christine McIntyre

Of all the supporting players who appeared in the Columbia shorts, Christine McIntyre remains the undisputed favorite. Her beauty and finely honed comic timing have endeared her to comedy aficionados, who are now beginning to realize that she was a vastly underrated comedienne. She was also something of a mystery woman, as very little biographical data is available on her.

Miss McIntyre received a Bachelor of Music degree from the Chicago Musical College. After trying her luck on radio, she entered films in the late 1930s. *The Rangers' Roundup* (1938), a Fred Scott western, is her earliest known movie credit.

She became a protege of short subjects producer Hugh McCollum and in 1943 she began appearing in the Columbia comedy shorts. Initially, she was merely a cipher used for decorative purposes. But within a couple of years she developed into a first-rate comedienne, playing innocent damsels and conniving vamps with equal finesse. Christine had a fine operatic voice and was given the opportunity to sing in a few of the films. Her best remembered role

The beautiful Christine McIntyre as she appears in the Three Stooges comedy *Micro-Phonies* (1945).

is in the Three Stooges short *Micro-Phonies* (1945), as an aspiring vocalist whose recording of "The Voice of Spring" is pilfered by the trio. She remained with the unit until 1954, although she was seen — courtesy of stock footage — in several shorts after that. She retired from show business around this time, when she married J. Donald Wilson, a pioneer writer, director, and producer during the early days of radio.

In addition to the two-reelers, Christine also appeared in feature films at Monogram, including *Partners of the Trail* (1947), *West of the Rio Grande* (1947), *Land of the Lawless* (1947), *Valley of Fear* (1947), *News Hounds* (1947), *Gun Talk* (1947), *A Modern Marriage* (1950) and *Colorado Ambush* (1951). Unlike the Columbia shorts, however, these pictures never took advantage of her comic skills.

"Of all the people I worked with, Christine was one of my favorites," says Emil Sitka. "She was so nice, so sweet; a real joy." Ed Bernds, who directed her many times, adds, "Chris would give you a performance that surpassed your expectations — and you always expected a lot from her. She had the rare ability of indulging in the zany antics and still remaining a real lady, which is what she was."

Christine McIntyre died of cancer on July 8, 1984, in Northridge, California.

Bob McKenzie

Robert B. McKenzie was born September 22, 1883 in Bellymania, Ireland. He had been a stage actor prior to entering films in 1915; his movie credits include *A Knight of the West* (1921), *Fightin' Devil* (1922), *The Desert Hawk* (1924), *A Six Shootin' Romance* (1926), *The White Outlaw* (1929), *Cimarron* (1931), *Tillie and Gus* (1933), *You're Telling Me* (1934), *The Little Minister* (1934), *The Bride Goes Home* (1935), *Hideaway* (1937), *Blondie Takes a Vacation* (1939), *Saps at Sea* (1940), *In Old California* (1942), *Jive Junction* (1943), *Tall in the Saddle* (1944) and *Duel in the Sun* (1946).

McKenzie appeared in Columbia shorts during the 1930s and 40s, most notably in a few Andy Clyde comedies. McKenzie's wife Eva (1889–1967) and daughter Ella (who was married to comedian Billy Gilbert) also had film careers, and were seen in a number of the Columbia two-reelers.

Bob McKenzie died of a heart attack on July 8, 1949, in Rhode Island.

James C. Morton

Born in 1884 in Helena, Montana, James C. Morton was a stage and vaudeville actor prior to entering films. Throughout the 1930s, he appeared in several Hal Roach comedies with Laurel & Hardy, Charley Chase, Zasu Pitts, Thelma Todd, Patsy Kelly and Our Gang.

Morton's feature film credits include *Follow the Leader* (1930), *Pack Up Your Troubles* (1932), *Our Relations* (1936), *Way Out West* (1937), *Rhythm in the Clouds* (1937), *Topper Takes a Trip* (1939), *Saps at Sea* (1940), *Never Give a Sucker an Even Break* (1941) and *The Boogie Man Will Get You* (1942).

In 1935 Morton began playing supporting roles in the Columbia shorts. His character was often embarrassed and exasperated by the removal of his toupee, as in the Three Stooges short *Disorder in the Court* (1936) in which Morton's toupee comes loose from his bald dome and is mistaken for a tarantula.

He died on October 24, 1942, in Reseda, California.

Eddie Quillan

Born March 31, 1907 in Philadelphia, Pennsylvania, Eddie Quillan started in show business at an early age. When he was seven, he was performing with his sister and three brothers. Their act, "The Rising Generation," was successful, and a subsequent screen test for Mack Sennett resulted in a movie contract for Eddie. After eighteen two-reelers for the "King of Comedy," Eddie objected to the off-color material in an upcoming script and left the studio. After two shorts for Jack White at Educational Pictures, he secured roles in feature films, with his big break coming in Cecil B. De Mille's *The*

Godless Girl (1929). He played the lead role in Leo McCarey's *The Sophomore* (1929) and starred with the rest of the Quillan family in *Noisy Neighbors* (1929).

With the advent of talking pictures, Eddie continued to appear in many feature films (in roles ranging from leads to bit parts), including *Big Money* (1930), *The Tip-Off* (1931), *The Big Shot* (1931), *Girl Crazy* (1932), *Broadway to Hollywood* (1933), *Gridiron Flash* (1934), *Hollywood Party* (1934), *Mutiny on the Bounty* (1935), *Fury* (1936), *London by Night* (1937), *The Flying Irishman* (1939), *Allegheny Uprising* (1939), *Young Mr. Lincoln* (1939), *The Grapes of Wrath* (1940), *The Flame of New Orleans* (1941), *Kid Glove Killer* (1942), *Priorities on Parade* (1942), *It Ain't Hay* (1943), *Here Comes Kelly* (1943), *Side Show* (1950), *Brigadoon* (1954), *Papa's Delicate Condition* (1963), *Viva Las Vegas* (1964), *Zebra in the Kitchen* (1965) and *The Ghost and Mr. Chicken* (1966).

Quillan was teamed with Wally Vernon for a Columbia comedy shorts series that ran from 1948 to 1956.

Eddie has also been seen on television, as a regular on *Julia* (1968–71) and as a guest star on several shows, including *Mannix, Police Story, Lucas Tanner* and *Baretta*. Still active in the business, he has recently appeared on episodes of *Little House on the Prairie, Father Murphy, Highway to Heaven, Hell Town* and *Moonlighting*. He resides in North Hollywood.

Arthur Ripley

Arthur DeWitt Ripley was born in the Bronx, New York, in 1895. As a youth he had artistic ambitions, aspired to dance, and played the trumpet. In 1909 he got a job cleaning negatives at the Kalem Studios for eight dollars a week. Three years later he became a film cutter at the Brooklyn Vitagraph Studio. Brought to the West Coast by director Rex Ingram in 1916, Ripley was eventually hired by Universal, where Irving Thalberg assigned him the monumental task of reducing Erich Von Stroheim's thirty-two reel *Foolish Wives* (1922) to a commercial length of eleven reels.

Ripley joined the Mack Sennett Studio in 1923 as a combination gag man and story editor. Along with Sennett alumni Harry Edwards and Frank Capra, he went on to join the Harry Langdon Corporation, coauthoring with Capra *The Strong Man* (1926) and *Long Pants* (1927). An argument between director Capra and screenwriter Ripley resulted in Capra's dismissal, whereupon Ripley codirected (sans screen credit) with Langdon three features: *Three's a Crowd* (1927), *The Chaser* (1928) and *Heart Trouble* (1928). All three pictures thudded at the box office. Ripley returned to Sennett's, this time as a full-fledged director. His notable achievements were the W.C. Fields shorts *The Pharmacist* and *The Barber Shop* (both 1933).

Ripley was one of the first members of the Columbia short subjects department to be hired by Jules White. There he was chiefly responsible for the recently inaugurated Harry Langdon series.

Finding his burgeoning artistic ambitions stifled by the time restrictions and subject matter, Ripley left Columbia in the late 1930s and spent the next twenty years promoting personal projects like the interesting noir thriller *Voice in the Wind* (1944), which, as he grumbled to a coworker, was rejected by the film industry because "everybody's too damn stupid to know what I was talking about." Says Sam White, a longtime friend of Ripley's:

> He was a little fond of the grape for the particular reason [that] he was frustrated. He was a brilliant guy but he had personality idiosyncrasies everyone did not cotton to.
>
> We used to call Ripley "The Antelope" because every time he'd get an idea that he thought was funny, he'd leap in the air like an antelope, and we used to laugh so hard; he was basically a funny man. He was long and drawn and skinny, with a face that was kind of sallow; he had a small head, almost like a pinhead, and he wore a mustache. I think he was about six feet, two inches tall.
>
> He adapted one of the great books of all time, Thomas Wolfe's *Look Homeward, Angel*, into a magnificent screenplay and he took it to MGM, but they didn't understand it the way Ripley saw it. He fought for principle, even to his own detriment. He fought for principle all the time. I think that was his undoing. He was too smart for his own good; he turned people off because his enthusiasm would drive them crazy.

In 1954 Kenneth Macgowan, a good friend of Ripley's, was organizing the theatre arts and cinema arts departments at the University of California at Los Angeles. (In addition to being an author and teacher, Macgowan was a film producer whose credits include *Little Women* (1933), *Anne of Green Gables* (1934), *Becky Sharp* (1935), *Young Mr. Lincoln* (1939), *Lifeboat* (1944) and *Jane Eyre* (1944).) Macgowan prevailed upon Ripley to become the first professor of cinema arts techniques. Ripley loved the idea of teaching students about editing, writing and directing, so he left active film production and became the founder of the UCLA Film Center (although he was beckoned out of retirement for Robert Mitchum's low-budget folktale *Thunder Road* in 1958). He made it a practical approach to learning how to make motion pictures. Instead of working out theories on a blackboard, Ripley saw to it that the students had all the necessary equipment at their disposal: moviolas, cutting rooms, and the like. When he couldn't get studios to donate what was needed, he begged the university to purchase the equipment. And he helped to build the university's motion picture library into an impressive collection.

Ripley eventually contracted lung cancer. Sam White recalls:

> My brother Jules and I were doing a half-hour comedy pilot for CBS titled "Oh, Those Bells!" with the Wiere Brothers. I wanted Rip to read the script and tell me what he thought of it. I called him at UCLA and he said, "Well, send it out; I'll be glad to take a look at it."
>
> And of course his reaction was the same as always: "That's the worst

bunch of shit I ever read in my life! How in the hell can they make that thing?"

I said, "Rip, they like it here."

"What the hell do they know about making motion pictures at CBS? They don't know anything! They're just a bunch of goddamned knotheads." And he went on cursing.

I said, "Tell me something constructive."

So he started breaking it down for me and told me we had things in there for no rhyme or reason. "There's no basis for any of the comedy whatsoever!"

So I contradicted him. We argued back and forth, and he finally said, "I'm not feeling well." It was then that he informed me that he had cancer. When I asked him what he was going to do, he said, "Well, I know where I'm going. I'm going to the Motion Picture Country Home and die." And he did.

Arthur Ripley died on February 15, 1961. An introspective, brooding man, he nevertheless possessed a keen insight into the worth of the cinema's past, and if his talent was often misguided, he was an original thinker in a typically plagiaristic business. "The nicest thing you could say about me," he stated in a 1944 interview, "is that you met somebody in this town who still has good intentions . . . to bring poetry and imagination back to the screen."

Gene Roth

Born Gene Stutenroth on January 8, 1903, in South Dakota, the actor used his real last name for several years before shortening it to "Roth." He appeared in supporting roles in over 190 films, including *Nightmare Alley* (1947), *Red Planet Mars* (1952), *Call Me Madam* (1953), *The Spider* (1958), *Attack of the Giant Leeches* (1959), *G.I. Blues* (1960), *Ada* (1961), *The Three Stooges Meet Hercules* (1962), *Young Dillinger* (1965), *Rosie!* (1968) and numerous "B" Westerns.

Roth began appearing in the Columbia comedy shorts in the mid-1940s and worked for the unit until it was shut down in 1958. He was usually cast as a comic heavy.

During the 1970s Roth was a popular guest speaker at western film nostalgia conventions. He died on July 19, 1976, in Los Angeles, after being struck by a car while crossing the street.

Gus Schilling

Born August E. Schilling on June 20, 1908, in New York City, Gus had been a stage and burlesque performer (at one time he was married to famed burlesque stripper Betty Rowland) prior to entering films in 1940. He played supporting roles in a number of feature films, including *Mexican Spitfire Out*

West (1940), *Citizen Kane* (1941), *It Started with Eve* (1941), *The Magnificent Ambersons* (1942), *Broadway* (1942), *You Were Never Lovelier* (1942), *Hers to Hold* (1943), *Chatterbox* (1943), *See My Lawyer* (1945), *Dangerous Business* (1946), *Calendar Girl* (1947), *Macbeth* (1948), *The Lady from Shanghai* (1948), *Bride for Sale* (1949), *Our Very Own* (1950), *Honeychile* (1951), *One Big Affair* (1952), *Executive Suite* (1954), *Run for Cover* (1955), *Glory* (1956) and *Bigger Than Life* (1956).

He was teamed with Richard Lane for a starring series of Columbia comedy shorts that ran from 1945 to 1950.

Schilling died on June 16, 1957, in Hollywood; although reports claimed that his death was due to a heart attack, Edward Bernds and Emil Sitka recall that Gus committed suicide.

Cy Schindell

Born Seymore Schindell in 1907, Cy had been a boxer before he turned to acting as a profession. With his thick features and punch-drunk style of delivering dialogue, Schindell played roles as heavies, first on stage, then in films. His movie credits include *The Face Behind the Mask* (1941), *Wildcat* (1942), *It's a Wonderful Life* (1946) and *Copacabana* (1947).

He appeared in Columbia shorts of the 1930s and 1940s, usually playing a comic adversary.

Schindell left the movie business for a while in the early 1940s, enlisting in the Marines during World War II. While serving on Guadalcanal, he developed a severe case of "jungle rot" (a general term for any fungus infection of the skin) under his arms. Cy returned to films in the mid-1940s. A mole had developed on his back; a medical examination disclosed that he had cancer. Ed Bernds recalls, "Cy always worked hard, giving his all, despite his illness."

Schindell died on August 24, 1948, in Hollywood.

Emil Sitka

One of the unit's most skilled and versatile supporting players, Emil Sitka brought a razor-sharp sense of comic timing to all his roles, weaving subtle nuances into the broadest slapstick antics. Thanks to his stage training, he was able to essay a wide variety of roles, playing everything from janitors and clerks to professors and millionaires, all with equal aplomb. Producer Hugh McCollum used to say, "Just leave it to Emil—he'll come up with the character."

As a teenager, Emil was raised in a Catholic convent in Pittsburgh, Pennsylvania. The convent was taken over by Father Cox, the leading priest in Pittsburgh; once a year, Father Cox supervised a performance of *A Passion Play*. Emil, who was studying to be a priest, appeared in the annual performances, with his roles growing in stature each succeeding year. When some of the

Cy Schindell (left) does a good job of intimidating the Three Stooges in *Fright Night* (1947).

better actors in the group were selected to play with the Pittsburgh Stock Company, Emil was one of the six actors (out of fifty) chosen.

The Depression sidetracked Sitka's acting pursuits, as he wound up working in a factory. In time, he ended up on the West Coast; he explains, "When Pittsburgh got flooded and the factory I worked at for two years was totally under water, I went to the Greyhound Bus Station and asked, 'What's the farthest destination you go to?' It turned out to be Los Angeles." With suitcase and all his savings in tow, he made the pilgrimage out to the movie capital.

One day, Emil, who had found work as a laborer, was walking by a little theater in Hollywood; stopping to look at the photographs of the latest stage production, the manager came out and invited him to watch a rehearsal. "He asked me, 'Why don't you take a little part?' and before I knew it, I was in the play. I had to work until three o'clock in the afternoon, so right after work I'd come to rehearsal and that night they'd put on a play. I wasn't going to do more than one, but when the theatre reviewers singled me out, the director said, 'See? You should work in some more.' "

Emil continued to work with small theater groups and stock companies in the area, playing every conceivable type of role, not only in comedies but productions of Maxim Gorky's *The Lower Depths*, Eugene O'Neill's *Anna*

Christie, William Saroyan's *The Time of Your Life*, and Upton Sinclair's *Depression Island, Roadside*, and *Pardon My Claws* as well. He was involved in about seventy plays, often serving as stage manager and director in addition to essaying a lead role. "This was all for no pay," he says. "None of these little theaters paid. I just did it because I loved to act. In 1946 I was selected as Best Actor by *Playgoer Magazine*. Even after I started working in films, I still worked in little theaters and stock companies."

While appearing in a play called *The Viper's Fang*, he was spotted by a talent scout from Columbia Pictures and was instructed to report to Jules White, the head of the studio's comedy shorts department. After meeting with White (for an in-depth account of this meeting see the "Casting" section of "The Comedy Shorts Department: A Close-Up"), Sitka was hired for a bit part in his first film, a Vera Vague short titled *Hiss and Yell* (1946). This began a long association with Columbia (he remained with the comedy shorts unit until its demise in 1958). Like Vernon Dent, Bud Jamison and Christine McIntyre, Sitka proved to be a valuable member of the stock company of supporting players. Although he worked steadily in films after that, Emil still held down an outside job. "That's one thing you have to know," he comments. "All my life I had an eight-to-five job while I was doing movie work. I had seven children, so I had to work every day. I used to take time off from these jobs in order to work in pictures."

The exposure he received in the comedy shorts led to roles in feature films for Columbia and other studios. His credits include *Fighting Mad* (1947), *Blondie's Secret* (1948), *Blondie Hits the Jackpot* (1949), *Rock Island Trail* (1949), *Feudin' Rhythm* (1949), *Beware of Blondie* (1950), *Kill the Umpire* (1950), *The Good Humor Man* (1950), *The Fuller Brush Girl* (1950), *Texas Dynamo* (1950), *The Well* (1951), *Bowery Battalion* (1951), *Fighting Coast Guard* (1951), *Gasoline Alley* (1951), *Let's Go Navy* (1951), *A Millionaire for Christy* (1951), *The Sea Hornet* (1951), *Gobs and Gals* (1951), *Sound Off* (1952), *Harem Girl* (1952), *Tropical Heat Wave* (1952), *All Ashore* (1953), *A Perilous Journey* (1953), *Private Eyes* (1953), *Geraldine* (1953), *Jubilee Trail* (1953), *Jungle Gents* (1954), *Three for the Show* (1955), *New York Confidential* (1955), *Carolina Cannonball* (1955), *Timberjack* (1955), *My Sister Eileen* (1955), *The Blackboard Jungle* (1955), *The Spoilers* (1955), *Gunsight Pass* (1955), *Over-Exposed* (1956), *Affair in Reno* (1956), *Crashing Las Vegas* (1956), *The 27th Day* (1957), *Who Was That Lady?* (1960), *The Three Stooges Meet Hercules* (1962), *The Three Stooges in Orbit* (1962), *The Three Stooges Go Around the World in a Daze* (1963), *The Outlaws Is Coming!* (1965), *The Mad Room* (1969), *Pendulum* (1969) and *Watermelon Man* (1970). Emil also made numerous TV appearances, on such shows as "The Third Man," "The Bob Cummings Show," "Father Knows Best," "Highway Patrol," "The Red Skelton Show," "My Little Margie," "Circus Boy," Schlitz Playhouse of Stars," "The Man Called X," and "Crusader."

Not only does Emil have the distinction of being the only supporting player to have worked with all four versions of the Three Stooges, he was to

Columbia supporting player Emil Sitka as he appears in the Hugh Herbert short *Honeymoon Blues* (1946).

become a member of the team for the fifth set. In 1971 Moe Howard asked him to replace Larry Fine (who had suffered a stroke the previous year and was partially paralyzed) for a production that was scheduled to be filmed on location in the Philippines. Sitka recalls:

Moe and I were good friends for years. He used to say that someday I would be one of the Stooges; I wasn't sure whether he was kidding or not, so I just took it as a compliment. When this Philippine project came along and the team had to be restructured because Larry was incapacitated, Moe came to me and told me to do a little soul-searching and really consider becoming a Stooge. I met with Larry and he approved of Moe's idea; Larry wanted me more than anyone else to assume the role in this and all other subsequent films with the Stooges.

However, this project never went beyond the planning stage. A recently published account of the meeting between the Stooges and a prospective producer claims that Emil demanded a limousine and said, "Well, I don't know if I'm available," implying that he was a contributing factor in the producer's withdrawal from the project. This story caused Emil a great deal of grief, and he remains unforgiving towards the source of this malicious distortion:

When I read that account, it hurt and shocked me. Especially when I was aware of dozens of capable actors eager to be considered for this opportunity. It's an entirely erroneous version of what happened. The truth is that even before we went to this meeting, Moe came to me and asked me to bring up a few questions that he himself wanted to know the answers to. He was a little leery about the whole deal, what with it being financed and produced, directed and distributed in a country like the Philippines. Mind you, this meeting was for the purpose of this producer okaying me as Larry's replacement. Because of Moe's uneasiness about the whole package, I agreed to make these inquiries.

During the course of this meeting, and in friendly course of conversation, I brought up the points that Moe was curious about: Was this production going to be within the guidelines and jurisdiction of the Screen Actors Guild? Were the film's finances deposited in a U.S. bank, as opposed to one in the Philippines? Was the distribution of the film going to include and guarantee showings in the U.S.? Moe had a hunch it would only be shown in foreign countries, and [he had] other misgivings. And what was going to be the method of payment? Deferred salaries, or whatever? Because Moe was no longer the strong voice for the Stooges in their business dealings, these are things he wanted me to ask, instead of himself. All were answered with "We're working on that . . . we'll see," and "Yes, that's being looked into," but no definite answer. Contrary to the false impression put forth, the atmosphere of this meeting was very congenial, very amiable. The producer not only accepted me, he said that he felt I might even do a better job than Larry. Moe was happy and we went away with high anticipations.

But this other story, in a book that purports to be true, complete and accurate, is totally false. It saddens and angers me, because my friends and fans who seek the truth about the Stooges deserve the real facts.

Moe told me shortly afterwards that the deal didn't go through. "We did not get the right answers to our questions. Be glad it didn't go through," he said. "But Emil, you're still going to be a Stooge," he predicted.

Four years later, to the month, Emil was indeed signed to be one of the Stooges for the Samuel M. Sherman production of *The Jet Set*. But Moe Howard died during the very week this new set of Stooges was due on location in Palm Springs, so the team was replaced by the Ritz Brothers, thus denying Emil his predicted role in the fifth set of the Stooges legend. (*The Jet Set* was eventually released under the title *Blazing Stewardesses*.)

Emil resides in Camarillo, California, and appeared in a comedy role in a new feature titled *The XYZ Murders*. After a sixteen-year absence from the screen, it's welcome news that he's back in front of the cameras with more of his wonderful contributions to film comedy.

Frank Sully

Born in 1908, Frank Sully had appeared in vaudeville and on Broadway prior to entering films in 1935. He played supporting roles in over 1200 films, including *Mary Burns, Fugitive* (1935), *Fury* (1936), *Some Like It Hot* (1939), *Grapes of Wrath* (1940), *The Fighting 69th* (1940), *Lillian Russell* (1940), *My Sister Eileen* (1942), *The Talk of the Town* (1942), *Thousands Cheer* (1943), *The More the Merrier* (1943), *Two Girls and a Sailor* (1944), *Father's Little Dividend* (1951), *With a Song in My Heart* (1952), *Pal Joey* (1957), *The Last Hurrah* (1958) and *Funny Girl* (1968).

Sully was seen in a number of Columbia shorts from the 1940s and 50s, playing supporting roles ranging from jealous boyfriends to irate neighbors.

He died on December 17, 1975, at age sixty-seven, in Woodland Hills, California.

The Three Stooges

One of the zaniest comedy teams in motion picture history was also the most indestructible. Throughout the years, the membership of the Three Stooges underwent a number of changes; Moe Howard and Larry Fine remained the steadfast members of the team, while the role of "third Stooge" was essayed by four different comedians, three of whom had their own comedy shorts series at Columbia.

Moe Howard was born Moses Horwitz on June 19, 1897, in Bensonhurst, New York. He entered films in 1909, playing small roles in several productions at the Vitagraph Studios in Brooklyn. In 1914 Moe joined a riverboat troupe, performing in *Ten Nights in a Barroom* and other melodramas of that ilk. During the World War I years, Moe and older brother Shemp (born Samuel Horwitz on March 17, 1895, in Brooklyn, New York) formed a blackface act and played the various vaudeville circuits.

Ted Healy, a boyhood friend of Moe's, had become a successful vaudeville comic; in 1922 Moe joined his act, serving as Healy's "stooge." Later, Shemp also joined the act.

In 1925 Larry Fine became a member of Healy's act. Born Louis Feinberg on October 5, 1902, in Philadelphia, Pennsylvania, Larry was a veteran of the vaudeville circuit, having been a member of Gus Edwards' Newsboy Sextet and part of a trio known as the Haney Sisters and Fine.

Ted Healy and His Stooges, as the act was called, fared well in vaudeville and on Broadway. In 1930 they appeared in their first film, *Soup to Nuts*, billed as "Ted Healy and His Racketeers." Shortly thereafter, Moe, Larry and Shemp parted company with Healy and formed their own act, "Three Lost Souls." In 1932 they rejoined Healy for a Broadway revue, *The Passing Show of 1932*; that same year, Shemp, disillusioned by Healy's frequently erratic behavior, left the act and embarked upon a solo career.

Moe's younger brother Jerry (born Jerome Lester Horwitz on October 22, 1903, in Brooklyn, New York) was selected to take Shemp's place. Christened "Curly," Jerry, who had limited experience as a performer, quickly adapted to the act's wild brand of roughhouse humor.

In 1933 Metro-Goldwyn-Mayer placed Healy and His Stooges under contract, where they appeared in two-reel shorts and feature films, both separately and as a team.

Moe, Larry and Curly parted with Healy in 1934; that same year they signed with Columbia Pictures, launching a series of two-reel comedy shorts that would make them world-famous.

The Stooges' offscreen personalities differed from their onscreen icons. Emil Sitka, who worked with all of them, recalls:

> Moe was very serious, very businesslike. He wasn't the type who went around cracking jokes. He was the brains of the team; he made all the business decisions. Larry was happy-go-lucky; he acted as though he didn't have a care in the world. As soon as the director yelled "Cut," Larry would be checking on the latest baseball scores and horse races. Curly was quiet, polite and introverted; not a show-off at all. But when the director was outlining a scene, you could tell he was thinking about what he was going to do. He was mulling over in his mind how he could fill in the scene with a "n'yuk, n'yuk" or "woo woo." Shemp was outgoing. He was always clowning and telling stories; you could always count on him for a good laugh.

In 1946 Curly Howard suffered a stroke that rendered him inactive; Shemp rejoined the act, taking Curly's place. In the years after leaving Ted Healy, Shemp had appeared in several two-reelers (including a series for Vitaphone) and feature films (he was under contract to Universal in the early 1940s). Just prior to returning to the Stooges, Shemp had his own comedy shorts series at Columbia (1944–47). Even though he remained a member of the team until his death, Shemp made a solo appearance in the 1949 feature *Africa Screams*, presumably as a favor to the film's stars, Abbott and Costello, with whom he had worked at Universal.

Though Curly never rejoined the act, he did appear briefly in two later

Stooge shorts with Shemp: *Hold That Lion* (1947) and *Malice in the Palace* (1949), although his sequence was deleted from the latter. Curly's health steadily deteriorated, hampered by a series of strokes; he died on January 18, 1952, in San Gabriel, California.

Shemp continued with the Stooges until his death of a heart attack on November 23, 1955, in Hollywood.

In 1956 Joe Besser (born August 12, 1907, in St. Louis, Missouri) was selected to assume the role of "third Stooge." Besser had been a successful comedian in vaudeville and on Broadway prior to entering films in the 1930s. In addition to his stage, radio, television and feature film work, Besser had his own comedy shorts series for Columbia (1949–56). He remained with the Stooges until 1958; by that time, the Columbia comedy shorts department had been shut down. Because of his wife's poor health, Besser quit the team rather than make the proposed personal appearances across the country.

When their Columbia shorts from the 1930s and 1940s were released to television in 1958, the Stooges found themselves thrust back into the limelight; it was one of the most successful comebacks in show business history. Later that year, Joe DeRita (born Joseph Wardell on July 12, 1909, in Philadelphia, Pennsylvania) became the "third Stooge." A veteran of the vaudeville and burlesque circuits, DeRita had starred in a brief series of Columbia shorts from 1946 to 1948. Nicknamed "Curly Joe," DeRita remained with the Stooges until the deaths of teammates Larry and Moe.

Riding the wave of their newfound popularity, the Stooges busied themselves with numerous projects. They did many TV appearances and a few feature films, including *Have Rocket, Will Travel* (1959), *Snow White and the Three Stooges* (1961), *The Three Stooges Meet Hercules* (1962), *The Three Stooges in Orbit* (1962), *The Three Stooges Go Around the World in a Daze* (1963) and *The Outlaws Is Coming!* (1965).

In 1970, during the production of a TV film entitled *Kook's Tour*, Larry suffered a stroke that rendered him inactive. Though other projects were discussed (with frequent Stooges costar Emil Sitka slated to take Larry's place), none came to fruition. Moe made solo appearances on television and in a science-fiction thriller *Dr. Death, Seeker of Souls* (1973) in addition to touring colleges, lecturing on his years with the Stooges.

Larry Fine died on January 24, 1975, at the Motion Picture Country Home in Woodland Hills, California. Moe Howard died of lung cancer on May 4, 1975, in Los Angeles.

John Tyrrell

John E. Tyrrell was born on December 7, 1902. Educated in Manhattan's public schools, he entered show business at age sixteen as half of the dance team of Tyrrell and Mack. The team "broke in" at Asbury Park, New Jersey; successful from the outset, they remained together for more than a decade, playing all over the United States (including several engagements at the

Palace Theatre in New York and a season as featured players with *George White's Scandals of 1926*) and Canada.

When vaudeville began to wane, Tyrrell studied acting, virtually beginning his theatrical career all over again. After two seasons with a stock company in Bridgeport, Connecticut, he journeyed to Hollywood in 1936 and was placed under a long-term contract to Columbia Pictures. He made his film debut in Columbia's *The Final Hour* (1936) and worked steadily for the studio, appearing in such pictures as *The Awful Truth* (1937), *Mr. Smith Goes to Washington* (1939), and *The Face Behind the Mask* (1941).

During the late 1930s on through the late 1940s, Tyrrell was seen as a supporting player in many of the Columbia shorts, usually cast as slick con men or officious types.

He died on September 19, 1949.

Elwood Ullman

Elwood Ullman was born in Memphis, Tennessee, in 1903. His family was Old South; they owned a distillery that produced Elwood Whiskey (Elwood was named after the same ancestor for whom the whiskey was named). Raised in St. Louis, Missouri, he wrote humor for several publications *(The St. Louis Post-Dispatch, New York World, Life, Captain Billy's Whiz Bang, Judge)* prior to his arrival in Hollywood, circa 1934. Through the efforts of Jack Natteford, an established western writer, Elwood began working with Bryan Foy, who was directing a series of two-reel comedies for the Thalians, a professional acting fraternity. Under the guidance of Foy and another director, Charles Lamont, Ullman learned the craft of writing for comedy shorts.

Jules White hired Ullman as a writer for the Columbia shorts department in August 1936; working for both the White and McCollum units, Elwood proved to be one of the finest gag writers on the payroll, providing first-rate material for the unit's sizable roster of comedians.

Ullman worked steadily for the unit throughout the 1940s, occasionally writing for feature films, such as the screenplays for *Honeymoon Ahead* (1945) and *Men in Her Diary* (1945).

"I enjoyed working on the two-reelers," says Ullman, "but there was no prestige in that field. I had to move on to feature films in order to stay alive in the business." So in 1951 he left Columbia for writing assignments at other studios, among them the adaptation for *Sailor Beware* (1951) with Martin & Lewis, the story for *Lost in Alaska* (1952) with Abbott & Costello, additional material for *The Stooge* (1953) with Martin & Lewis, and the screenplay for *Ma and Pa Kettle in Waikiki* (1955). He also joined writer-director Edward Bernds, another Columbia alumnus, at Allied Artists for a series of Bowery Boys comedies, including *Loose in London* (1953), *The Bowery Boys Meet the Monsters* (1954) and *Bowery to Bagdad* (1955).

During the 1960s, Ullman wrote the screenplays for *The Three Stooges*

Meet Hercules (1962), *The Three Stooges in Orbit* (1962), *The Three Stooges Go Around the World in a Daze* (1963) and *The Outlaws Is Coming!* (1965), and cowrote the Elvis Presley musical *Tickle Me* (1965) and the Beach Party entry *The Ghost in the Invisible Bikini* (1966).

Elwood Ullman died on October 11, 1985, in Hollywood.

Vera Vague (Barbara Jo Allen)

Barbara Jo Allen was born September 2, circa 1904, in New York City. During her high school years, she was active in student theatrical productions. After studying at the Sorbonne in Paris, France, she returned to New York and began her career as a serious actress on Broadway. She moved to Los Angeles in the mid-1930s and found work in radio, on such programs as "One Man's Family," "I Love a Mystery" and "Death Valley Days."

Miss Allen conceived the spinster character of Vera Vague in 1939. Vera was an instant hit with radio listeners, and eventually the creation eclipsed the creator; within a few years, Miss Allen was billing herself solely as Vera Vague. She had her own radio program and soon became a regular on Bob Hope's Pepsodent show.

She entered films in 1939, appearing in a few Leon Errol two-reelers at RKO, a series of one-reel comic travelogues called *Vera Vague Laff Tours* at Columbia, and thirty-nine feature films, including *Melody Ranch* (1940), *The Mad Doctor* (1941), *Kiss the Boys Goodbye* (1941), *Design for Scandal* (1941), *Priorities on Parade* (1942), *Henry Aldrich Plays Cupid* (1944), *Snafu* (1945) and *Born to Be Loved* (1959).

Her Columbia comedy shorts series ran from 1943 to 1952.

During the 1950s she made television appearances; in the 1960s her book, *The Animal Convention*, which dealt with ecology, was published.

She died on September 14, 1974, in Santa Barbara, California.

Phil Van Zandt

Born on October 3, 1904, in Amsterdam, Holland, Phil Van Zandt had been a stage actor prior to entering films in the 1930s. His feature credits include *Those High Gray Walls* (1939), *Citizen Kane* (1941), *The Hard Way* (1942), *Air Raid Wardens* (1943), *The Big Noise* (1944), *House of Frankenstein* (1945), *Night and Day* (1946), *A Night in Casablanca* (1946), *Life with Father* (1947), *Walk a Crooked Mile* (1948), *Ghost Chasers* (1951), *His Kind of Woman* (1951), *Viva Zapata!* (1952), *Knock on Wood* (1954), *Three Ring Circus* (1954), *The Big Combo* (1955), *To Catch a Thief* (1955), *Our Miss Brooks* (1956), *Around the World in 80 Days* (1956) and *Man of a Thousand Faces* (1957).

Van Zandt was a supporting player in many Columbia shorts of the 1940s and 1950s, almost always playing a comic villain. In the 1950s he also appeared on television and tried to initiate an acting school bearing his name.

Phil Van Zandt (right) played a variety of adversaries. Here, he and henchman Tom Kennedy terrorize Norma Randall in the Three Stooges short *Spooks* (1953).

Despondent over his flagging career, and having squandered most of his money through compulsive gambling, Van Zandt committed suicide (an overdose of sleeping pills) on February 16, 1958, in Hollywood.

Wally Vernon

Wally Vernon was born in New York City in 1904. He started in show business at the age of three, and his career spanned minstrel shows, stage, vaudeville and burlesque prior to his entering films in the 1930s. His feature credits include *Mountain Music* (1937), *You Can't Have Everything* (1937), *Alexander's Ragtime Band* (1938), *The Gorilla* (1939), *Reveille with Beverly* (1943), *Outlaws of Santa Fe* (1944), *King of the Gamblers* (1948), *Always Leave Them Laughing* (1949), *Everybody's Dancin'* (1950), *What Price Glory* (1952), *Affair with a Stranger* (1953), *Fury at Gunsight Pass* (1956) and *What a Way to Go!* (1964).

Vernon was paired with Eddie Quillan for a Columbia comedy shorts series that ran from 1948 to 1956.

Vernon was killed by a hit-and-run driver on March 7, 1970, in Van Nuys, California.

Dick Wessel

Born in 1913, Dick Wessel had a lengthy stage career prior to entering films in the mid-1930s. He played supporting roles in many feature films, including *They Made Me a Criminal* (1939), *Gentleman Jim* (1942), *Dick Tracy vs. Cueball* (1946), *On the Town* (1949), *Beware of Blondie* (1950), *Strangers on a Train* (1951), *Gentlemen Prefer Blondes* (1953), *Francis in the Navy* (1955), *Around the World in 80 Days* (1956), *Pocketful of Miracles* (1961) and *The Ugly Dachshund* (1966).

He played supporting roles in the Columbia shorts from the mid-1940s through the 1950s, usually cast as a jealous husband or oafish brother-in-law.

Wessel also worked in radio and television. He died of a heart attack on April 20, 1965, at his home in Studio City, California.

Jack White (Preston Black)

Born March 2, 1899, in Austria, Jack White entered the film business in 1909 as a child actor. The White family (real last name: Weiss) had moved to America in 1904 and settled in Edendale, where the motion picture industry began in California. "The picture people came to Edendale from New York to take advantage of the beautiful weather," Jack recalls. "Mack Sennett, Tom Ince, all those big names came out here, and my brothers (Jules, Sam) and I got in the business that way. They couldn't find any actors, so they made actors out of us; they came to us, we didn't go to them."

In 1912 Jack landed a job as switchboard operator at the Mack Sennett Studios ("Keystone Comedies"). There he rubbed elbows with the likes of Roscoe "Fatty" Arbuckle, Ford Sterling, Mabel Normand and Charlie Chaplin. "When he was at Keystone, Chaplin was about to give up the picture business and I talked him out of it," says White. "I said, 'Stick around, you'll be alright.' If I hadn't done that, he might have gone back to England and you would have never heard of Charlie Chaplin."

Jack's stay at Sennett's ended in 1914 when, one day while he was at the switchboard, a messenger came in with an important communication for Ford Sterling, a top Sennett comic who had gained fame as the chief of the legendary Keystone Kops. Jack personally saw to it that Sterling got the message, which was an offer from a rival studio for Sterling's services. Ford accepted the offer, and left Keystone. Sennett, in a rage, wanted to know how the message got onto the lot. When he found out that it was Jack White who delivered the message to Sterling, he fired Jack.

Jack eventually got a job in the cutting department of the Fox Studios. Before long, he was editing the Fox "Sunshine Comedies." One day in 1917, when all the regular directors were busy and some additional scenes were needed for one of the comedies, Jack went out and shot the required scenes. The end result was better than anyone had anticipated, and so, at the ripe old age of seventeen, Jack White became a comedy director for William Fox.

Jack White (right) clowns with comedian Lloyd Hamilton in this Educational Pictures gag photo from the 1920s, celebrating Thanksgiving.

While at Fox, White struck up a personal working relationship with comedian Lloyd Hamilton. Shortly thereafter, when the two left the employ of Fox, White would become one of the leading figures in comedy production.

White is best known for his tenure with Educational Pictures, an association that began in 1920. Says Jack:

> I had made a picture off the cuff and previewed it. It was a smash. Sol Wurtzel, the head of Fox, happened to be at the preview and he wanted the picture. I said, "Sol, you can have a series but it's going to cost you X amount of dollars per unit." He didn't take me up on the offer, so I sent a representative to Earle Hammons, the founder and president of Educational Pictures, in New York. He liked the picture and gave us a contract for six. He kept increasing the number each year thereafter until finally they bought a studio for us on Santa Monica Boulevard.

They bought it from Sol Lesser and we made our comedies there. We saved a lot of money because the principal amount of rental money went into the purchase of this studio.

Jack was in charge of his own comedy unit, "Mermaid Comedies," which were distributed by Educational. Jimmy Adams and Lige Conley were among Mermaid's comedy stars, but it was White's felicitous collaboration with Lloyd Hamilton that established him as one of the premier comedy producers of the era. The Hamilton shorts were heralded as some of the funniest and most original comedies of the 1920s; tragically, the majority of these pictures are unavailable today due to a fire in the Educational Pictures warehouse, which destroyed most of the negatives.

White remained with Educational until 1933; he then journeyed to New York and produced a stage show. "It wasn't very good," he recalls. "I had a deal with the Shuberts; they wanted to bring it down to Broadway but I wouldn't let them. They had no investment as I had produced it on my own." During this time, Jack also produced a musical comedy at the Al Christie unit housed at the Long Island–based Eastern Service Studios. *Poppin' the Cork* (1933), a three-reel short, was released through Educational. A musical tribute to the repeal of prohibition, it was Milton Berle's first sound film, and featured a musical score by James Hanley and Benny Davis, with Henry King's Orchestra.

Returning to Hollywood around 1935, Jack went to work for Columbia Pictures in a varied position: to write, direct and help produce films for the comedy shorts department of which his brother Jules was now in charge. At this time, Jack worked under the pseudonym Preston Black. He explains, "I was having divorce trouble and the lawyers were hounding me everywhere I went to work. So I changed my screen name so they couldn't tell who the hell it was. I worked under the name Preston Black for, on and off, ten years." At Columbia, he directed two-reelers with the Three Stooges, Andy Clyde, Harry Langdon, El Brendel and Walter Catlett.

With the coming of World War II, Jack went into the service. "They didn't have a film unit where I was stationed in Florida, so I had to take the toughest kind of abuse. Finally, somebody discovered I was from Hollywood and they decided to send me to Wright Field in Dayton, Ohio where they had their headquarters. But that's another story—that was murder. I eventually got sick and came home." Back on the West Coast, he went to work for 20th Century-Fox. "I worked there as an assistant director—third assistant—and I learned a lot that I hadn't come in contact with before. I had a deal with the studio; I was to stay there until the war ended, at which time the regular guy whose job I had would be able to reclaim his position. When he returned, I went back to Columbia." Jack remained with the Columbia comedy shorts department until it was shut down in 1958.

Jack White died on April 10, 1984. With a career that spanned more than four decades, he has earned a place in motion picture history as one of the most influential comedy creators of his time.

Jules White

The man whose name is synonymous with the Columbia comedy shorts department was born Jules J. Weiss on September 17, 1900, in Budapest. In 1904 his family came to America and settled in Edendale, California. At age nine, Jules started appearing in small roles for the film companies that were springing up in the area. He had bit parts in such milestone pictures as *The Spoilers* (1914) and *The Birth of a Nation* (1915) (of the latter, Jules comments, "I was one of the children running down the street cheering the Ku Klux Klan. Imagine that—a Jewish boy cheering the Klan!"). He worked with directors Colin Campbell and D.W. Griffith and actors Hobart Bosworth, Bobby Harron and Blanche Sweet.

In his late teenage years, with film roles growing fewer, Jules worked in a produce market. In the meantime, his older brother Jack, who had also been a child actor, had built a reputation as an astute producer-director of comedy shorts. At age twenty, Jules joined Jack at Educational Pictures, where Jack was in charge of his own comedy unit. At Educational, Jules learned his craft inside and out, working as an assistant film editor, purchasing agent, still photographer and assistant director. In 1925 he became a full-fledged director for the unit; the following year, he left to direct comedies for William Fox. Returning to Educational in 1927, White continued to direct comedy shorts until 1929, when he went to MGM to help organize their short subjects department. During his MGM stint, Jules directed several of the early *Pete Smith Specialties* and, with director Zion Myers, created the *Dogville* comedies, spoofs of then-current movies featuring an all-canine cast. He and Myers also directed the Buster Keaton feature *Sidewalks of New York* (1931).

While serving as associate director on the Paramount feature *King of the Jungle* (1933) starring Buster Crabbe, Jules was contacted by Columbia Pictures. Studio chieftain Harry Cohn wanted to form a comedy shorts department, and White had been recommended as a good man to organize it. Cohn met with White, and hired him on the spot; Cohn could not have made a better choice, as White's instincts for comedy were infallible. Hiring a truly remarkable staff of writers, directors and performers—as well as serving as a producer and director himself—Jules made enormous incalculable contributions to motion picture comedy. Suffice it to say that he and his associates were, for a number of years, the sole purveyors of the slapstick art. What is certain is that White has never really received full recognition for his efforts.

Harry Cohn died in 1958; soon after, the short subjects department was shut down. White had been with the studio a record twenty-five years, a staggering achievement in a town where producers' careers have the longevity of the proverbial snowball in hell. When Ralph Cohn, Harry's nephew, organized Screen Gems, Columbia's television subsidiary, he wanted White to join him, but Jules declined the offer. "I could have been a millionaire," says White, "but with all that pressure, I would have never lived to enjoy it."

In 1960 Columbia released *Stop! Look! and Laugh!*, a feature-length compilation of excerpts from Three Stooges shorts. Jules directed new sequences with ventriloquist Paul Winchell, which served as a framework for the older footage. That same year, Jules and his brother Sam created and produced a half-hour TV pilot for CBS. "Oh, Those Bells!" starring the Wiere Brothers, was an attempt to bring old-fashioned, freewheeling slapstick comedy to the home screen. CBS was enthusiastic about the project at first, but the thirteen episodes commissioned were shelved and didn't receive airplay until May 1962, when a filler was needed for the summertime schedule.

Jules retired after that, settling in Sherman Oaks, California. On January 18, 1982, the Academy of Motion Picture Arts and Sciences held *A Salute to Jules White*. With White in attendance, an audience of several hundred warmly greeted representative samplings of his work: excerpts from his Andy Clyde, Schilling & Lane, Buster Keaton and Three Stooges shorts, and complete screenings of *The Dogway Melody* (1930), one of the celebrated *Dogville* comedies, *Free Rent* (Collins and Kennedy, 1936) and *Half-Wits Holiday* (The Three Stooges, 1947). Though appreciative of this latter-day acclaim ("The critics looked down their noses at our pictures"), White takes it all in stride. When we visited Jules while preparing this book, he said, "I'll show you the award that means the most to me." The prolific producer-director, whose work has garnered Academy Award nominations, then brought out a certificate presented to him by his grandchildren. It read "World's Greatest Grandpa."

Some time after the writing of this book, Jules became ill and was eventually diagnosed as having Alzheimer's Disease. He passed away on April 30, 1985. We will always be grateful for his help and support of this project.

Jean Willes (Jean Donahue)

Born in Los Angeles, Jean spent her childhood in Salt Lake City, Utah, then moved to Seattle, Washington, when she was around ten years old.

The lovely, dark-haired actress played supporting roles in Columbia shorts from the mid-1940s through the mid-1950s. She acted under the name Jean Donahue until she got married in the late 1940s, at which time she became Jean Willes. Says Ed Bernds, "I never met her husband, but I understand he was a professional wrestler. So if anybody on the set got any notions about Jean, someone was probably very happy to tell him that she was married to a big, rough guy who could tear him limb from limb."

Her feature credits include *Here Come the Waves* (1944), *The Winner's Circle* (1948), *A Woman of Distinction* (1950), *Son of Paleface* (1952), *From Here to Eternity* (1953), *Abbott and Costello Go to Mars* (1953), *Five Against the House* (1955), *Bowery to Bagdad* (1955), *Invasion of the Body Snatchers* (1956), *A King and Four Queens* (1956), *The Revolt of Mamie Stover* (1956), *The FBI Story* (1959), *Ocean's Eleven* (1960) and *Gypsy* (1962).

Throughout the 1950s and 1960s Jean made more than 400 television appearances, guesting on such programs as "Boston Blackie," "The Jack Benny Show," "The Burns and Allen Show," "The Bob Cummings Show," "The Twilight Zone" (in an episode titled "Will the Real Martian Please Stand Up") and "The Beverly Hillbillies."

Bibliography

Capra, Frank. *The Name Above the Title*. New York: Macmillan, 1971.

Everson, William K. *Classics of the Horror Film*. Secaucus, NJ: Citadel Press, 1974.

_____. *The Films of Hal Roach*. New York: Museum of Modern Art, 1971.

Fine, Larry, and James Carone. *Stroke of Luck*. Hollywood, CA: Siena Publishing Company, 1973.

Fitzgerald, Michael G. *Universal Pictures*. New Rochelle, NY: Arlington House, 1977.

Forrester, Jeffrey. *The Stooge Chronicles*. Chicago: Triumvirate Productions, 1981.

_____. *The Stoogephile Trivia Book*. Chicago: Triumvirate Productions, 1981.

Grossman, Gary H. *Saturday Morning TV*. New York: Dell, 1981.

Halliwell, Leslie. *The Filmgoer's Companion*. New York: Avon Books, 1974.

Howard, Moe. *Moe Howard & The Three Stooges*. Secaucus, NJ: Citadel Press, 1977.

Jewell, Richard B., with Vernon Harbin. *The RKO Story*. New York: Crown, 1982.

Jones, Ken D., Arthur F. McClure, and Alfred E. Twomey. *Character People*. Cranbury, NJ: A.S. Barnes, 1976.

Keaton, Buster, with Charles Samuels. *My Wonderful World of Slapstick*. Garden City, NY: Doubleday, 1960.

Kerr, Walter. *The Silent Clowns*. New York: Alfred A. Knopf, 1975.

Lahue, Kalton C. *World of Laughter*. Norman, OK: University of Oklahoma Press, 1966.

_____ and Samuel Gill. *Clown Princes and Court Jesters*. Cranbury, NJ: A.S. Barnes, 1970.

Lamparski, Richard. *Whatever Became Of...?, Fifth Series*. New York: Crown, 1982.

Lenburg, Jeff, Joan Howard Maurer, and Greg Lenburg. *The Three Stooges Scrapbook*. Secaucus, NJ: Citadel Press, 1982.

McCaffrey, Donald W. *The Golden Age of Sound Comedy*. Cranbury, NJ: A.S. Barnes, 1973.

McCarthy, Todd, and Charles Flynn. *Kings of the Bs*. New York: E.P. Dutton, 1975.

Maltin, Leonard. *The Great Movie Comedians*. New York: Crown, 1978.

_____. *The Great Movie Shorts*. New York: Crown, 1972.

_____. *Hollywood: The Movie Factory*. New York: Popular Library, 1976.

_____. *Movie Comedy Teams*. New York: New American Library, 1970.

_____. *The Real Stars*. New York: Curtis Books, 1973.

Mast, Gerald. *The Comic Mind*. Indianapolis, IN, and New York: Bobbs-Merrill, 1973.

Michael, Paul. *The American Movies*. New York: Garland Books, 1969.
_____. *Movie Greats*. New York: Garland Books, 1969.
Truitt, Evelyn Mack. *Who Was Who on Screen*. New York: R.R. Bowker, 1974.

Index

Numbers in boldface indicate photographs.

251